Sublime S

A Journey to Love in Thailand

By: C. L. Wilson

Dear Lenora,
Thanks for shining!
Love Cassandra
Oct 2014
#3.

Sublime Surroundings
A Journey to Love in Thailand

Published by One Day Publications

This is based on a true story. Some of the names of characters, places and circumstances have been changed. Any resemblance to any persons living or dead is purely coincidental.

The author wishes to acknowledge the support of the Vancouver branch of the Canadian Author's Association during the writing of this book.

Createspace Template Cover Design by: Cassandra Wilson

Cover Artwork by: Cassandra Wilson

Contact Information at: sublimesurroundingsthebook@gmail.com

ISBN# 978-0-9880400-2-1

Acknowledgements

First of all, I would like to Thank God, Mother Earth and the Universe.

I would like to thank all the special people with whom I have shared the story of this book. I would like to thank my parents John Charles and Beverly Joan Wilson for listening and faithfully abiding with me through the years of its gestation. Thanks to my brother Kevin Shaun and my sister Carol Ann who believed that one day it would come to light.

Thank you cousin Kent Wilson very much for his brilliant edits and thoughtful hours to make this book more accessible to readers.

I want to thank Kaurina Danu, Shelley Klassen, Joceline Heersink for reading this book and providing feedback.

I would like to thank all of the characters in this book who played with me during this time in my life inspiring me to forge onward. I have created images of them from my point of view.

I would also like to thank Jo K. Eitrheim who showed me love, generosity and kindness in helping make this book a reality.

And to all who love, this one's for you.

Table of Contents:

Sublime Surroundings

Chapter 1 – Turquoise Eyes

I awoke in the middle of the night. Our bus was hurtling down the highway at high speed. I sat upright and looked out the front. White headlights approached us directly ahead. At the last second the bus driver swerved back into our lane, jostling passengers with the sudden movement over uneven concrete. Mark was asleep in the seat beside me, his eyes closed as we raced haphazardly through the heat of the night travelling south on the Thailand peninsula from Bangkok to Samui Island.

"Mark, wake up," I breathed. "He's driving in the wrong lane."

"Don't watch, Kid," he murmured, twisting in his seat.

Tossing and turning while sitting upright, wedging my head against the window, I stared into the night as groups of fluorescent lights occasionally popped out of the darkness, illuminating roadside restaurants. Around 2 a.m., we pulled over and were waved inside for a stretch and something to eat.

Thai men played cards at patio tables, smoking and laughing while refuelling with speed induced sodas, their trucks parked along the side of the road. A buffet counter warmed vegetables and curries, emanating exotic scents from under red heat lamps. The sound of clanging metal chairs and voices rang off cement walls while we chose plates of warm food and ordered drinks. I noticed a handsome man from our bus with brown eyes and sun-kissed brown hair, sauntering into the restaurant. His tanned skin, confident, relaxed manner aroused my curiosity. After we finished our pack re-boarded the bus and we were quickly lulled back into a hypnotic state by the resounding hum of the bus engine. We rolled on with it anticipating the following day.

In the clear, early morning light, a new day dawned as we parked and were directed off the bus into a restaurant filled with other tourists. We were moved into the seating area as fellow travellers milled about awaiting buses to faraway island destinations. Just north of the Malaysian border, the scent of seaweed carried by a moist breeze told us the shore was nearby. We mingled with others, eyeing them curiously, ordering breakfast over the metal and glass counter.

"It smells like fish for breakfast," Mark chuckled.

"Mmm," I responded, making eye contact with the staff, "it smells delicious." I elbowed Mark gently as I admired our Thai servers: suntanned skin, loose clothing, and casual repose. Choosing from the array of curries we ordered vegetables and rice, and sat amidst the crowd of foreigners.

My desire for cereal and toast unabated, we sipped coffee while enjoying the delicious food, if a little too spicy for our morning meal. Tourists ate breakfast at nearby tables eyeing one another for tans and tattoos, in flip flops or tank tops, breezy dresses or sport shorts. Beautifully tanned and relaxed people smiled easily to one another as they talked, some tying their hair back as the heat of the day began to rise. The sound of unusual birds and foreign languages captivated us as the exotic breeze swept across our moist skin.

Soon we responded to a call from a uniformed Thai bus driver, who said "Koh Samui", and boarded another bus to the ferry.

"I hope this island is worth all this travelling," said Mark.

"It will be. The adventure is only beginning," I replied. We had been in Bangkok for three days, hot and busy touring many sights. The heat was intense and we needed somewhere comfortable to relax and unwind. I had convinced Mark that the islands were where we needed to be, having taken the word of our friend Connie passing through the city on her way back to South Korea.

"Oh, you will love the islands," she said. "Koh Samui is the best. There's a lot of action happening there. Beautiful beaches, fun places to see. Trust me."

We followed the cues of Thai people and were herded along the way, sticky tickets in hand, hoping our destination would fulfill its promise and render this excursion life-changing and delightful. Mark was sceptical by nature, his dry wit and sarcasm entertaining as I jollied him into enjoying the vast differences of life between Thailand and Canada.

We had met teaching English in South Korea and developed a friendship while spending a year under contract at different schools. Socializing was on weekends only at the International Pub, fondly called the IP. One night feeling carefree while riding home on my scooter with only weeks to go on our sojourns, we cooked up a plan to travel to Thailand to see elephants. The wind in our faces, the wide road clear and the sky dark, the whole world felt like our own. We were now making true on our agreement.

Our friends had made similar plans and travelled to China, Vietnam, Laos and other South Asian countries. After working full time for a year, with a lump of savings untouched, we needed a break to relax. Most expats went south after their years were complete, South East Asia being a well loved destination with its inexpensive travel, tropical beaches and beautiful exotic sights.

Sitting together on the creaking and weaving bus as it coursed through the jungle, I inhaled the rare breeze through the open window, wedged between the passengers as the heavy bus rocked along a dirt path. Pulsating energy beamed from surrounding trees and bushes as we drove through thickening jungle. Vibrant with life, greenery enveloped my senses as my vision stayed glued to the flicker of colour through the window. Thickening tropical foliage rolled past as branches swept across the windows, encircling us in leaves. I stared out awaiting the flutter of bird wings or the glitter of cat eyes, certain they perched or crept just inside the jungle edge.

"Looks like we're arriving at the work camp," Mark jested, causing a brief moment of speculation.

"Yeah, right," I laughed. "Elephants live in this jungle. And wildcats. I hope we see some fascinating creatures," I said, my eyes glued to the window.

"They're waiting for you, too," he laughed, "salivating."

Soon the foliage receded and we entered onto open tarmac at the Surat Thani pier, rolling toward a large ferry packed with tourists. The bus careened to a halt and we were ushered aboard. Mark led me forward through masses of passengers to a spot in front of the cockpit window.

"I hope he doesn't need to see," I said, sitting down with a glance at our drivers who seemed to be enjoying the chaos, preparing to depart at the instruction of someone on deck checking the view. Tourists piled onboard as bags slumped down onto every space of deck, people squeezing in beside one another, jousting for position. At this point the tanned, handsome man from our bus sat down beside Mark and they began conversing. Introducing himself as Damian from Sydney, he shook our hands and spoke with Mark about the geography of the area.

When our boat pulled away from the pier there was a loud cheer onboard. Mark and I exchanged smiles. The dazzling blue sky and glowing white sun warmed our skin while the salty sea breeze caressed us. From behind my sunglasses, I watched couples apply sunscreen, men open cans of beer all amid the hum of many voices. Beautiful bodies reclined against backpacks, bare male chests everywhere as women revealed colourful bikini tops in the sun. I leaned against the cockpit window and pulled up the edge of my shorts.

Mark turned to me. "Damian says we should go with him to the next island north of Koh Samui called Koh Phangan. He says it's just as beautiful as Samui with fewer tourists and it's less expensive." I leaned into the conversation.

"Koh Samui is full of girlie bars and its noisy," said Damian. "Koh Phangan is cheaper than Samui and it's only another hour on this boat. Come with me, I'll take you where I'm going."

Mark and I exchanged glances while I quickly reviewed the option in my mind. I had made one promise to myself in preparing for this journey and that was to do things I had never done before. I wanted an adventure, and already the plot was thickening.

"Sure. Let's check it out," I smiled, feeling excited.

"Okay. We'll go with you," Mark said to Damian, who smiled and seemed satisfied. They continued to talk and laugh while I settled back to take in the view.

We docked at the pier for Koh Samui and watched as most of the boat emptied around us. I shifted uneasily, hoping we were making the right decision.

"Clearly our destination is remote," Mark said, causing my heart to thump. The boat sailed for another hour in the clear, glistening light before we arrived at Koh Phangan. Docking at a long pier, I grabbed my small red backpack and Mark his duffle bag and we ambled alongside

Damian as he and Mark continued to converse. Damian led us down the dock to a small parking lot filled with truck taxis. We chose one and threw our packs on the top rack, piling in with seven others. We smiled to one another.

Careening out of the parking lot we rolled through dusty streets into a village with shops, tiny markets and second level abodes closely lining the road. Children played while elderly watched from wooden stools, relaxed, their eyes following the scene. Soon the paved road gave way to dirt tracks into a field of towering palms, with tropical birds swooping from tree to tree. The sights and scene gripped my attention as the jungle crackled with energy through the thickening palm grove, raised platform lounges secured between trees and thatched roofs over wooden huts. Glimpses of sparkling sea shone between trees in the distance as I stared in awe of the beauty, a peaceful feeling permeating me. The truck rolled to a stop as we dropped people off along the way, leaving them wandering down hidden byways and gently worn paths with heavy packs on their back. I wondered where they were headed as we rolled on.

Ambling along the bumps of the uneven road, the truck cruised leisurely as we swayed within it, mesmerized by the enveloping scene. Sitting in awed silence, we delivered many of our counterparts until Damian tapped the side of the truck.

"This is it," he said, hopping out. The three of us grabbed our packs from the top rack and started down a long pathway into a field of swaying palm trees, as the truck rolled on, disappearing from view. The sound of palm leaves rustling high over our heads drew our attention up as the buzzing jungle swallowed us. Narrow trunks bended to the breeze, as clusters of green and grey coconuts proliferated the treetops.

"This is paradise," Mark said, beaming.

"It's breathtaking," I echoed.

"Welcome," Damian said.

"Thank you," we chimed.

"There are many types of bungalows here: some are beside the beach,
some are back in the jungle. There are about fifteen in all. I'm staying in a grass hut right on the beach. It depends what kind of setting you want."

As we walked, I could see the shimmer of water up ahead.

"You can explore the jungle by taking the trails. There are waterfalls, beaches, and many natural places to explore. You can't get too lost, because the island is small - about 10-15 kms wide. Haadrin is just over in that direction. That's where they have the Full Moon parties." He gestured to the left sending my sight through thick palm trees as I tried to orient myself on the island.

"We are on the south side of the island. You can see Koh Samui across the water." I could see a narrow foot path weaving through the trees from yard to yard as if there was a jungle sidewalk, just far enough away from the houses to maintain privacy.

"Tourists only started coming to this island about 20 years ago The Thai families here have been living in the jungle for thousands of years, and many of them have never been off this island." Looking more closely I saw people sitting on platforms built into trees in other yards, high above the ground under shading of large palm leaves. They appeared relaxed as their gaze followed us.

"The nature is very diverse for an island. There are many breeds of

insects, spiders and snakes. Only some are dangerous. Just be careful.

"I've heard they have cobras here, and even King Cobras," I ventured.

"Yes, there are cobras here. You can see cobra shows in town. They live in this jungle. There are also King cobras but they mostly stay in the middle of the jungle and eat other snakes. They're not a big threat to people because they are so reclusive." Mark and I exchanged looks.

Damian padded along easily as Mark and I contemplated the crunching leaves underfoot more resolutely.

As we approached the main building we were met by a pack of barking dogs announcing our arrival. Sniffing at our knees, they soon moved on after rendering us non-threatening. We left our shoes in the pile at the base of the wooden steps and ascended into the open-air restaurant, with a view over tables and chairs to a beaming stretch of beach. The whisper of an exotic breeze caressed me, calmed my senses with scents that told me I was very far from home.

There was a wooden front counter and small windowed office on the right with a desk and old style telephone with some posted signs about local destinations with maps of the area. The only person in the place was a thin Thai man, who looked at us from his relaxed position while reclining in a chair. The serene vibe floated us into passive appreciation, as we gazed around, held by the moment.

"Hello," he softened, smiling.

"Hello, I'm back. These two need accommodation," Damian nodded at us, then padding off.

"One bungalow or two?" the man from the chair asked without shifting position. Mark and I looked at each other, measuring the moment with an inhale.

"Two," I spoke in the blushing moment.

Only then, the man turned in his chair, pointing to the end of a row of wooden bungalows. "Take your pick of those two beside the beach." We gazed over at two wood cabins, each with a hammock and a porch.

"Two hundred baht a night. You can pay later," he said, retiring from our conversation.

"Thanks," we said, smiling, then tiptoed across the soft floor to put on our sandals, chuckling at the ease of the transaction. Walking across the velvety, white sand, under towering palm trees we realized we had been given the choice of the best location on the beach.

"I'll give you the sea view, Kid. I'll be next door," Mark said, climbing up the steps into his bungalow and moving inside.

"Thanks. See you soon." I scampered over to mine and mounted the steps of my new abode: a small sun-bleached wood and rattan room raised up by pillars, right beside a slope of inviting sand and gentle waves lapping at the beach. Across my grey planked porch hung a white canvas hammock, two washing lines and two benches: one under the front window and one built in across the end. Inside the cozy room, the walls were made of rattan plywood and the ceiling was corrugated metal. A tad rustic, I could see lots of tiny openings where light poured in. I placed my bag on the soft double bed with fresh flowered sheets, two fluffy pillows, and a rolled up mosquito net. There was a wide headboard I could use for a shelf. It was clean and neat and I liked the cozy feeling. Inside the tidy bathroom down three cement steps into a concrete room lined with decorative cut outs, there was a shower head, a pressure toilet with a small water bucket and a sink.

I opened the bedroom window over the bed to the beach, mesmerized by the breathtaking view. Clear blue water lapped gently at the shore, as a soft breeze rustled palm leaves way up high. The other window opened to a view across the beach.

The last one opened toward Mark's bungalow and I could see him inside, grinning. "Hey Mark, let's meet on the beach for a swim."

"Yeah, I'm ready," he replied.

As I changed into my blue and white bikini in the bathroom, I smiled at our simple success. The space was perfect for relaxation – compact, comfortable and inexpensive. I happily unpacked my things lining up my candle, walkman, speakers and water bottle on the headboard/shelf under the window. I knew it was going to be perfect.

In a moment, I heard Mark shuffling on my porch, so I went out to join him. We walked over the sand to the shining beach, admiring the beautiful view in shades of teal, blue and white. The warmth enveloped us as I lay my purple sarong on the icing sugar sand, kneeling to adjust my bikini, feeling the sunlight bathe my skin. The velvety beach spread generously to the shore where gentle waves lapped under the spotless blue sky. Palm trees lined the glistening white all the way into the distance, waving fingered green leaves up high. We tiptoed down to the shore where the clear, shallow water sparkled, inviting us in.

"Ooh, it is lovely," I said, slowly moving into it.

"It's a good thing we listened to Damian or we would be listening to thumping disco music right now," he chuckled.

"Instead we are here," I replied. We grinned at each other. "This place is incredible!"

The tranquil glowing beach stretched as far as we could see, almost bare of tourists, wrapping around distant bends. I inhaled our idyllic utopia, as the shimmering sea sparkled all the way out to the horizon where the island of Samui rested in a grey green haze.

"It's shallow," I said. "Let's sit down." Finding a soft bottom, we swayed gently with the current, the water up to our waists. Appreciating the astounding beauty of lush jungle, glowing sand and the serene watery oasis, the deep silence lulled us into quiet contemplation. I could see other bungalow shapes behind the tree line along the shore, lying in the shade beneath the palm trees. The places beside ours were similar and I could see a few other guests lounging in hammocks.

"This is everything I could have dreamed of and more. We are n paradise."

"We sure are, Kid. This is it." Rolling back into the water, I felt peace. The gentle flow of the waves and glistening light resonated clarity, relaxing me with every breath.

"This may be the most beautiful beach I've ever seen," I finally said.

"Yeah, me too," said Mark.

"What happens on a beach this beautiful? Do people fall in love? Does God come?" I asked.

"God is already here," he answered. We laughed.

"Yes! Just look at this beauty! Surely people experience something spectacular here," I said, my eyes wide with anticipation.

"I guess we'll find out," he answered.

I relished the feeling of wonder about how this beautiful place would change me. It seemed gentle and generous, and I began to feel more open just by being in it. Tranquil perfect sights delighted our senses, as we laughed, having fun in awe of our newfound home.

Finally, Mark checked his shoulders. "My skin is burning. Let's go in and get a cold beer to start the celebrating."

"Sounds good." We rose dripping from the water and strolled through the crystal clear waves. The sandy bottom stirred with each step, making me want to skip over it to maintain its perfection.

"I'll go get the beers." Mark padded off, hanging his towel over the railing of his porch on the way. I retreated from the heat, sipping water from my capped plastic bottle with blue Thai writing, taking in the view from my porch. Mark returned with two Singha Thai beers, and we clanged our bottles in cheer.

"This is worth waiting for," I ventured, as Mark and I cooled our throats with beer.

"This is what its all about, Kid," Mark replied.

"Its so quiet and peaceful. Its the perfect place to unwind."

"Paradise found," he said, reclining into quiet contemplation.

The sun warmed my skin and I shifted to divert the light from burning me. My sarong covered my legs but I couldn't move myself from the sunshine. It felt so nurturing, so what I needed.

As the sun began to lower in the sky, we stretched from our relaxed positions on my porch, our stomachs beginning to rumble. Mark suggested dinner.

"Brilliant idea, my friend."

"We will soon see," he chuckled.

We strolled up to the restaurant for something to eat. Reading the list of extensive menu options, we elected to eat the most popular choice as recommended by our smiling Thai server, pad thai noodles and coconut shakes.

Served on large plates, each meal was filling and delicious. Spicy chillies punctuated the dish and added zip. When we stood at the counter to pay, we were told to come back and pay for it in a few days. Mark and I laughed at their unprecedented trust and agreed to return.

Drifting over the sand on the way back to our bungalows we began to feel attuned to our unique, blissful space and walking more slowly. Other bungalows were scattered over the sand with inhabitants similarly reposed. Stepping up to my bungalow door, I unlocked the latch and went inside to open the windows. The calm feeling deepened in me as I sat on the bed, contemplating our luck.

Mark came over after he had changed into dry clothes and reclined at the end of my bed, leaning against the wall. I sat at the top of it, leaning on my pillows at the headboard. We laughed, reminiscing about our good times in South Korea, where we had met working as English teachers and formed part of a small tribe of expats.

"So, how did you get here, Mark? Did you always want to travel and work overseas?" I asked.

"No, I didn't plan on leaving Canada. I wanted a good paying job and a change of scene, so I started researching my options. Saskatchewan only has so much to offer."

"I heard the wheat fields there are breathtakingly beautiful."

"They are. The fields can be really stunning at times. They have a saying in Saskatchewan, Never get in trouble because even if you run, you can be seen for miles." He laughed his infectious chuckle, his moustache wiggling, making me laugh.

When the sun started to set, we moved out onto my porch watching the dog pack come down to the beach, frolicking and playing in the sand. Hammocks swung with embracing couples and people formed small clusters on the beach. Deep gratitude for this special place was evident in our lowered voices as we sat beneath changing colours, anticipating the setting of the golden sun. The Thai family who owned the restaurant moved out onto the sand, joining us to watch.

The sunset played a colourful message across the sky as pinks, oranges and purples moved into each other like I had never seen before. Sweeping bands of colour stretched across the sky and poured over the horizon. They leaked back behind us over the treetops covering the entire sky, silencing us with beauty. At the precise moment the sun set, the glowing yellow ball moved behind Koh Samui, honorary silence was an unspoken rule.

In what seemed like only moments, the light dimmed, then was gone. Creatures began tweeting and chirping around us as the beautiful scene disappeared into darkness. Stars shone from the blackened sky, glistening in our view. Palm leaves rustled as the winds picked up, causing my sarong to flutter in the candlelight. Barefoot on the porch, I reclined on the bench while Mark relaxed in the hammock.

"It got cooler," I said, wrapping my sarong over my bare shoulders.

"Breeze is blowing in from Siberia," he replied, making me laugh.

"It smells sweet and pure," I inhaled, lifting my nostrils to identify the scents.

"It smells like flowers and seaweed," he said.

"Yes, it does!"

Relaxing on my porch, a few more hours passed until I yawned, stretching, and checked the clock.

"It's only 10 o'clock, but it feels late. I'm tired so I'm going to bed, Mark."

"You got it," Mark said, rousing himself from my hammock.

"Sleep lightly," I teased, "just in case."

"You'll be fine, Kid. I'm right next door. Call me if you need anything," he said, reassuringly.

"I will. Thanks." I smiled, relieved that he understood.

"Goodnight," he said, stepping down onto the sand toward his bungalow.

"Goodnight, Mark," I said, moving inside and shutting the door. I locked the tiny latch from the inside and closed all the windows. I looked around at my cozy candle lit abode. It was rustic with only the necessities, but it was perfect. I pulled out my journal and sat by the candlelight to write some words about the glorious place we had found. I had bought it in Bangkok at a tiny corner store. The cover read, 'The Quiet Notebook'. When I closed the journal, I went into the bathroom turning on the light. A few insects scurried undercover, none large or looking too threatening. I checked under the sheets before climbing in. Everything clear. I switched off the light, got under the covers and lay awake listening to unfamiliar sounds emanating from in and around the bungalow. Captivating my attention, I wondered then worried about what could be joining me as I slept. Something was busy clicking and shifting so I got up and turned on the light. The holes I had seen during the day was now cause for concern but upon further inspection I saw nothing. There were no creatures appearing. I turned off the light and got back into bed, but the sounds kept me awake as I stared into the darkness. Finally, I fell asleep.

Morning sun warmed the bungalow and light came in through the cracks. I reached up to open the window over the bed letting in fresh air and the glorious sea view. It was calm and beautiful, just as the day before. Ah, blissful.

I turned on the shower and cool water poured from the nozzle, smelling of the sea. I gradually moved into the full stream, using my tiny bottle of shampoo and bar of soap. Birds called out and flew past the concrete cut outs around the top of the room, while small green geckos darted here and there. I could see vines on the outside wall, questioning what other creatures might be appearing in my space.

A troop of red and black army ants traversed in single file across the floor to a hole under the sink, circumventing droplets of water en route, a moving highway across the bathroom. I stepped over them while towelling off, watching their progress as I moved up onto the wooden floor. Narrow openings between the floor boards allowed sand to fall through but only the tiniest of creatures could make passage.

Dressing in my bikini, shorts and a tank, I prepared to spend the day on the beach. A tranquil setting greeted me when I opened the door, bungalows scattered lazily over a sea of white sparkling sand among tall grey palm stalks reaching up to the sky.

I looked over at Mark's bungalow. He was reclining in his hammock, grinning.

"Ready for breakfast?" he asked.

"Sure. Let's go eat!" I answered.

There was a blue sarong with orange flowers hanging over the porch beside Mark's. The door was open and two pairs of sandals lay at the entry as we walked across the sand past the few other bungalows. Putting our shoes in the pile, we stepped barefoot into the open air café with only a few others in sight. We followed the smooth floor to a small platform jutting out over the sand, where two tables stood in the partial shade of palm leaves. We sat at one and picked up the menus already laying there. The sunlight dancing over our skin as we read the breakfast menu and chose coconut shakes and banana pancakes.

A thin Thai man approached our table wearing a t-shirt with a clock on it that read, On Time. He introduced himself as Dang and we smiled.

"I'm Mark. And I like your t-shirt!" said Mark. We laughed.

"Yeah," he said, grinning.

I introduced myself.

We reclined in the chairs, the early morning sun light and warming. The whole place was quiet and serene. She returned with our coffees, honey and cream. We stirred, smiling at one another, exhaling with relief.

"Ah, we have found paradise," I reaffirmed.

"This is the most peaceful place I have ever been!" he laughed, as we shook our heads, still digesting our great discovery.

"Wow, its so beautiful. I never imagined a place like this existed. And here we are." We sipped our coffee until our food arrived. It looked delicious, with honey drizzled over the banana pancakes. We ate everything enjoying every bite. We left a tip, then pushed back our chairs and walked back to the bungalows.

Mark approached my hammock trying a new method for mounting it, one that would be more graceful. He struggled for the right positioning, wriggling between the folds of fabric until it opened and he was sitting safely inside. He breathed a sigh of relief.

"This is great," he started. "No schedule, no pressure, just relaxation. Our food is here, our beds, shade, the beach - everything we need. I could really get into this."

"I am into this," I said, spreading my sarong across the bench at the end of my porch. Sitting high up I could watch over the scene, with a view of the water, the beach and the horizon. The peaceful serenity made me feel calm, calmer than I could remember feeling. The breeze caressed us, gently resounding peacefulness and I sighed with relief.

"Mark, this place is having an effect on me. I feel so calm. It's a new feeling to be this relaxed."

"I know. Its new for me, too. I've just been sitting in the hammock enjoying the view since we got here. I thought it would be boring but I'm finding so much to think about, so much to consider, things that I never had time to consider before. I'm catching up on all the things I wanted to think about."

"That's how I feel. Finally, no pressure. I can just be myself. Its kind of strange that I've never felt this relaxed. I guess it's this place." I inhaled deeply, feeling the beauty of everything around me.

We sat for hours talking and laughing, observing the placid scene, barely moving except to change the music in my walkman. Tracy Chapman and Bjork sang for us while we rocked back and forth, lulled by the natural surroundings.

"I'm so happy we are taking this time to listen to ourselves. I've been busy for so long, my whole life! Its nice to get a chance to just be," I realized.

"I've been busy for so long, I forgot what it is to just be, just exist. 'Got to make the money'," he repeated.

"Yeah. Just hearing that stresses me out. It sounds like pressure." I laughed, and it rolled through me.

"It is pressure. Schedules are pressure. This, on the other hand, is bliss," he said. "Let's just be here, and think about this."

"It must have been fun growing up on a farm. Isn't that a relaxing lifestyle?"

"Life on a farm is a lot of hard work. Everyday you have to work, get up early and shovel and lift and transport. Its no picnic."

"I imagined it to be idyllic."

"When you are raised on a farm, its different. I have two older brothers and we all work on the farm."

"I love farms. I love the fresh air and all the animals."

"The air isn't always fresh," he laughed. "And we didn't raise livestock. We were grain farmers. My Dad is gone now, so my brothers are responsible for all the work. I hope my mother will be okay. She still was in shock when I left on this crazy trip with you."

"Tell me about your Dad."

"He was a hard worker. Saskatchewan born and raised."

"Were you close?"

"Yeah. I was the youngest." He paused, feeling his emotions. Tears welled in his eyes. "I miss him."

"He's probably with you now, somehow," I said.

"Like a ghost?" he asked, twisting in the hammock.

"I believe in life after death. I think loved ones stay with you somehow, maybe in spirit form," I ventured.

"Well, I hope he's okay, enjoying himself." He chuckled at the thought. I was happy to see him smile.

The greenery around the bungalow shone with vibrant energy. The pulse of the scene filled my eyes with light as the sensation stimulated me. I could feel the space beaming.

"I feel something here, like I am radiating the same energy I see around me as if I were being enveloped."

"I can feel that its peaceful," he said.

"It feels like love somehow, like I can hear love in this place." I pondered more on the feeling, searching for words.

"Hmm. That sounds nice," he said.

"Can you hear it?" I asked.

"I can't hear anything, but I feel relaxed."

"At last I'm at a time in my life when I can search for something beyond myself that has meaning, that makes sense to me," I exhaled, stretching my legs.

"What about religion?" he asked.

"I was taught religion, my parents are Protestant. But I could never pay attention in church. The words didn't make sense to me. I tried to understand what they were saying, but I got the feeling they didn't even know. I made every excuse not to go, even babysitting the toddlers in the hallway while the sermon droned. But I feel something watches over me. I believe in God, although I haven't had much time to explore the meaning. Now, I have some time, so maybe I will understand more by being here."

"I hear you. I was taught religion too. Everyone in my small town goes to church. If you don't, you're an outcast. Its all about the Sunday social." Mark said, laughing.

"I believe something bigger than myself loves me and protects me. I want to believe that. It feels good to think that, its reassuring," I explained.

"Why do you feel that something cares to protect you?" he asked.

"I guess because I've always been taught that. But now I can explore faith in my own way. I want to know life from my experiences."

"What makes you think you can know through your experience?"

"How else would I know it? It's my experience of life. Surely, if there's something to know, I can know it. I'm here, living it."

"That's brave, Kid. Most people don't really consider their life. They just live it and don't think much about it," he laughed. "Like I do."

"This place is perfect for exploration because it is already beautiful. It feels easy to be here. It's the perfect setting to unfold ourselves and see what life can be!" I said, urging him to join me.

"Yeah, you're right about that. This place is beautiful," he said, looking around.

"I am feeling this amazing-ness within me. I want to know more." I felt myself opening, holding more exuberance. I stretched my arms upward.

"Did you study philosophy at University?"

"Yes. I took an introductory course in my third year. But I felt like I had to turn my brain on its side to understand what my professor was saying. It was the only course I dropped."

"What degree did you get?"

"A Bachelor's in Sociology, with a minor in Psych."

"Ah, right. I've read some philosophy books. It sounds like you are interested in philosophy," he said, reaching for his water bottle.

"I don't know what you want to call it, but I want to know more about what is possible. This is the perfect place to explore." I smiled.

"Let's go for a dip, Kid. Enough of this deep talk."

Mark peeled himself out of the hammock and we waded into the azure water. Soft sand rippled underfoot and squished between my toes. Puffs of it swirled beneath the surface and tiny sparkling minnows darted underneath.

"They are so cute! Tropical minnows."

"They're running from jaws," he joked.

"Sharks probably don't come in this close to shore," I swallowed.

"They're out there waiting for one of us to swim out." I looked at him and shook my head, laughing.

"Don't freak me out."

We sat down on the sandy bottom, peering into the clear water Tiny fish and bottom feeders scurried along in the current while pieces of seaweed floated above.

Mark leaned back on his elbow. I sat crossed legged, gently lolling in the current. The horizon looked just as peaceful. Everything was calm and serene.

All of a sudden Mark leapt into the air like lightning, landing on his feet. A giant piece of seaweed had floated onto his shoulder and he flung it into back into the water amidst my roar of laughter. I couldn't stop laughing.

"Funny," he said with a straight face, trying to regain his composure.

"Are you afraid of water creatures, Mark?"

"I'm from Saskatchewan. I've only swum in lakes," he answered, sitting back down, eyeing the approach of other seaweed pieces floating nearby.

"I had a thing about turtles when I was younger, toothy creatures moving toward me underwater," I said.

"Turtles?" he chuckled.

"Yeah. My brother and I used to camp during our summer holidays at my great aunt's place on a river. We caught lots of different turtles for inspection – painted turtles, mud turtles, even some snapping turtles - before returning them to the river. My brother told me stories of turtles biting off fingers and toes, conjuring my fear until I began to have nightmares about our camper rolling into the water, seeing them swimming through the windows. I would wake up in the middle of the night to the snoring of my elderly relatives, lying completely still from the fearful dream, staring into blackness until I fell asleep again sometimes hours later."

"Sounds eerie."

"It was," I laughed, reminiscing. "I never quite shook the fear."

"Its fairly unusual to be attacked by a turtle, isn't it? I've never heard of any turtle casualties." He tried to hold back his laughter.

"I know," I said, laughing too. "I just like to keep my eyes open."

As the moments drifted along, I considered the relationships with my family members during silent breaks of conversation. I remembered fun times we shared appreciating them more so as I gazed across the blue water, mesmerized by beauty. Subtle vibrations came through my eyes as I stared at the scene. It felt good, attuning me to observation as I sat appreciating the eloquent setting, and the details of the natural community. Something seemed to be in the moment with me, witnessing our enjoyment.

"Mark, do you feel like something is watching us?"

"Thieves in the bushes near our bungalows," he jested.

I laughed. "No, like we're not alone."

"Hmm." Mark gazed around us, trying to connect with my feeling. "I don't know what you mean by that."

"It's just so beautiful. How could we be here all by ourselves? Look at how beautiful this is."

"You're probably right. But I don't sense anything."

"Its just beautiful, so beautiful."

"Wow, Kid. You are really affected by this place."

"Yeah, I think it's the most beautiful place I have ever seen."

"Agreed. Can we go in now? I think my shoulders are burning."

We walked dripping into shore. I wrapped my purple sarong around me, smiling at fellow tourists on the beach. The amazing character of the place was starting to be revealed. We found ourselves in the midst of a bevy of seasoned travellers from across Europe and Australia, gauging from their accents.

We gathered our things and moved across the hot sand to settle comfortably on my porch. Popping the tops of our water bottles, we doused ourselves in cool clean water. We settled into our spots: Mark in the hammock and me on the bench.

"Do you have any desire to really know what's really happening, Mark?" I asked, feeling the space within me opening even wider.

"No. I just like to let things be. Too much thinking complicates it," he said, retracting from the offer.

"But what about your feelings?" I asked, as mine began to expand.

"My feelings are telling me it's time for another beer. Can I get you one?"

"Not now, but, I'd love a bottle of cold water, thanks." Sand fell from Mark's clothes as he padded off to the restaurant. My thoughts continued to launch out beyond my regular patterns of thinking, titillating me. I became excited at new possibilities of what my life could become.

"I'm exactly where I always wanted to be, Mark," I started, when he returned, handing me a bottle of chilled water. I was sitting upright on the bench.

"Tell me about it," he said, cracking his beer, then climbing back into the hammock with one hand.

"All my life what I've dreamed of is this exact setting, getting to a place just like this. And now I'm here." I said, exhaling gratefully.

"For your whole life?" he asked.

"Since the days of high school I wanted to escape to somewhere like this. I remember drawing palm trees on my notebooks, daydreaming about tropical paradise, an X on a treasure map. And now I'm here. Amazing. I live on this incredible beach, found by following the guidance of a total stranger. And now I'm having the time of my life. Of course, its even better that you're here." I smiled.

"Wow, this is big for you," he said, sipping. "Nice to know I'm appreciated." He looked into my eyes.

"I want to explore my mind now that I have the time and the right place to do it. Are you ready for it, Mark?"

"I'm ready, Kid. I may not always get what you're saying but I'l listen to you and your kooky ideas." He laughed. "I'm just joking."

"I know. It may sound strange to you, but this place is really opening me. I don't know what I'll find inside myself. It feels kind of daunting."

"I don't mean to make fun, Kid. I think you're awesome. You know that." He smiled, a blush sweeping over his face.

"Yeah, Mark. What would I do without you? I wouldn't be here without your help. We found this place together. And for that I will always be grateful."

"Aw," he said, smiling.

We adjusted in our seats and sat quietly for a while, enjoying the peace and quiet. The calm environment drew my attention to what wasn't calm inside me. Before I realized what was happening tears came to my eyes. I was reviewing old stories, old memories of hurtful moments, words said and actions done. My mother had challenged me so much in life and these memories began to emerge. I realized how I had internalized these painful images and the associated suffering. I exhaled, expanding, letting go of a wave of bottled up emotions.

"Are you okay, Kid?" Mark asked kindly.

"Yeah. Whoa. Just reliving a memory about my mom and the black feelings surrounding it. I let it go, washed it away. Holy." I used the corner of my sarong to dab my eyes, feeling relieved and happier. I laughed and looked at Mark.

"Incredible. I feel clearer now," I said.

"Its old stuff, bottled up inside. Maybe you should think of something else," he said.

"No, I think its good to let it go. It was intense dealing with it but now its gone. I don't feel the same. I feel relief."

"Hmm," he said. We were quiet for a while.

Then I felt him shuddering, his shoulders moving. Tears rolled down his face. I just looked at him.

"I miss my Dad sometimes," he said, sniffling.

"Its okay. You can cry in front of me. I did already," I laughed.

"Yeah. It just came up. Not such a tough guy."

"I think its good."

The silent thickness of the afternoon held us glued to the spot. A breeze blew gently ruffling leaves as the perfect setting enveloped us.

The depth of feeling seemed to resound across the sand as everyone remained quiet. A breeze blew in changing the tone and we shifted. I got up to visit the bathroom, not sure what was taking place. Our real feelings were revealing themselves, and I was curious to know why. It felt exhilarating.

When I returned to the porch I had a question for Mark.

"What did your parents teach you about life?"

He paused, thinking. "That life is hard. And you had to work hard to earn money," he seemed to retract as he said it, feeling guilty to be relaxing on a hammock, as though his father's words now rang in his ears.

"My parents told me to do what I wanted to do, whatever made me happy. It was assumed I would find a good job and make enough money to support myself, and find a husband who would take care of me." The words fell between us in the moment. I wondered if we would be with one another.

"My mother's words of advice always were, 'Only you can make yourself happy.'" I thought of my mother and the discord we had endured in our efforts to understand one another. My throat began to tighten, recalling the kind words. "And now I am happy, feeling more in harmony with myself and this dream I've had my whole life, my primary goal. Isn't it amazing, that it was to get here, to a place?" I wanted her approval, I wanted to be a good daughter. A feeling of guilt rose up in me as I considered whether I was doing the right thing, if she would approve of me doing absolutely nothing all day long. I exhaled, not wanting anything to shadow my bright feeling of bliss. I turned on my seat to face Mark.

"I never had a goal like that," he said. "We never thought that way in Saskatchewan. I was taught to make money to provide for a wife and family. Life on a farm is pretty much set up. It is a lifelong occupation. And now, I've left the work for my brothers."

"Do you feel guilty?"

"Yeah, I do. Some. But I had to get out. They understood." He was silent, emotion welling up inside him.

"Its okay, let it out. This is the place."

He laughed to hide it. "Yeah," he choked.

"This place is making me feel things I've never felt before. I'm exploring the inner me. Its like I can't help it! Its so quiet here that I can hear the voices inside, telling stories that I've forgotten. Its like their words are in my head, telling me what to do."

"We get programmed to act a certain way. No one cares how you really feel. They want you to produce and contribute to society. There are expectations to live up to. We get taught from kindergarten," he said.

"You are right! And my parents were taught by their parents. Think of all the things we have been told! No one ever said, Hey Kid, how do you feel? I can't remember anyone saying that to me!"

"They didn't. They didn't even think about it."

"Its crazy. Well, that's going to stop. I'm going to hear what's going on inside so I can release these old ideas, other people's ideas, and hear myself! Coming here has been the one goal in my whole life. I wanted to come to a place like this, and now I understand why. To hear myself think! I didn't even know that I couldn't! I didn't have to go and DO something to live a dream, I was supposed to FEEL something! Its amazing."

Mark was attempting to sit upright in the hammock when Damian approached, sauntering barefoot towards us. "Not so fast there, Mark. Be careful on the hammocks. People have been hurt falling out."

"Yeah, I'll be alright," Mark said, as he paused, considering the dismount more resolutely. "Now, may I have my beer?"

I handed him his beer and he sat down on the bench. "How often do you come here, Damian?" Mark asked.

"About once a year for the past 10 years."

"Hmm. Amazing."

"It's the same every time. Incredible beauty, peaceful vibe and tourists from all over passing through paradise. Some of them stay because they fall in love with this place."

"Who has been here the longest?" I asked.

"Debra, the woman in the bungalow next to Mark. She has been here for about six months. She was a nurse in England and came here for a short vacation but ended up staying. She gave up her job to be here. She lives on her savings right now, but it's going to run out. She'll have to go back sooner or later but not of her own choosing."

I had seen her blond shoulder length hair bobbing about. She appeared relaxed and peaceful. I was curious about someone making such a bold move. I wanted to speak with her.

"Is there work on the island?" I asked.

"No. There aren't really any places for a foreigner to work on this island. Industry is very small, so there's not enough demand for foreign labour."

"So people come here and their life really changes," I offered.

"This place is so different from where they're from. It is paradise to most people."

"Yeah," Mark echoed.

"I feel incredible here. My thoughts are changing so much. I'm having thoughts I've never had before."

"It happens here and some people stay to try to figure it out. They think they can define the experience. Its tough. Most just move on to another place." He reclined lazily on my porch, while I pondered his words.

Mark and I exchanged glances.

"I bet its possible to understand more here. Its so serene and beautiful. It feels like love."

"Yeah. Enjoy it. I don't know any other place on Earth like this."

As the hours passed on, we enjoyed watching the sun moving slowly across the sky. The colours came and slid down over the horizon, a symphony of delight.

The sky dimmed and soon it was pitch black. I lit candles on the window sill as Mark went to get beers for Damian and himself. I sat on the porch in the calm evening breeze, smelling the warm salty air. Mark returned with the beer. Then something large swooped past the roof. Mark jumped back.

"What was that?" he blurted.

"I think it's a bat!" I said.

Mark and I moved away from the candle light to see dark forms flapping over our heads. We watched as bats of various sizes used the roof as a flight path, zooming around through the palm trees. They flew low causing Mark to bend over and run back to my porch.

"Are those things poisonous?" Mark asked Damian.

"No, but watch out for the smaller ones. Some of them are vampire bats."

"The bigger ones look more daunting," he said.

"The big ones are harmless," Damian said, as Mark and I raised our eyebrows at each other.

"All the creatures here are amazing. Cassandra, did you find the two geckos living behind your bathroom mirror?" Damian smiled to me.

"Are you serious?"

"They're big. You don't want to try to catch one."

Mark and I went to my bathroom and turned on the light. Peering behind the mirror mounted on the cement wall, I saw a large green speckled gecko. It stared back. Mark and I returned to the porch.

"They're waiting for spiders or anything they can catch," Damian said.

"I saw a big spider yesterday. I think I got a bite on my foot," I said, scratching.

"There's a wasp nest in my roof," Mark confessed, laughing.

"What?" I asked.

"Yeah. I've heard buzzing and seen them flying around. I think there's a nest in the roof."

"Oh, Mark. Do you want to move to another bungalow?" I consoled.

"No, they haven't bothered me. Hey, get this," he said laughing, his shoulders shrugging. "I woke up last night with a cockroach crawling on my face. At least, I think that's what it was. I hurled it at the wall and heard a crack, but this morning there was nothing there."

"Oh!" Damian and I exclaimed and burst out laughing. "It's probably better to have that then something else."

"Yeah," I said, trying to hold back my laughter.

"The creatures here are territorial, but they live harmoniously with the humans for the most part. Try to preserve that. Debra had a green snake hanging from her rafters a couple of days ago. We just moved it outside with a stick. Just be happy you don't have snakes. Geckos are a great thing to have because they eat spiders and other insects and keep other predators away. They are harmless to humans unless you try to corner them. Then they can give you a nasty bite," he said, padding off to bed. "Goodnight, sleep well."

"Goodnight," we echoed.

"I'm going to bed too, Mark," I said.

"I'll be up for a while," he replied, perhaps spooked by the stories. "I'll be watching the bats."

"Okay," I said. "And don't let the cockroaches bite. If they do, bite them back."

I went inside and closed all the windows, trying to push fretful thoughts out of my head. I washed my face and turned in.

I lay awake, just as I had done the night before, listening to strange sounds. What was I really afraid of?

The next morning I showered and tidied my room, then swept the front porch and steps. I had seen Debra sweeping at her bungalow and I liked her style of housekeeping. It was only sand I was clearing, but I enjoyed making the bungalow feel like home.

Mark was waiting for me in his hammock and I smiled over at him. He grinned widely. We flip-flopped over the sand to the restaurant for breakfast and sat at our secluded table. His giggles told me he was high, and when he removed his sunglasses, I laughed at his glassy eyes.

"Dang showed up at my door at 7 a.m. with a packed bong," he said.

I burst out laughing. Mark could hardly contain his laughter. "The guy's got a three foot high bong he straps to his back. Hilarious! I was so stoned all morning, all I could do was just sit in my hammock and stare at the sea. It was unbelievable."

I laughed, feeling glad that Dang wasn't knocking on my door at 7 a.m.

A breeze caressed us, rustling palm leaves as we awaited our food. The breeze blew gently through the restaurant as soft music played on the overhead speakers. The whole place was serene and felt like a different reality than I had ever known. It was hard to imagine the rest of the world going on as usual with a place like this existing in absolute peacefulness and ultimate beauty.

After finishing our meal, we walked back to my bungalow across the cool velvety sand shaded by the palm leaves. We sat on the porch.

"My old life has just faded away because there is nothing here to connect or refer to it," I said.

"I know what you mean," Mark replied.

"I'm not having the same thoughts I had before. The old thoughts and worries have disappeared." I wasn't sure where I was headed in my thoughts.

"Me too. I'm thinking about things I never thought before," he replied. We sat in silence.

"It's like my mind is opening up to a new part of myself, or I'm creating a new part. Something is changing and I feel peaceful." I stretched my arms up and out, as we relaxed in the shade.

"Mark, do you think that life is knowable?"

"Knowable? Sure. We know we're living."

"There are many people like Damian who think life is unknowable. They go along, they don't ask questions and just take what comes."

"Life is a grind. That's just the way it is," Mark replied, glumly.

"People are suffering because they don't know what else to do with their lives. They live the same routine, but they aren't happy. Something has to change. We deserve more," I said, convinced there was a better way.

"I don't know what to say, Kid. Life may always be this way."

"The characteristics of life must be identifiable. There must be something we can learn about living it better. You know, if I can change one person's life by showing them a viewpoint into this incredible beauty, then this whole trip is worth it for me." My feelings poured open.

"That's very generous of you."

"People deserve to know what is waiting for them and what is possible." Emotion moved up my throat and into my eyes as tears rolled down my face.

"Wow, you're having an experience. And it's riveting to watch, Kid. You've really got something going on over there."

"I don't know what it is, Mark. I just feel alive and invigorated. I feel like there is something more I can understand, something valuable that I can find out if I just keep looking."

Around me, the warm and comforting beach with its gentle water and perfect sky enveloped me in beauty. "If something so breathtakingly beautiful as these trees and this sea and this life are sharing the space with us, then obviously we are missing something in our unenlightened perspective because this experience is incredible."

"Sure it's amazing, more beautiful than anything I've ever seen. It's nice to be sharing this with you, Kid," Mark said.

"Thanks. I feel the same way. I'm so glad we travelled here together," I said, smiling to him.

"It sure beats the IP!" he joked.

I inhaled deeply. "This place makes me feel more energized, and I want to experience more of it. I want to share myself with life. It's sharing its beauty with us, Mark."

"I know, Kid."

"Everything around us is not just a backdrop for our experience, but a living, breathing organism. Earth is alive!" I exclaimed.

"It sure is," he beamed.

"I want my life to be different now. I'm ready to know life. I want this feeling of bliss in my life everyday, Mark. I'm ready."

"Okay, Kid. Just don't go too far. I need to get you home in one piece."

"Life can be amazing. If this feeling exists here, it can exist anywhere," I said.

"But life will always be the same. Even our parents had to deal with these issues, you know. They are longstanding. Society has been dealing with the same problems for centuries: hardship, homelessness, war, poverty, hunger. Life will always have its trials."

"I want to see beyond that negative acceptance perspective. If I reach upward higher than before, surely there will something incredible that will transcend this idea of obstacles. Surely, there is something bigger."

"Good luck with that, Kid. I hope you can find something better. I really do."

Damian walked over the sand to Debra's cabin and went inside. Within moments, the door closed.

Mark and I were curious about the other guests staying in the bungalows but most people were only seen passing by because the row of bungalows in front of us obscured the view. Often, the residents were inside resting or taking a break from the heat. The afternoon was serene as our gaze meandered over the empty beach. As our bungalows backed onto the edge of the property, we could see the back walls of four other bungalows and partially onto one deck where we could hear some activity. A woman with a flowing skirt was on the porch talking with a man. He had a British accent while hers was Russian. As they spoke, she set up an easel on the porch then sat down to paint. They had been quiet until now, surprising us with their presence.

Hours of introspection came to a close with hunger pangs, and I skipped over the sand barefoot to the restaurant as Mark strode beside me in sandals. When we entered the restaurant, we caught a gentle breeze from the field of palm trees on the other side of the building. English tourists lounged on the large raised platform at the side of the restaurant, off the floor by a few feet, where soft cushions and pillows lined the wall. Leaning back with a cigarette or beer against the cushions, they smiled courteously as we walked in. Playing backgammon and drinking beer, their bellowing laughter rang out in the room, and we smiled over. Mark chose a quiet corner table at the edge of the restaurant jutting over the sand in the shade of palm leaves. We opened our menus.

"I think we have found our perfect table," I said.

"This is it," he echoed.

We ordered coconut shakes then watched the scene of the other guests. A few more barefoot Europeans shuffled about ordering fruit shakes from the counter, exhibiting tanned torsos and a few tattoos. Reggae played over the speakers, enlivening the vibe. We were in a hot spot.

A while later Dang came to our table with two beautiful blended white coconut shakes in clear mugs. He put down the mugs and straws, then took our meal order. Thirty minutes later, he returned with our food. It wasn't what we ordered, but he was smiling so we smiled and thanked him. Finishing up our meals, we said goodbye to the other visitors.

"Come join us next time," a boisterous Englishman called after us. I smiled and waved back.

"Sure thing," Mark replied. I wanted to connect with nature so much that socializing took a backseat. I wanted to know paradise, and

Mark echoed agreement as we hopped up on my porch. Mark attempted to mount the hammock with such seriousness that I laughed out loud.

I went inside to open the windows and turn on music. I popped the speakers on the window frame, put on Bjork, and returned to the porch to see Mark reclined comfortably in the hammock.

"You need to try this," he said.

"I will. The view is good from here, too. I like this space." My spot on the bench at the side of my porch, next to the calm sea, was perfect for me. Sitting comfortably on my sarong, I leaned back against the wall of my bungalow catching the gentle sea breeze. By mid afternoon as the heat permeated the shade we began to feel hot.

"Let's swim, Markus."

"Whatever you say, Kid."

Frolicking in the shallow water, sitting on the sandy bottom, I could feel the rising intensity of joyful emotions. I inhaled deeply to feel them as if they were swirling all around me.

"The sun shines down on us from above everyday without fail. And those hills, they're covered with lush, vibrant trees and bushes living in peace and harmony with all of the creatures. And we can see them! Look at them Mark. Look! And the sand, feel how soft it is and the breeze as it tickles us. This is life Mark, this is love!"

I felt energized, feeling lights turning on all over the place within my consciousness. Basking in the warmth of the water, vibrant sun and blue sky shining brilliantly, the glowing vista drew me into expanding appreciation as the pulsating scene enlivened me. I gazed into the jungle feeling my focus deepen. I felt something very close to me, inside me, open up. From this place, I began to speak.

"Be who you are and don't think of anything else." I inhaled deeply and continued, "Love is all around you and inside you." Something changed. "Love yourself; life is in you." My feelings expanded. "The beauty that is outside of you, is inside of you."

I was riveted to the spot, my eyes wide with focus. Gentle, positive energy poured through me. I felt incredible. What was happening?

"Be what you want, do what feels right for you. Listen to yourself and release your fears."

Words poured from a font within me that continued to flow. I spoke words I had never spoken before.

"Pay attention to your wishes and dreams; they will guide you." I stared into beauty and felt love. "There is wisdom in your desires." Something brilliant and powerful within myself opened up as new answers began to emerge from me. Every question that ran through my mind was answered in my words. My body was erect and light as I sat upright, attuned to a higher frequency than I had ever known. My mind opened, my eyes widened, while just stared at me.

"Kid, what's happening to you? Where did you get those answers?"

"They're inside of me," I replied, stunned at my own revelation. Something had changed with me, something deep within had shifted. I talked on with myself, opening within, my observation yielding powerful results. Mark witnessed the transformation and couldn't believe what was happening.

"Kid, are you okay?"

"I feel incredible. It's new and amazing. Its so good." My breath was high in my chest as I reached through the water to the sand, wanting to feel solid ground.

"Let's go in," he said, helping me up.

"I'm fine. I feel good." I was lucid, delighted and elated, but stunned at the same time. I walked with him to the shore as the words continued.

"Look deep inside to your love and let it out through you and into a glorious feeling always in your life."

Mark turned to me and said, "Hey Kid, you gotta write this down. This stuff is brilliant!"

Inside my bungalow, I moved slowly, changing into dry clothes in awe of my inner transformation. What was happening with me? I sat on my bed half laughing, half crying because there was so much I was beginning to see and feel, more than I had ever experienced before.

Mark came over and sat beside me on the bed.

"Are you okay? What happened?"

"It feels like something is listening to me and answering my questions." We sat silently, trying to process this wave of information.

"What gave you answers? God?"

"I don't know! But I feel amazing. Whatever it is, it loves me, and I can feel it."

The messages of wisdom continued within my thoughts, as I moved about, just watching myself in space. Mark went back to his hammock while I stayed inside, writing in my journal and trying to comprehend what was happening. I felt like I had opened a door within me that would never again be shut. I listened intently to this source of information that seemed obscure, yet present. Where was it coming from?

I moved onto the porch and felt openness within, the awareness of depth inside me. As I continued to ask questions within my thoughts, the answers came, responding to me in a private way within my thoughts. The concepts were so complete and so personal that tears poured down my face. I felt relief that something cared so much about me to listen and respond to my yearning to know. Something could answer me back.

This awareness was life changing, and I sat for hours in communication with this new source. I laughed and cried as I journeyed inside myself, and whenever I wanted to know something, I posed a question in my mind and waited for the answer. Information rolled through me, convulsing me with laughter as I listened to this new internal voice. It was so close to me, within me, and I had never known it was possible. Enchanted by my transformation, I guarded my personal time and spent hours on my bed writing about the revelations coming through me. Mark checked on me and sat with ears open, giggling with me at my profound shift, trying to comprehend my experience.

"Kid, do you think you are losing your mind?"

"Part of it, yes! The old part that didn't know much about life! This is amazing. I feel incredible!"

"How is this happening, Mark? Is there something gigantic, watching me, listening to me and helping me?" I stared at him wide eyed, wondering if he could believe it. "Do you know what this means? It means we have help! From something invisible and huge and beautiful! Its life-changing!"

"I don't know what to say, Kid. This is deep." He smiled uncertainly.

"Are you feeling any of this? Is it just me?"

"It's just you," he said, a flash of worry over his face.

"This is amazing. It's a miracle!" I exploded.

Damian walked over to us.

"What's all the hubbub?" he asked.

"Cass is tripping out," said Mark. "I'm just kidding. It sounds like she's having an experience of awakening."

"Something brilliant is talking to me, through me," I said.

"Whoa," he responded, eyeing me then Mark.

"Information is coming through me, to me, in my own mind, like I've tapped into something huge and magnificent. Its unreal!"

"Tapped into what?" Damian asked.

"I don't know what to call it." I answered.

"I've witnessed the whole thing and it's pretty amazing," Mark said. Damian looked from Mark to me, incredulously.

"She's speaking very wise words, like those of a sage on a mountain. I've never heard her talk like this before."

"Just don't fall off the deep end," said Damian. He retreated, cautiously.

The voice within receded, calmly, safely. I went inside to my journal again while Mark went to his hammock. I began to write about the miracles unfolding in my life, changing the way I experienced reality – forever. As I considered my thoughts, I received responses as if something helped me consider them. I began to look more clearly at what was going through my mind.

I realized that most of what I thought were patterns and memories of past experiences. Habits of thinking and answering. Why not choose something larger, a bigger perspective? I could see thoughts dimming some windows of my mind like spots on a kaleidoscope. I could see that most of the ideas I held previously were taught to me, from my parents, school, friends and from life. I found myself repeating the words of others in my mind, just out of habit, and stopping there. Now I was seeing, thinking new things, I could take my mind past these places of limitation. As I opened and explored my thinking, brilliant revelations continued to pour through me. Sometimes tears were released because of the heaviness of the content. I breathed, shifting my position on the bed as I sifted through my thoughts and beliefs, seeing my own uniqueness emerge from within them.

I saw that my thoughts were my beliefs, practiced thinking that led to practiced outcome, limiting my experience of life. So I began to consider the value and usefulness of each belief I uncovered. I began to objectively examine the thoughts I was thinking, seeing them rise up in me for inspection.

This process was gentle and gracious, and made me feel powerful. Seeing many incomplete thoughts, I carried on with the exploration of each one that came up until a crystallized conclusion appeared in my mind. The unfinished business of my thought processes had been a result of my busy lifestyle, and not seeing the importance of understanding the way my mind was working. I declared to myself that there must be a better way to think, and charged with this new energy, I was going to find it.

Chapter 2 – Phosphorescent Blue

I floated, feeling surreal now even more self absorbed, listening only to my inner voice. I followed the feeling as much as I could, trusting more and more the nudges that provided insight. Mark's voice faded into the background at times as I evaluated the truth that we spoke. Postulating the essence of our existence tired him at times.

"Talking to you is like answering a multiple choice question," he finally confessed.

I laughed, and tried to simplify my wording. I wanted to understand all that I could.

"This is our chance Mark! It can be different from here, life can be different."

Taking turns between the shallow water, the sandy beach and the porch of my bungalow, we explored our minds together. I focussed on my pursuit of understanding, asking for guidance along the way.

Insight and information flooded my awareness as I recognized wisdom in the expressions of life. Like opening a birthday package, I peeled back the layers and beneath the wrapping paper I could see more and more depth, beauty and perfection. It was all I ever wanted. I wanted to understand what was around me, as well as who was talking to me through my mind. And most importantly, What was it trying to tell me?

I lost track of calendar days as Mark and I expanded our awareness, deep within the treasured moments of feeling at one with our natural surroundings. Sitting quietly in our familiar positions in my bungalow, we moved through our feelings and reflections, sharing our emotions of times past. Sorting through our feelings, we found they needed release. I moved into parts of myself that felt stuck in a moment, and began to wipe away the dust within like an archaeologist mining for treasure. Often finding a new realization, we shared our new understanding, laughing and supporting one another in our own personal journeys. This search of the self caused tears to fall at times, their release palpable, and then an exhale to let it go. "This is amazing, Kid. I'm releasing pent up emotion; I can feel myself letting go. It feels great and now I feel lighter."

I smiled. "Me too. Its amazing," I replied.

"Since my father died, I didn't realize I was carrying all that emotion, until I started sitting here with you staring at the sea everyday. I'm facing those feelings, moving through them, and letting them go."

"That's so good, Mark. I'm doing the same thing. My painful memories are from years ago, living at home arguing with my mother. The heated exchanges took a toll on me, I can see now, and made me retreat within myself. I wasn't living my true potential, just replaying these hurtful happenings in my mind, keeping me trapped inside myself." I exhaled. "So much I made of our arguments, and now all that energy is finding its way to the surface. Its exhilarating. Imagine if everyone could do this, how much more peaceful the world would be."

"Its true, Kid."

"And every time you let go of something, I feel a shift too and I release something in me. Its so cool."

"You have to write this down, Kid. Keep at it. Get it down in words." I wrote more and more in my journal, putting into words what we shared as we became more in tune with our surroundings. The peacefulness of the place drew us in, carefully holding us while we explored ourselves. Something within my experience wanted me to know more, wanted me to succeed, and encouraged me to continue looking more deeply.

As my understanding grew, I began to spend more time alone, recording ideas. Mark spent more time alone in his hammock, and always smiled from behind his sunglasses when I looked over or waved.

I basked in the vibrant beauty around me, filling with appreciation as I strived for a deeper understanding of life. This new awakening tested my will and strength to believe, to follow the instruction of the words in my head, release my doubt about what was happening and to trust in what I was beginning to know. I was opening into something loving, but still did not know what. Yet, I knew I wanted to follow wherever it would lead me because it felt so good.

When the sun neared the horizon, Mark rose from his hammock to join me on my porch. "I feel more relaxed now than I ever have before. Letting go of that emotional stuff helped. It's amazing. Laying in the hammock, staring at a perfect sea for hours every day, I'm taking time to consider my life. It's overwhelming at times because it's so real. Whatever we are doing, we are onto something good, Kid."

I nodded and smiled.

Melding into the view, we relaxed and enjoyed the sounds of nature. I focused on it until I heard the buzz of insects humming in unison. "Listen to the music!" Riveted to the natural symphony, we burst out laughing at exactly the same moment, as if there had been an ending point in the piece.

"What musicians, the crickets! Delightful!"

"Until one's in your bed," Mark teased.

"Thanks, Mark."

I listened intently for hours until my hearing became tired from my intense focus. A cool breeze blew over my shoulders, sending me to bed.

"Mark, I'm toast. Going to bed."

"Okay, goodnight," he said, pulling himself upright out of my hammock.

As I closed the door to my porch, ending one of the most amazing days in my life, tears came to my eyes. I had tapped into something bigger than me, and it was helping me. I knew it. I settled happily into my bed, trusting I would be safe and turned out the light. Then, I fell fast asleep.

The next day, I woke up and pushed open the windows. "What do you have for me today, wonderful world?" Just then, a beautiful bird flew to the tree in my view. It sang a song, tilted its head at me, then flew away. I sat back on my bed in awe.

When I met Mark for breakfast at the restaurant, we spoke in lowered voices as more eyes were on us. Word travelled fast in such a small place and soon someone was standing at our table.

"Having a good time, are we?" a blonde man with a bare chest and brush cut said in an English accent, smiling at us.

"Yes, we are." I gazed into his eyes, wanting to share my feeling with him.

"I'm William and our gang is usually up there in the afternoons," he said, motioning to the backgammon platform and a table of regal postures. "Come round and see us sometime."

He nodded and went back to his table, his tanned legs showing beneath fitted shorts.

"I would love to chat with everyone, but I'm so fascinated about this feeling now that I don't want to stop exploring it for anything."

"We'll see them again," Mark said, and we finished breakfast in the dappling sunlight.

"That was perfect."

"Seems to be the order of the day."

"I'm going to pay my bill so I'll see you back at the bungalows."

"Sure, Kid," Mark said, heading over the sand. I walked to the counter. In a few minutes someone arrived, checked a penciled account of my total then asked for the payment. I smiled back at the ease of the transaction then paid in full. The next moments seemed surreal as I bent down to put on my sandals at the base of the steps. Someone stood nearby, then took my arm to lead me out of earshot of the others. A woman in decorative clothing spoke quietly as I gazed downward to the sand as she spoke.

"Things are being said about you. There is a wave of love coming to change our world. Only those directly involved can hear the call. You are one of them. You'll be led to where you need to go, follow your heart. Trust in the feeling. Stay strong." Her hand dropped from my arm and she moved away, letting the worlds roll over me, bringing me face to face with the truth of the moment. She turned and walked away, leaving me speechless. Soon, the exchange faded from my awareness as I returned to appreciation of the nature I was calling home.

Later, Mark and I sat together on my porch playing a game of chess, talking about relationships that had made an impression on us.

"What is it with women? They love you one minute, then before you know it, they're off with the next guy," he complained.

"Maybe they're not the right woman, that's all." I replied, imagining being on the other side of this story.

"Well, why all the pretending and false affection, then 'poof' they're off to the next guy they have pretend to like you, then go to the next guy."

"I don't know if that's always the case, but maybe they aren't sure what they are looking for in a guy. Tell me some juicy stories."

"Ah, you want one from the archives?"

"Yeah, tell me about the ways that women behave."

"Okay, let's go inside. I've got a few ear benders." We went inside and reclined in our favourite positions.

"I met this girl at a bar," he started.

"Okay, here we go," I laughed.

"I dated her a few times, but she was wild. I never knew what to expect. One night, we were on the floor in front of the fireplace. I had my shirt off, and you've seen me, I have hair on my chest."

"Yes," I said, waiting for more.

"Well, everything was really hot and I was liking it, then she picked up a candle from the mantle and poured hot wax on my chest!"

"Oh my God! What did you do?"

"I kept going, I couldn't stop there. But it burned. It left red marks. I saw her a few more times after that but it ended."

"No kidding!" I laughed.

Mark chuckled.

"That's a wild one. She doesn't sound like a typical girl. Obviously she wasn't your type."

"Yeah, well, what is my type? I just want someone I can get along with, someone I can be close to. No S&M please," he stated.

"Maybe she was trying you out to see if you fit her lifestyle," I offered.

"So, they're testing me out, seeing if I'm good enough?" he asked.

"Well, yeah. It makes sense. Guys do the same."

"No, they don't. A guy will go for a girl he truly likes."

"That's true." I admitted.

"Another girl I liked ended up dumping me for my friend," he winced.

"Ouch," I replied, seeing that his pain was palpable. I was humbled at hearing how the female gender had affected him.

"Women are different creatures than men," I defended.

"But we want the same things in life: intimate companionship and perhaps a family."

We heard two voices from the people at the bungalow with the easel. Then, the man left with a backpack, and she went back to her easel.

"I'm getting hot, Kid. Let's go for a swim."

"Okay. Meet you on the beach in five."

I changed into my red bikini and wrapped a sarong around my waist. Then, I put on my sandals to walk to the beach. Sitting upon it and waiting for Mark, I eyed a couple down at the end of the beach. They were entwined in each other's embrace, watching the horizon, as they kissed and caressed.

Mark sat down beside me and caught sight of my focal point.

He laughed, eyeing me. I looked down to the sand and poured some through my fingers. The moment became thicker as silence hung in the air. I got up to dust off my bottoms and invited Mark to join me in the water.

We strode out leisurely, the water at our calves.

"Let's sit," I suggested and found a soft spot in the sand. Mark sank down to his bottom, then dropped it into the sea. The sand flushed into waves around him. The gentle ebb and flow of the waves lulled me into relaxation. The tan on my body was developing well and I enjoyed looking at my body through the shimmering water. We enjoyed the glow upon us.

"You look very fine," he grinned.

I smiled back. We watched the vibrant colours surrounding us, observing the light as the sun beamed high in the sky. As my skin began to turn pink, I sat up.

"When do you want to explore the town?"

"Let's go to town tomorrow. Or the next day," I said, leisurely.

"We've got to check this place out."

"Sure," I said, not wanting to go anywhere.

Playing with the sand under the water, I tried to build a hill, but the waves kept moving the sand. We sat for a long time without saying anything. The beauty absorbed our attention.

"What's happening with the wisdom transmissions?"

"It comes and it goes. But if I have a question, I just ask inside. I get the answers. I think I need to be feeling really great for it to pour out of me."

"I like hearing it, so when you're ready I'm all ears."

When we returned to the shore, we sat on my porch. Reclining, we watched as a plump Thai woman walked around collecting coconuts lying on the sand. Gracefully squatting to scoop the grey coconuts into her apron, she moved with comfort and ease, as if she were walking through her garden. She embodied contentment, bonded with her surroundings in a supportive, committed relationship. Here I was - just coming alive to the point of view she had been living her whole life.

When she finished, she wanted more coconuts so she called to someone at the back of the restaurant. A lean Thai man appeared, youthful and grinning, and scampered up the tree trunk with great dexterity. We watched in awe as he levelled several green coconuts. "Sweeter and softer meat inside," he explained to us. As they banged on the ground randomly, she kept us at safe distance.

"Enough?" he asked, and when she said yes, he smiled and shimmied down to our amazed expressions. They laughed, collected the coconuts and walked back to the restaurant.

We watched from the bungalow while the resident multi-coloured dogs frolicked on the beach, a pack of about eight. A new one arrived, a puppy, and we watched as the dogs playfully challenged it, rolling it over in the sand. The puppy sprang to his feet, again and again. A strong youthful Thai woman came to the beach scolding the older dogs for rough play.

Revellers lay in the sand and in hammocks, basking in the warm sunlight, easing us into the evening. The breathtaking beauty engulfed us all as the beaming sun began its colourful descent, a glowing orange ball in the centre of the horizon, taking all of us with it. A breeze blew gently and I wrapped my purple sarong around my waist, taking ballet steps across the porch, dancing to the beat of the music. Mark sat pensively, his eyes fixated on the chessboard on the bench, as the candlelight flickered. Warm breezes surrounded me with luscious scents of an exotic paradise.

As the sky darkened, I heard the shift in sounds of the creatures of the night, a different symphony but equally as beautiful. Mark made his move, inviting me to respond but something glowing on the shore caught my eye.

"Hey, Mark. What is that light?" Mark looked up from the board to gaze at the glow. We moved over the sand to the shore, where tiny pebbles rolled back and forth in the bubbling waves, shimmering blue light beneath the water. I scooped up a handful of small pebbles but there was no light. Placing them back in the water, we watched as the waves moved back and forth, delighting us with phosphorescence.

"I have never seen this before. This is amazing."

"I haven't either," Mark said.

"Phosphorescence," said a passerby, his face escaping the candlelight.

Returning to our spots at the bungalow, Mark said, "Life sure is showing us a good time, Kid."

"It keeps getting better." I responded.

"Where do we go from here?" he asked. "This is the best place I've ever been." We laughed.

"Me, too."

Mark's eyes twinkled at me, and his shy smile poked through his moustache.

The next day, the blue light on the shore was gone! The warm sun and gentle breeze greeted me as Mark and I walked over the sand to the restaurant.

Soon, a server arrived at our table.

"Hello," she said, smiling at us. "What can I get you?" she asked, her eyes taking us in.

"I will have coffee, a banana pancake and a coconut shake, please."

"Make that two," Mark echoed.

"Good choice," she said and sauntered like the waves back into the kitchen. We shared breakfast in peace and calm. The stillness around me was inside me. We delighted in our breakfast, drizzled with honey and topped with icing sugar.

"This place is like a cocoon," he said. "I'm transforming."

"It's a love cocoon. This is all love."

"There is a lot to see on this island. We should make a plan to visit some sights," he said.

"Maybe later."

"Let's just do what we feel, and when the mood moves us, we'll go."

We moseyed back toward our bungalows. Mark climbed up into his hammock and I went inside my bungalow, opening windows and turned on some music.

Once I relaxed on my bed, I began by deep breathing connecting with my body, until it began to suggest movement. Opening my chest cavity and lifting my spine, I felt the release of some energy that had gathered there. Feeling more lucid, I worked through more kinks, eliminating knots from my muscles. I naturally began to move and stretch my body, appreciating the way it moved. Beautiful and supple skin, golden bronze and red in places, it looked healthy and youthful.

Tracy Chapman played Revolution Song, as I pondered the meaning of her words. Notebook and pen in hand, I reflected on the life I lived that was changing, but into what?

A million bugs shared the bungalow with me. I discovered one after another in my bathroom, where it was wet and damp and connected to the outside. So, I told myself they all wanted to be in there and not in my bed. I confronted a fear of mine by staying in that bungalow, and falling asleep without worrying was getting easier as I became more familiar with my space.

There were small spiders and big spiders inside and outside, ones that I'd never seen before, and the last place I wanted them was on me. I decided to live in harmony with them because it was their home, too. I wanted to appreciate the differences between myself and the tiny creatures. I did get a few bites on my ankles and feet that itched for a while, but I tried not to let it bother me.

Within my feelings were answers to my questions, because the more I looked at something, the clearer it became. And if I wasn't afraid of the feeling, the crying or upset, I could go through it to the other side and watch it disappear.

My introspection turned to my home life when growing up had not been so easy. I found the pain of quarrels with my mother inside me as memories and tears poured down my cheeks. On one occasion, she forbade me to see a certain person with whom I was discovering the best form of friendship. I liked a boy of whom she did not approve. After meeting him, she promptly grounded me from spending lunch hour at school. In this and other ways, processes were halted by her command and I was forced to abide, so this I later resented. But now I cried as I released the blame from her interference. I lifted and lightened. The pain was leaving me.

Wiping away tears, I brightened with the shifting of my body and exhaled, refocusing on the beautiful beach through my window. What were the birds chirping? What were the waves waving? I was so grateful to have found such a place, where I could toss away the old and make way for the new. I moved off the bed to check on Mark, reclined in his hammock with a steady grin on his face.

"Time for lunch?"

"Sure thing," he replied. On our private patio that was always available, we ordered pad thai noodles with spicy coconut tom yum soup, and coconut shakes. As we paid at the counter, a Thai boy buzzed up on a scooter. He offered everyone sticky coconut rice packed in bamboo, which we purchased on the advice of our server.

As I looked into her eyes, I saw depth of vision beyond what I understood. The Thai people, having lived on the island for perhaps thousands of years, echoed depth in their gaze. The Thai boy hopped onto his scooter and made his way back along the path through the coconut grove, buzzing along to the next resort.

As the light of the day shifted, my mood changed with it, as if called to certain action. It was a hot day, so hot that people stayed in their bungalows for hours with the fan blowing. We heard hysterical laughter that went on and on. We knew that others were having a good time too, as their laughter rippled out along the beach. We were all enjoying the space and freedom.

Many of the tourists were on extended vacations, travelling throughout the region on six or eight month breaks. Our moments together were precious, as we shared the best of our stories with one another, learning about the region and the experiences that delighted or astounded us. We talked about journeys to Vietnam, Cambodia, Laos, Malaysia, Indonesia, Singapore and Australia. Where I would go from here?

Without any clocks or time pieces except the one at the restaurant, we lived in concordance with the natural cycle. I rose at nine a.m. with the heat of the sun, and settled down for six at sundown. I ate when I felt hunger, and drank when thirsty. This unique freedom from a schedule was my everyday life, and it was more freedom than I had ever known.

In the heat of the day, Mark said, "Let's go for a walk. Its cooler in the jungle under the trees." We walked along the path into the palm grove we came through when we arrived. I saw the family's rooms behind the restaurant with cloth doors tied back. Inside, I saw soft beds and colourful blankets neatly arranged. The swirl of incense moved out from a room with a pair of tanned legs splayed comfortably on a colourful grass mat. A large pile of coconuts lay at the back of the restaurant, one pile of bulbous grey ones and another of green ones. A massive machete lay against the wall beside a chair and a tall homemade tool with a sharp hook at the top stood leaning on the thatched house. Just then we heard a howling sound through the trees.

"Is that a monkey?"

"Orangutan," he joked. "We're in the jungle, now."

"Welcome to the jungle, are you sure you want to stay? Welcome to the jungle, you can't run away."

"It's true. I can't run away. How many weeks are we going to spend here?"

"I can't even imagine leaving right now. I'm opening a whole new part of myself. I don't know how long I'll be here," I smiled, feeling joyful at my admission.

I could feel Mark thinking about his next destination, but my experience was too deep to even think of moving. We strolled leisurely through trees that grew close to one another, a path weaving through leading off into the distance. We stepped off the trail and entered into the untamed garden. The ground was littered with grey, crispy leaves and branches in between shrubs.

"I think it needs some pruning," I noticed.

"They don't have gardening here. That's a Western concept. This is raw jungle," he reminded me.

"I guess so. This is true nature - Breathtaking."

"The snakes must love to wend through this jungle. It's covered in leaves," he said, as he inspected the forest floor.

"Let's not talk about snakes," I requested.

I rubbed my hand along the smooth trunk of an arching palm and looked up to a nettle of grey coconuts, big green leaves and blue sky beyond. I inhaled a complex medley of scents mixed with a hint of salty seaweed.

"Imagine discovering this place after being ship wrecked, crawling onto this island full of coconuts and fresh fruit with freedom everyday, beauty and serenity everywhere. Living on this island could transform your life," I speculated.

"It would transform it immediately when you came face to face with the natives and their machetes," he laughed.

"Yeah, right. But let's imagine they were friendly and we never had to go back to civilization, we just ended up here for the rest of our lives. Imagine what that would be like? I keep thinking of that."

"Maybe we were here before, Kid, in another time."

"It's possible. The image keeps returning, as if I have done this before. Maybe we did end up here, or somewhere like this, and now we've returned for a little more of paradise."

"That would be cool, Kid."

"Mark, I love this place." I said, gazing around me, spellbound. "All this time in my life, I have never seen nature like this, but here it was all along."

"Shimmy up that tree and get us a coconut, Kid."

"No. You do it."

"Come on. You know this is where they grow mushrooms out of elephant dung."

I looked around to imagine elephants walking through this jungle. "I guess they could fit through the trees in some places," I said.

"Damian said people have elephants as pets here."

"They have cobras as pets, too," I said, cringing.

"Let's get out of here and go have a beer," Mark suggested.

"Back to the beach," I directed.

As I sat on my porch and gazed out to the sea, I realized this place enriched my being. I could feel clarity in lasting moments, like the steady calmness of the sea. This resounding tranquility was new for me; its intensity more than I could ever remember feeling. More bubbles of memory rose up within me, as I uncovered things inside myself. I wanted to live in harmony with my surroundings, and I liked the feeling of serenity. I wanted to live in peace. This was the first time in my life I had this much peace and I knew I never wanted to give it up.

I reclined on my bed, the surrounding windows open, and lifted up my notebook. I could feel something stirring inside me, wanting recollection. I reviewed my life at University, my busy days with no time for reflection. I never even paused for myself, aside from activities at home, like cooking or cleaning. Even during a year in South Korea, my life was always busy, scheduled. So I had repeated the life skills I had learned as a child – get through it. Now, it was the complete opposite. I was relishing every moment of this new life where I could listen to silence and hear a voice within me that spoke just to me. I could feel peace instead of trying to block out the sounds of life that came from city chaos, stress, and my hectic lifestyle. Stretching my body to release the tension of the memory, I wrote the nuance on my page, then looked back out to the sea.

Every day, my desire to understand my life experience grew. Engaging my whole being with diligent concentration, each new realization proceeded toward the whole truth of me, each insight illuminating like a small light bulb shining down a darkened corridor. I was understanding more by talking with Mark, developing my questions, then seeing the answers appear before me. Looking at situations from this opening perspective, feeling safe, I could explore myself in these surroundings.

"My parents were over protective. They sheltered me 'For my own good'. But they limited me because of their fears," I complained.

"I think most parents do that with their kids. Unless, it's the exact opposite, and they don't care at all." A new appreciation stirred in me because I had never thought of it that way.

"You're right. I could look at it that way. It would feel better to," I laughed.

"Sure. It sounds like you had good parents. You're a good kid, Kid," he winked.

"My Dad is someone I have always admired. I could always understand him, even if he was mad. I think he carries on in life with dignity and humility, learning from his mistakes and sharing those lessons with us."

"That's great."

"My family can laugh easily, sharing stories and entertaining each other like well paid comedians."

"That sounds like fun," said Mark.

"My Mom was the tough one for me to understand." I paused to reframe the picture in my mind. "I can choose to see my mother as the jumping off point, having taken me as far as her abilities would go, then it is up to me to make something good of what she gave. Does that make sense?" The emotion spun upward inside me, and I inhaled releasing it by not holding onto it anymore. "The definition of her treatment of me was the tie that bound me to the feeling, and if it's not good, I can change it."

"Wow, that is profound," he remarked.

"Thanks," I said, "like driving me to baseball every summer and ringette every winter, supporting me at my games and cheering me on."

"What is ringette?"

"An awesome sport on ice for girls who play with a cut off hockey stick and rubber ring. Its like floor hockey."

"So, she was there for you. Some kids don't get that."

"Thanks, Mark," I said, feeling a new way to appreciate her care, wanting to free her from my condemnation, knowing I could feel better about it. The story was all there woven in the fabric between the threads of memory that made up my life.

"I feel better than I ever have. And that's the truth. I'm even thinking about making a big change," he said.

"Really? What?"

"The moustache," he grinned, stroking it. It was always perfectly maintained, and it suited his character complimenting his wry humour and twinkling eyes.

He choked up, and I could see the smile was hiding some tears. "I've had it since I was eighteen."

"You've never shaved it?"

"This would be a first. Your crazy talk has made me think about just shaving it off and starting fresh." He was trembling.

"I think that would be a great idea. Then I can see more of your face."

"It used to work for me when I was in private investigation."

"Really, you were a private eye?"

"I worked on a job with a guy for a few weeks to try it out. It wasn't for me but I learned a lot about the strange things people do. That's for sure, like the kind of parents you could have."

"Tell me your craziest story."

"This guy and I had to follow a man who was married to the client. It was a typical situation in marital disputes, but this woman really loved her husband and wanted to know where he was going two or three times a week with a gym bag, not returning until very late, sometimes the next morning. She could not get an answer out of him, so she had him followed. We were the guys she hired. Two nights went by and no luck. Then on the third night, we saw him go into a seedy bar. By the time we went in, he was gone. The next night we followed him into a club on the dodgy side of town. He's got his bag in hand and disappeared inside. Thirty minutes later he came out wearing a pink fedora, feathered scarf and a long, black trench coat. He was a pimp!"

"That is shocking!" I laughed. "What did she say?"

"She was shocked too. We left without knowing the outcome. But can you imagine? He was living a double life."

"Wow. Crazy."

"When it comes to marriage, we have to make a good choice."

"Exactly!"

We moved onto the porch before sundown to witness the others gathering on the beach as we played chess. Then, we watched a new man wearing a backpack approach the bungalow with the easel. The woman excitedly ran toward him for an embrace and they spoke in Russian. Mark and I exchanged surprised glances.

The sun set with the usual fanfare on the beach, and Mark and I reclined to watch. After another chess game, we were tired and ready to sleep.

"Goodnight, Mark," I called after him, watching him pad to his bungalow.

"Goodnight. Call me if you need anything." I closed the door and set the tiny lock, appreciative that it did the trick every night. Candles glowed and the moist air coursed through my window. I filled up another page of my journal, recording the transformation I was going through. Then, I closed the window and sat on my bed to breathe and take it all in.

"Thank you for this great life," I said, hands clasped at my heart, looking up. "Thank you for being here with me, helping me know myself. I love this experience, this journey, and I really feel I am growing. I am so grateful to be here. Thank you, God."

I tucked myself in and fell fast asleep.

I awoke to the steady ping of rain on my roof. It was just before dawn so I got up and opened the door, ushered into a sacred moment. The light had just begun to appear as I moved silently onto the porch in my pyjamas. The sweet scent of damp sand and pinging palm leaves enchanted me, as I joined the trees in taciturn appreciation. The feeling comforted me as I shared a special moment with time. In my journal I wrote, Beauty is all there is, and it is always there waiting for me and all I have to do is open the door.

The rain's visit remained a secret as the morning heat dried the sand, bringing about a new fresh scent. Birds sang and waves tinkled upon the shore. After my customary morning knocking to shoo any creatures, I entered the bathroom to see a large brown spider circling on the cement wall. Then, it paused. Wanting a closer look at such a large insect, I approached carefully. The body was the size of a small grape, and its brown hair was meticulously groomed. The legs were long and magnificent, perfectly manicured. The head was erect as its eyes looked directly at me. Startled, I pulled back, laughing at my fearfulness and left the bathroom.

I went back in later and it was gone, so I began my daily cleanse.

After breakfast, Mark reclined on the hammock and I sat on the bench across the end of the porch in our usual positions. We could see the whole beach but still remained in the shade. A beautiful Thai man with smiling eyes who worked at the restaurant approached barefoot, followed by a gaggle of tourists heading for a boat in the shallows. "Do you want to snorkelling?" he asked.

"Yes. I would love to!" I beamed.

"Have fun, Kid. I'm staying here," was Mark's reply.

The long boat floating in the shallows with the protective red sash tied around its nose, filled up with flippers, masks and tourists. As we motored out into the bay, the water became deeper and darker and I looked back to shore. Our bungalows were barely visible under the shade of coconut trees as the temperate water begged me to plunge in. At the right moment, the engine was shut off and we started grappling with gear. One by one, the others jumped in as I leaned over to peer into the deep clear water. A startling vision from my childhood came back, flooding me with fear, as I remembered the sight of a large snapping turtle below our boat.

Pinned to my seat, I took in shallow breaths while the boat emptied around me. The driver asked, "Why you wait?" Finally, I jumped into the water staying close to the boat as I nervously positioned my mask, wrestling with my fear that shouted, 'What about a shark? A hungry shark!' My thoughts raced as logic struggled to the forefront. Soon, it was time to go and I hadn't seen any fish at all.

As the boat made its way to the next snorkelling site, I repeated to myself, 'Nothing stands in my way because I won't allow anything to.' I felt empowered and when we got there I was first to jump in.

The white sandy sea bottom twenty feet below us extended to a ledge then plunged into dark blue water. Larger fish were swimming below and my thought of something emerging from the deep had to be pushed aside. I focussed on the sun's rays through the water, then I saw a few more fish nearby as curious about me as I was about them.

When we were called back to the boat, I casually waited for my turn to board and looked beneath me to see clear, non-threatening water. Relief filled me. We boarded the boat and it whirred back to shore. Padding to the bungalow, I felt satisfied that I had overcome my fear. Mark was in his hammock when I returned.

"How was it?"

"Life changing," I replied with a grin.

"Marvellous."

Back inside my bungalow, my thoughts drifted to people in my life who had an impact. There were many people who fascinated me or helped me change by giving me new ideas to see a better way. I recalled them, one by one, and thanked them in my mind. Each person, each friend, was taking a new place in my life. I loved to think of them and I recalled our laughter. Mark heard me giggling and called over from his hammock.

"Hey Kid, need some company?"

"Sure," I replied, grinning.

"Meet you on the beach."

"Perfect," I laughed, getting up to put on a dry swim suit.

Like reeds gently moved by the current, Mark and I became attentive to nature's brilliant expressions blooming in harmony, speaking a truth we couldn't ignore. "Can you feel it, Mark? What is that feeling, that buzz that tingles me all over?"

"I don't know."

"I've never felt anything this good coming from the environment before. Have you?"

"No. Not like this, but I'm sure there are other places that feel this good."

"Imagine that."

"It's tranquil, yet vibrant."

"How far does this system go? Why was it that only here that we are realizing this?"

"I think because we are taking the time to listen."

"What else is it trying to tell us?"

"Good question," he laughed.

Waves of energy moved through the space, with the same current as the sea: gentle and measured. My thoughts raced higher. "Subtle vibrations speak to us through expressions of nature, displaying interconnectivity of the natural environment. The grandness of the systems give way to the realization that everything we can see around us is connected."

"Where are you getting this information?"

"Something within this beauty has incredible power and is speaking to us in natural symphony." I sat erect, attuned, focussed on the beauty. "Trust in life and yourself. Open up to the love you feel around you. You are always safe."

"How do you know this, Kid?"

"Everything is connected. Do you get that, Mark? Do you understand the power of that?"

"Not exactly."

"If what is over there is here, then we can adapt here to affect over there. It just makes sense. The power is in our hands to create the life we want."

"That sounds like false promises I was fed in fairytales."

"Exactly! Except it's not a false promise. We can make it whatever we want! The information is there, rather here. We just have to use it. It's all connected. Just as you drop a stone in the water, it ripples out causing an effect. Your thoughts are the same."

"That is amazing, Kid. I think I know what you are saying."

"Yes, incredible. I would never have dreamed of knowing that yesterday."

"Let's go back in so you can write it down." I got up off the sandy bottom, elated with the feeling in my body and I beamed a smile at Mark. His face was bright and glowing. When we got back to shore, we went to our own pads to relax. After an hour or so, I came out to see Mark without a moustache on his hammock.

"Come over! You look amazing." With a wide grin and a fresh smile, he showed his dimpled boyish face.

"Well done," I commended, patting him on the back.

"Thank you." The sun set as Mark and I talked about the day. "What a spectacular time it has been here with you."

"You have been a blast too," I smiled.

"I don't know how much more I can take, how much more hair can be removed." We laughed and stayed on my porch playing chess until bedtime. The candles flickered as the day came to a close.

"Goodnight, Mark."

"Goodnight, Cass." I settled into my cozy bed for another night of enchanted rest with the calm ocean lulling me into sleep.

The morning began with rising heat in the bungalow, a good preventative measure for sleeping in. At nine in the morning every day, the bungalow became an oven until I opened the window to let in the breeze. Morning sunshine coasted in from the calm sea. The blue, peaceful sky held the scene. I rested my eyes until joy filled me and I was reminded that my journey supported me, just like the beautiful, steady surroundings as shadows of doubt faded away.

Staring through holes at the top of the shower while I rinsed myself with cool water, I could see 3 inch geckos and birds flicker by. I reminded myself each morning while I prepared for the day to appreciate everything in those moments because now was the time in my life that my dream began.

I swept off the porch and the steps, looking over to see Mark reclined in his hammock watching the sea.

"Good Morning."

"Good Morning," he grinned.

"Hey, Mark! How's the view?"

"Great, Kid."

"Are you learning anything?"

"Tons."

After breakfast, I reclined on my bed with my journal. I lit a candle and put on soft music. Something within everything seemed to be aware of what I was experiencing. I could feel the need to connect to something, teaching me to continue with my desire to learn more about myself and life. The answers to my questions were easily apparent to me, like opening a treasure box full of everything I had ever wondered about.

As a child, I was sent to bed hours before I slept. During those hours, I quietly contemplated and entertained myself with various thought processes and counting games. I felt comforted by the presence of something as I used the time until I fell asleep. It was this union with something beyond me that I now began to recall.

I sat back on my bed and let my eyes lift up to my window. Gazing through it, I stepped back from my thoughts with the idea to observe them passing through my head. Detaching myself from the content and watching them float like balloons, I immediately learned more about myself from the types of thoughts I was having. It was exhilarating to be a voyeur, watching them as if they belonged to someone else.

I put my notebook down to interact with my beautiful surroundings. The day shone with the same intensity I felt inside, as beauty pulsated from life around me. I walked over the sand to the plants and trees, touching the leaves, wanting to feel a connection. I wondered if they could hear me, feel me or even see me.

Each day I was learning how to use my mind as a powerful tool, to use creatively to take me where I wanted to go, and into what I wanted to feel. I wanted to feel good. The choice was easy, but the practice of feeling good required dedication. Doubt would fly in to land on my shoulder. 'Who could think such a thing, that your thoughts could teach you?' 'Who would believe you that it was happening?'

Feeling calm, I was embraced by an essence of love staring me in the face, daring me to believe. Edging forward toward it was frightening! What if I was wrong? What if I was making it up?

Thankfully, Mark was around to share time. His stocky solid manner and dry wit sparked our conversations, sending me into fits of laughter. It poured through me, bringing me to tears, and him too. It was good to cry from happiness.

I had the sniffles. "Ah, I'm so glad we are getting this chance. Most people don't have this luxury, to take weeks off in a tropical paradise, all expenses paid."

"True, the exchange makes it that much more valuable," he said.

"We can live, eat and drink all day for about 12 dollars! And it is paradise. It's amazing that paradise comes this cheap."

"Ironic. Well said, Kid."

He revealed his tender side in exquisite moments of sweetness, as he peeled back the layers and began to show his true self. He was looking for love, just as I was, and our precious moments together begged for a clarification of our individual intentions.

"Mark, you are an amazing guy. I know just the kind of woman you need. You need a rugged kind of girl to take home to Saskatchewan. I'll come visit one day, and we'll tell her all about the time where you lost your mind."

"What do you mean a rugged girl? And more like, you lost your mind."

"Yeah, it kind of feels like that, like I've given up old thoughts and found new and better ones. What I mean is, a strong girl, a worthy travel partner."

"Maybe, I'll just stay single. It's easier that way, no one gets hurt. Right, Kid?"

"Mark, you will be scooped up for sure. You're so handsome and funny." Our friendship, in this very romantic setting was confusing for sure but platonic in nature.

"You'll get scooped up, too, Kid. You're a beautiful girl," he said, with emotion in his voice. I could see his vulnerability in glimpses under his big coat of camouflage. He held it tight against him, but once in a while he would show a piece of himself, then he was translucent, like an angel.

"Let's go for a swim, in paradise," I suggested, getting off the bed.

"Sounds great. Meet you out there."

I changed into my bikini and walked to the beach. Mark soon arrived and we strolled into the water. I watched him as he settled onto the bottom, seeing more of his true nature.

"I love watching you unfold and look at yourself. It's so beautiful to witness."

"This isn't what I normally do, Kid. I'm staring at the sea for hours, and this stuff comes up inside. I am appreciating my life like I never have before. And it's because of you and your starry-eyed talk."

"I'm having so much fun. I love that we're having these moments together. I wonder where this trip is going to take us?"

He laughed. "Only time will tell, Kid."

Lounging at our bungalows, sunning my legs over the edge, it was like being absorbed into love. Everything around me was perfect and beautiful, a miracle. I breathed in the scents with stories travelling from foreign lands I had never explored. But I wanted to. Where would I go from here? Where could I go from here?

A beautiful tanned girl with short brown hair, shorts and a tank walked across the sand toward the beach. She approached for a chat at my porch.

"My boyfriend and I have been on the island for a couple of weeks. We're staying in that cabin." She pointed to the end of our row, beside the restaurant. "He left for a few days to stay on the north side of the island. We need a break sometimes because we've been travelling together for six months." She twisted her foot in the sand as she talked.

"Wow, it's great that you can trust each other like that," I said.

"We give each other the freedom to do whatever we want. When we return to the city, we have a lot of opportunity."

"Nice," I smiled, not sure what she was referring to. "What is the north side of the island like?"

"Beautiful, like this, but there are more snakes there. For some reason, because of the sun or something, most of the snakes live there. So, it's more dangerous. There are deep jungle parties for foreigners, and one is tonight. Do you want to go with me?"

"Tonight?"

"Yeah, after dinner we can take a truck taxi to the party where they have it all set up with speakers so we can have a big dance party in the jungle. We can go together, then when we want to leave we walk or maybe we find a drive home."

I imagined us walking home alone through the jungle at night.

"I think I'll pass tonight."

"Okay," she said, and padded off as I wondered where her life would lead her.

In the afternoon heat, I saw the blond woman with the easel walking across the sand holding three puppies. By now, her Russian partner had left.

"Oh, where did you find them?" I asked, moving off the porch to pet them. They were only a few weeks old, white with orange and brown patches.

"I found them. I'm going to nurse them to health and feed them until they are big enough to take care of themselves."

"That's very kind of you. Can I take a picture of them?" I sat down with three little puppies who whined for her as Mark took the picture. We watched as she carried them back to her bungalow.

I went inside to retreat from the heat, revelling in appreciation for my present experiences. I sat on my bed, focussed in concentration while gazing out the window. My thinking culminated in a brilliant conclusion just as a beautiful butterfly danced into sight. The timing was perfect punctuation. Instantly, I wondered, Why did there seem to be a connection between my thoughts and visual experience?

After asking the question, something within me opened and I wanted to know more. Then, my doubt spoke, 'Now, wait a minute, what makes you really think that's happening? Who would believe that?' It was the same doubt I had listened to many times throughout my life. I wanted to toss it aside because it just got in the way, shading the light of bittersweet moments, pushing like a bully in the playground. It took my voice and used it as its own.

What was real? What was really happening?

"Mark, are you over there? What do you think?"

"I don't know what you're going through, Kid, but it sounds pretty amazing to me."

"It's scary at times. I don't even know what's happening. The one thing I know is how good it feels. It's amazing."

"It must be a good thing, then."

"I want to share this feeling with the world."

The cause and effect relationship between my thoughts and my experience played on in my mind. I worked at drawing metaphors and paradigms in my notebook to describe it. I saw it as a relationship that had always existed and of which I was only becoming aware. Something encouraged me on a personal level, challenging me to trust in what I was coming to know in spite of doubts from my rational mind. The more synchronicity I saw, the more passionate I became about understanding what was behind the elusiveness of its nature. The experience began to reveal something deeper.

"Keep going," said someone in conversation, passing my window.

The ideas I was entertaining were familiar, yet undiscovered by my conscious mind. It was like going into a storage area and recalling all that had been stored there, many years ago, the hopes, dreams and wishes on a journey of a life of my dreams. And here was I, living them, more fully than I had ever known.

I moved more into feelings of blissfulness as I inhaled and exhaled joyfully. I was feeling good, so much better than I could have ever imagined, so I listened. I wanted to understand all that I could here, translating magical experiences into words and stories to help me find myself in the experience. The characteristic of the relationship between my thoughts and my experience were within reach.

Mark and I rolled forward by the push of the waves.

"I've got it!"

"Got what?"

"I know what to do!"

"Kid, you're shouting."

"If I can understand this relationship between my thoughts and the experience, then I will be able to understand how to live a better life!"

"Wow, that's deep."

"Yes, but it can be done. There's nothing to do here but listen tc the beauty until it opens you, naturally. This is a natural process. And the life I have lived is so different from this! Now, I appreciate everything, a butterfly, an ant, a flower. It's all coming alive for me!"

"This is a beautiful experience. Write it down. Keep going with your writing."

"Mark, this is totally amazing. There is something to know and understand and it's inside all of us. It has to be! It makes perfect sense. You don't have to travel all the way to Thailand, you only have to travel all the way to.... yourself."

"I think the silence here makes it possible to hear yourself."

"Yes, this beautiful beach is a magical ingredient. I could have never heard these things in the city. Life in the city for me was about blocking out sounds. Now I can hear myself think about what I'm really saying and wanting. I can hear me."

"Yeah, its life changing." Our eyes met and our smiles came from deep within.

Back at the bungalow with my notebook, my contact lenses were sticking to my eyes. As I got up from the bed, I ventured a silent question into space about whether I should take them out or whether there was a better solution to my problem. Immediately, I felt as if this helpful source was too big to insert itself into such a miniscule problem, but would wait for me while I tended to it.

Getting to know my self in this way felt so natural. But why did I have to wait this long, and be on a tropical island in South East Asia to discover myself? Why was society working so hard all the time? Surely they would be happier with more time to know themselves.

I decided to swim on my own and waded into the shallows. The breeze delightfully stroked my skin, while the sun kissed my shoulders. The quiet scene was enchanting, even though without anyone on the beach. I rolled back in the warm water, ears in, for a float. God stared down, I was sure of it, seeing me on a tiny island in the sea. I exhaled then inhaled, my body bobbing. Blissful.

When I felt my face getting warm, I returned to the beach to sit under the shade of palm leaves. The warm sand heated my bottom as I sat on my colourful sarong in my bikini, thinking about the person I had become, on the most incredible beach I had ever seen. I smiled at my success and inhaled the beautiful tapestry of colours that shifted warmth and light in eminence of this surreal setting.

I drifted back into memory about events in my life, worrying if I had made irreparable mistakes. I felt so alone. Taking a deep breath and stretching my body, I released the worry as Mark joined me on the sand.

"I've never taken so much time to consider myself. It's very revealing," I said.

"Me, neither. I'm learning things that I didn't know I had the answer to."

"Self-introspection. The key to life."

"Hey, I found out something interesting from Damian. They have mushroom tea here that they can make with one day's notice so they can go pick the mushrooms. Are you up for a Thai style adventure?"

"Tell me everything."

"Magic mushrooms grow here naturally in elephant dung."

I laughed.

"Damian said the locals have used them for thousands of years, like going on a vision quest in the native tradition."

"So people here have used the same ones you're talking about?"

"Yes, and they make a mushroom tea. You eat light meals that day then drink it at sunset. The colours are supposed to be incredible."

"Cool. So we will stay here on the beach the whole time."

"Yes." Mark grinned.

"Okay. Let's try them."

"Okay, I'll figure it out."

I looked up at tall, swaying palm trees and sparkling blue sky. Glimmering velvety sand held me while I admired all the expressions of beauty, revisiting my vision of a tropical paradise where life would reveal its secrets to me. My dream had come true along with answers to my questions, unfolding like some big familiar mystery story of which I seemed to be the anonymous author. It felt surreal, as if I had somehow been secretly planning these events my whole life without being conscious of how my hopes and dreams were shaping my future.

"It's so simple, Mark! Follow your dreams and become fulfilled! Do what you want! Happiness lies where you think it does. Make your dreams a reality!"

"I am," he smiled.

"I have to tell the people about this!"

"Are you writing this down?"

"Yes, but sometimes I just want to enjoy it myself. I do think of the others in the world, working right now, never taking the time to get away from their lives. They don't know what they want; only what others want from them. They can't hear themselves because of the noise of the city or they think they can't afford it. Thus, they are trapped. I hope this story will help them realize the potential they have inside, if they allow themselves to feel like this, to feel blissful." A magical feeling permeated through me, something unlike I had ever experienced before. Everything was perfect. Tears came to my eyes for release as I sensed something equally as happy as I was, about me. My own feelings became magnified by thinking of it.

I wondered about the source that had become known to me in free flowing expressions through my words and my thoughts. It seemed to be helping me now with intensity. I wanted to hold onto the feeling so

I could explain it to others, but it was elusive. And sometimes the words rang through loud and clear.

Listen to your heart about getting over yourself and your worst fears. Have Truth, Love, Light. Believe.

Pure, electric feelings surged through me, filling me with appreciation for everything that had brought me to where I was now. I felt so much love for my parents, seeing how their loving support really had helped me reach my dreams. I could see how I had blamed them in the past, giving my power away to make changes.

What was teaching me to trust? Who was helping me to explore myself? Then, I heard the melody of a tree frog singing a song for me. Step by step, each moment reassured me that I what I felt was real. I was encouraged to realize what was happening, as I turned and gazed at life with new eyes.

Mark and I resumed our positions in my room. He reclined against the wall at the end of my bed, and I reclined against the headboard on pillows. Sitting comfortably with the surrounding windows open, I could see clearly over the sea to capture the beautiful scenery within the window frame.

Uncovering secrets that had lain hidden within our minds, we talked until tears rolled down our faces. We let go of painful memories, breathing through it, until we laughed and felt much better inside. My thoughts led me to consider worries that shook my serenity, as I tensed physically, experiencing fear, dread, and anxiety of the unknown. I was left in the darkness with doubt and worry where there had been joy.

"I want to be free of fear. Witnessing it inside me makes me angry. Why can't I feel pleasure all the time? Why can't I just let it go?" Mark sat silently without the answer. I tried to have faith that I would overcome the powerful insidiousness of fear, but that seemed to be a considerable lesson to learn.

When I moved from fear into surrender, I exhaled the anxiety of the previous moment. The thoughts let go easily, as if there wasn't really anything to be afraid of in the first place. I was learning that I held the font of power in my own hands, like the gas pedal of a Ferrari, and I sat in the driver's seat feeling the steering wheel. In this moment, I began to call forth the power within me, feeling it whoosh up inside me ready for action. I stated my desire for this power, affirming it for myself. How could I help others struggling with fear? How could I help others come from where I had been?

Teach everyone to open their hearts. You know how, teach them.

Something wise responded with encouraging words, as if my introspection was being observed by something wonderfully persistent at helping me understand my life. How did these ideas kept coming to help me, urging me to make them part of my own understanding?

They're in you, that's why they keep coming back to you.

I began to trust in the availability of constant blissfulness. I began to trust that the feeling was there, it was only a matter of my awareness if I connected to it. I just needed to exercise my own faith and trust that it is there, feeling as I reach deeper into it, that it expands.

"Are you ready for an excursion?"

"What have you got in mind?"

"Let's go into town."

"You got it."

Mark and I waited at the edge of the road for the truck taxi to Thong Sala. After some time one arrived and we piled in with other tourists. The conversations were mundane and lacked the depth and clarity Mark and I had created at the beach. We silently watched the passing view, then hopped out when we got into town. We meandered from shop to shop as I eyed each Thai person I came across. I wanted to see more of this depth, and understand what kind of wisdom they embodied.

Not being able to share their language, I depended on eye contact and smiles to interpret what was happening with the locals. They seemed reserved, but happy, and somewhat curious about us as well.

We walked into a few shops and I admired the bright colourful clothing and decorative items hand carved and prepared by the locals. I picked out some colourful tye died pants and a flowing white top. Mark wandered nearby, taking in the sights.

"Don't you want to buy something?" I asked.

"I'm not buying pants that look like I'm wearing a diaper." I laughed out loud. He was referring to the local style of casual pants, with a cotton waist tie and lots of extra fabric.

We returned within the hour, our excursion complete. I longed for the silence and serenity of the beach. We motored back into the jungle in the back of another truck taxi and hopped out at our stop with relief. The journey had challenged us to engage with the business of life and we needed to unwind on my porch. Laughing at our desire to return to our safe haven, we realised the deepening effect of our past time and that our sensitivity needed to be respected.

Enraptured in my pursuit of understanding within the realm of beauty, I opened more and began to feel more with pen in hand and mind in thought. Watching the sunset was a luxury that I regarded from the bungalow. Staying up late to share candle light and bask in the calm quiet, Mark sat in my hammock so I scampered out to join him. I sat on the bench wrapped in my purple sarong.

"Come on, let's go sit on the sand."

We sauntered down to the beach, whispering in the darkness to sit and stare up at the stars and bats. Mark was disconcerted by the idea of a bat attack, then they seemed to fly closer to him, dive-bombing within inches of his head. I laughed as he scrambled to get lower under the hasty approach of the one meter wide wingspans, falling back onto the sand.

Staring up at the clear night sky for a long time, I wished upon falling stars. "Are you wishing, Mark?"

"Wishing for what?"

"Wishing on a star? For something good to happen when you see one shooting across the sky."

"That's for girls."

"Don't guys want anything? They'll just take whatever life gives them? That's what I'm talking about here Mark, asking for more, being ready for more. You deserve it, too."

"Thanks, Kid." I detected blushing in the dim light.

Just then, the wind picked up and licked our faces, blowing in off the warm water, moist and fresh. "The wind is telling us it's time to call it a night."

Mark and I went back up to the bungalows. "Good night, Mark. Sleep tight and don't let the cockroaches bite!"

"Thanks."

"You're welcome."

I closed the windows and locked the latch then lay in bed reviewing the day. I was living the perfect life, surrendering to my every whim, eating when I was hungry and changing the scenery at will. I was relaxed and at ease. The weather was perfect, sunny and clear everyday. But at the same time, I was facing some of my biggest fears - living with spiders larger than I had ever seen and countless unknown insects; swimming in a large foreign body of water, with the possibility of approaching large toothy creatures; sleeping alone with only a tiny lock holding my door; surrounded by various openings in and around the bungalow for possible snake passage. I exhaled.

It was a delicate dance and I fumbled with the steps, while turning and gazing at everything around me, appreciation bubbling inside. Wondering about life's beauty and meaning, secrets were being to be shown to me, in glimpses that intrigued my mind and senses. I struggled to accept that something much bigger than I could put into words existed in my life and showed me evidence that I was being heard.

Chapter 3 – Clear Skies

The next morning after breakfast I sat on my porch with a coconut shake. Gazing upon the beach, I smiled realizing I had found something entirely worth looking for. I had somehow opened a door inside myself that poured forth brilliant expressions of insight.

Each insight inspired me to ask more questions and pursue more understanding. I felt that something grand wanted me to succeed, wanted change as much as I did and was teaching me that I had the answers to my questions. Each idea was the next step in my understanding and because of this, I knew I wasn't just imagining. It was as if I were waking up from a long, deep sleep becoming aware of a magical world that existed around me.

"Kid, I'd like a beer. Do you want one?"

"I just finished my coconut shake so I'll pass."

As Mark headed off to the restaurant, the breeze blew rustling palm leaves way up high in a relaxing shuffle. The balmy surroundings pulsed, drawing me into quiet contemplation. The leaves splayed lovingly, touching the sunshine, messaging serenity.

Something moving across the sand caught my eye. A small, green lizard with great strides from its hind legs was bounding across the sand as a larger lizard gave chase. The little one picked up the speed, clamouring up a tree trunk with one eye looking down. The larger lizard started up the tree just as the smaller one bounded off, turning in the air to land on the sand and sprinted out of sight. The larger lizard stood stymied on the tree trunk, foiled. I giggled at the sight of pure enjoyment in wonder of all the creatures that lived in harmony around us. Life in various forms was thriving all around me, running through foliage into hiding places in yet to be discovered places.

Mark returned with his beer and sat on my porch.

"Living a happy life is about getting in touch with the part of the self that knows how to play the game of life. There are rules and principles upon which life operates. If we can decipher them, then a wider perspective will allow us to play the game with more skill. The tools to learn are always inside us. We can play with brilliance."

"You're beautiful, sexy and smart," he said.

"Thank you, Mark," I smiled. "The information is for all of us."

After finishing his drink we waded into the shallows, appreciating our sublime surroundings. I sat on the sandy bottom, just like sitting in nature's bathtub and filled with appreciation.

"We all have the potential to experience our own heaven on earth. I know that because if I can, anyone can. We are all able to find love inside and give it out. After all, feeling the goodness of life is everyone's choice."

"Some people may not choose goodness. They may want to be miserable."

"But why would someone choose to be miserable? They would only choose it if they didn't know this existed."

"Good point."

"Which is why we have to tell them, Mark."

"I just don't know if I'm cut out for it. I'm not as much of a trailblazer as you," he laughed.

I could hardly believe what I was hearing. "You mean now that you know life is loving you back, you're not going to tell anyone?"

"I never said life is loving me back. You said it."

"But you have witnessed it. You have seen the unfolding in your eyes. Doesn't that mean something for you?"

"It means you are having a nice experience. I'm still the same person."

"You let go of a lot of emotion."

"I let go of it, and I feel better, but I'm not having an awakening like you." I rolled back in frustration. Was I really alone in this? Would I have help?

When we returned to my bungalow, I went inside and wrote words in my notebook.

Follow your heart, put it out there, give it to the people. Channel it, this feeling of love. Channel it like you have been doing. Talk about it. It is so true. Don't fight it, no matter what anyone tells you. Don't listen about how to dislike yourself, your surroundings, or your life.

The next afternoon Mark showed up with two clear mugs of mushroom tea. We cheered our mugs together, giggling about the texture and taste of the unusual mixture. Sipping lumpy, floating mushrooms with green tea, I gathered my things for the evening. I had in my bag, my sarong, a water bottle and a Mars bar. Damian padded over barefoot to see our perspective expand before his eyes.

"Make sure to stay on this beach all evening. Don't go wandering off. I'll keep an eye on you."

"Thanks," we echoed, then he padded off to his rattan hut.

"This is going to be a night to remember, Kid. I can feel it."

"Me too. Think of all that I've been asking to know."

"Let's stay together. On the beach."

"Yes, we'll stay together, and both bring water. I'm bringing my sarong to sit on the sand."

"I'm fine. I'm really fine." Mark's hand moved past his face as he laughed, causing me to laugh.

Moving with the music between sips and swallows, I watched Mark's obvious facial expression change as he tasted the concoction. I laughed.

Then we locked up and crept down to the beach to watch the sunset. The white sand was almost bare and we sat down upon it with an unobstructed view of the sky. I spread out my sarong and placed my water bottle beside me. Mark settled into the sand on my left side and we both reclined in the velvety chair.

Watching the sky become a glorious tapestry of moving colours, our perceptions became enhanced. Colours swallowed my attention and drew me into the changing scene. My hands looked increasingly alive and interesting as the scenery and sounds invaded my senses. Details I hadn't noticed previously enveloped my awareness. Everything I could perceive became hilarious. We laughed and laughed until tears rolled down ours faces.

The sand held us in a soft, velvety embrace as colours danced before my eyes. Then, a more serious tone overtook me. I felt enormously important and loved. In this space of deepening resound, I reached a question within. "What am I doing here?"

This acute perceptual awareness caused laughter to come again. What was I doing there? Why had I come? More profound feelings emerged within me as I breathed deeply to steady myself, awareness rolling in waves. I touched the sand and felt its truth: a glistening mound of fun softness. My hands appeared strong and capable, my beautiful skin was smooth and supple. The ground beneath us cushioned us lovingly as we watched the colours of the sky moving before our eyes. What were they saying?

Life glowed with brilliant energy and euphoria overcame me.

"What is going on? What is life about?" I spoke aloud to the sky, stretching my arms up as the beautiful colours drew me into a feeling of deep peace. I could hear Mark chuckling, although my visual field had narrowed to the colours of the sky and the sand beneath me.

"Give me what you've got! Show me what this is all about!"

Silence enveloped me while something beyond vision called my attention. Then my conception of lying in the sand disappeared as life transformed into lightness - I was floating, weightless, as rich gentle feelings poured through me and sweet whispers of love seduced my hearing. A lasting moment coloured my life with truth beyond anything I had known.

Awakening again to the colours of the beach, I realized I had gone somewhere within my mind. I had left my reality to venture somewhere unknown, all the while held in a loving embrace. A secret door within myself had led me to another place as if I had removed a blinder worn all my life and stared into power too great to comprehend.

Whoa. This is huge.

I could feel the presence of something greater than myself, something more loving and lenient that loved me unconditionally. A beloved sense of truth, energy and brilliance joined me in the moment.

Amazing.

What was happening? Where did I go?

Relax, go with it.

Like sitting on a swing, I went into the colours into a greater knowing, far beyond what my eyes could see. I witnessed all there was about me, facing my strengths and weaknesses, exploring myself more, feeling with my environment. Life whispered to me, 'Look, you are all of these wonderful things and you can do anything you want!'

I thought of my family as I watched my hands wave about, just like my Dad's. I could see my father in my mind's eye as if he were teaching me there in that moment. I awed at how much of his ideas I had incorporated, realizing how I had taken his words and made them my own.

I saw the strength that my mother had brought forth in me, her lessons shown to me in bouts of indifference, that held timeless value. 'Only you can make yourself happy,' she had often said. Or, 'Do your own thing, regardless of what others are doing.' At times, her message had seemed redundant, but it became what I valued most.

I began to understand that I was on a journey in this life, a special journey where I brought to myself the words and advice I needed to fulfil my destiny. What I did was best for my individual growth. I had chosen what I remembered so that I could understand it as my own, as if there were some principle operating behind the scene recording the advice of others, helping me in my own quest for realising myself. It was a beautiful experience, and it filled me with love to look so deeply at myself.

I realized that I was the one just now realizing the connection, as if this had existed around me always and of what I was only beginning to become aware. Something larger than me, something loving was beholding me as I journeyed inside myself.

I questioned my experience and the answers came into my mind, more deeply and profoundly that ever before. It was like my thoughts were bouncing off a mirror but the mirror was the inner me. I felt a reverberation of the selves as if a very close friend lived inside my being and was helping me see myself and love myself, a loving someone who had been watching me and being with me all my life, someone just like me. And we were friends.

I was reassured that I still existed in physical reality, coming back into awareness of the beach evident in the feeling of sand and colours of the sky. I could see the same beauty and truth manifested around me in the trees, birds, insects, and waves, as I stared into space with my mouth open in surprise.

Upward, outward into somewhere light, I rode on the swing into where I could see that everything was inherited, learned and accepted from the ideas of people around me as they served to guide me to be my greatest self. I recognized my ability to help others and saw that I had done so in many ways, fulfilling my destiny before I even knew what it was.

I came to realize that I was a teacher in this life, and I shouted it out in excitement for realizing my purpose. I began to hear the dogs from our bungalows barking, and Mark's voice saying, "Kid, stop shouting."

I exhaled, and shifted my position. Then I relaxed into it again.

Go with it, feel it, it's right.

I wanted everyone to feel this feeling, to experience this moment with me, brought together on a beautiful beach to be told everything's all right. I reached out to feel humanity and felt surprise when sadness came over me like a wave. In the moment I witnessed the sadness of people in the world and tears began to stream down my face.

I knew then that sadness was entirely without reason and that we were only wasting time feeling sadness.

Give it up, get through it, take love and let it be a filter for you. Use it and show others. Think of and use the Supreme Guidance, my Love.

Mark was in conversation with something invisible to me, as if a teacher stood in front of him. I went back into my own journey assured he was okay.

Just breathe and let go.

Embraced by a black tapestry of stars, I saw light shining through holes of the black velvet blanket that wrapped itself around the sky. I learned that my most powerful tool was faith and that my answers were there as always inside of me, and that I would never be alone again.

I looked over to see Mark jolt upright exclaiming, "I can't believe it. I was just talking to my relatives." He repeated himself, until I reached for his arm.

"Mark? Are you finished? Are you ready to go in?" It was late. I got up from the sand smiling, feeling content. I folded my sarong and put my water bottle in my bag.

"Yeah, I'm ready," he said, then felt around on the sand to collect his things. We had stayed in the same spot for hours, just watching the sky. We padded to our bungalows.

"Goodnight, Mark," I said, climbing the steps.

"Goodnight, Kid," he said, heading toward his bungalow. I heard his door close and I closed mine, lit a candle and prepared for bed.

The next morning I awoke with the rising sun, and felt calm and presence like I had never known before. As I rose for the day, I concentrated on each moment as newfound peace and clarity resonated through my being. During my shower, I focused on each element of the task, taking in every morsel of richness in each moment. My attention to each moment was a new experience for me, but it felt natural and I enjoyed it.

When I finished, I went outside to sit on my porch in my lucid state, and sat on my bench to watch the sea. It was calm like my thoughts. Words felt unnecessary with the knowing that nothing really mattered. Everything was alive. Bees buzzed and insects chimed, a symphony of music played in the beauty and perfection in every event. My awareness began to bring me to tears in a feeling like I was waking up to what always existed, to what was patiently waiting for me to notice.

Reverence remained as I moved slowly and purposefully through my day, back straight and shoulders square. The serenity of gratitude resonated within as I witnessed the sacred space, flowing gracefully with the motions of my day. I knew that my experience of life had changed forever.

Mark was in his hammock, smiling behind his sunglasses, when I looked over to check on him. I waved, smiling, but now I felt that we each needed time alone to process our experience. I knew Mark was feeling new spaces within himself, too, because he didn't speak very much either. We walked across the sand to the restaurant for our meals, but something bigger had taken our focus. I didn't know where we were headed.

The resonant stillness began to give way to thoughts as days passed. My concentration began to move from topic to topic as my inner silence began to slip away. The pendulum of thinking began to swing, slowly at first, then more widely as I questioned and postulated upon the conditions of my experience. Moving back into my scientific evaluation, I gave way to speculation, and serenity began to recede into memory.

I was in the bathroom looking behind the mirror at the two geckos resting on my wall. They were fluorescent rainbow coloured with beautiful blues and greens, and green sparkling eyelids. They just looked at me with round perfect eyes.

"Kid, are you having flashbacks?" Mark called to me from the porch. I laughed.

"Check out these lizards. They are so beautiful!"

"I want to talk with you about something," Mark said, sitting down on my bed, a quiver in his voice.

"Do you remember what happened the other night on the beach?" he started.

"I think so," I said, sitting down. "Why?"

He continued to look at me as if waiting for a specific answer.

"What is it?" I asked.

"Well, I was sitting on the beach and everything was groovy. Then later when it was dark, I was talking to some relatives including my father, all of whom have died."

I looked at him, stunned.

"And you were saying the words," he said staring at me.

"Tell me what happened!"

"At first, I was talking with my relatives. Then my Dad spoke to me, in your voice, reassuring me everything was okay, that he was fine on the other side. We talked about things only he and I knew. There is no way you could have known what you were speaking. We talked about personal things. And the whole time, your body was writhing on the beach, as if in absolute ecstasy." I rolled back onto the bed to absorb his words, shaking my head at being involved in such a precious experience.

"So, I channelled your Dad. Well, I've never done that before."

"I had no idea I could have an experience like that. Why do you think I've been walking around here for days like a zombie?"

"That experience was life changing. It was so amazing."

"I'll never be the same!" he said, somewhat frightful.

"I'm sure its fine. You know you're Dad is fine. Don't worry about it. I'm fine too." I smiled at him reassuringly, then gave him a hug.

Mark and I moved onto the porch in a feeling that our relationship had changed. We had changed. I watched him recline in my hammock without the usual commentary.

"Where do we go from here?" I asked, rhetorically.

"Good question," he answered.

"There is something amazing about this place. The beauty here is surreal."

"I'm sure in a place like this we aren't the only ones having unusual experiences."

Just then Debra, Damian's friend and the woman who stayed beside Mark walked across the sand toward a moored boat floating in the shallow water. As I watched her pass, blue eyes nearly hidden beneath sun bleached blond hair, she met my gaze. "Care to join me?" she asked, swaggering by my porch.

"Sure," I said, hopping up.

We tiptoed into the waves and waded out to the boat.

"I'm Debra," she said, checking to make sure her items wouldn't get wet before climbing in.

"I'm Cassandra. It's nice to finally meet you. You're a friend of Damian's?"

"He's a little bugger," she said, lighting a cigarette. "What about that guy you're with?"

"Oh, Mark's just a friend," I explained, sitting on my sarong. The boat rocked gently in the water, moored to a rock on the sandy bottom.

"Right. So how long are you here for?" she asked.

"I'll be staying at least another week." I had no future plans.

"Great, so you'll be here for the full moon party."

"Yes," I said, looking in to shore. "Have you been to one before?"

"Yes, they're a smashing hit with everyone here. That's why the bungalows get full around this time as people travel from all over to the island."

"Cool. I can't wait to check it out. Hey, I heard you used to be a nurse."

"Yeah, technically, I still am. I just left my job. When I got down here I just unfolded and haven't been able to leave." She took a puff of her cigarette.

"Sounds like what I'm experiencing."

"I see you with a notebook a lot. Are you writing something?" she asked, exhaling.

"Yes. I'm writing about this experience," I breathed, just beginning to share with others my plan.

"That's a great idea. You have to publish it, so I can read it."

"Thanks for the encouragement," I smiled. Reassurance noted.

After floating and sunning ourselves in the gentle waves, we splashed into the water and doused our bodies. Then we headed back.

In the afternoon, Mark and I joined others in the back of a truck taxi for a trip back into the port village Thong Sala. Hopping out of the truck taxi we made our way to the little shops along the dusty roads of the village. We were hungry and decided to go to the only restaurant that made spaghetti with tomato sauce. Other tourists at our bungalows had found the place and shared the knowledge of where to get comfort food. It was delicious and slightly spicy, just what we needed to feel at home. After our meal, we browsed shops where I chose a small red pottery vase and two identical sarongs - a rare find, and a white cotton long sleeved shirt for the full moon party. It would glow in the florescent lights and keep me cozy during the long night away from the bungalow.

Riding back, the excitement of the party reverberated as the tourists made jokes about what we were in for. When we returned to our beach stop, a curly haired blond man hopped off too. As we walked down the path together he asked, "Does this go to Pink's?" in an English accent. "I've come for a vacation. My friends from Jersey told me about this place and I'm here for a month or more if I like it. I'm David by the way." We introduced ourselves.

"You're at the right place. Where's Jersey?"

"Jersey is one of the Channel Islands, next to Guernsey between England and France. It's actually closer to France." Under the majestic palms, we walked through the grove until we could see the water and the beach. Soon, the dogs stirred and came running toward us, barking.

"Welcome to the beach. Don't mind the dogs," I said, as they sniffed us and then went off into the palm grove.

"Thanks," he smiled, and headed off to rent a room.

Reclining on my porch, we watched as David crossed the sand toward the bungalows at the edge of the property and next to a creek.

"I wonder what creatures inhabit his bungalow."

"Creatures from the creek. I'm glad we're not staying over there."

Mark and I ate dinner as the sun was setting. They lit candles in the restaurant while Bob Marley played over the speakers.

"This full moon party is going to be a trip." Mark said, laughing.

"Yeah, I know." When Dang came to our table, we ordered pad thai and banana shakes.

After we finished, Mark and I went to our own bungalows. I lit candles and was sitting on my bed, deep in thought, pen in hand. All of a sudden, there was a large, brown bat hanging upside down on the edge of my roof. I moved off the bed and backed away from the window with images of it flying in to flutter in my face. But, it finally picked up and flew off as I laughed to myself.

As I was drifting off to sleep I heard the muffled sounds of something large moving under the bungalow. I sat up in bed listening to movement from side to side, a large creature was dragging its body across the sand. Feeling captive in my fear and wanting to break free, I opened the door to the porch. It was black outside and everyone was asleep. The movement stopped. With no porch lights to see, I shut the door and again went to bed wondering what it was.

The next morning Mark and I entered the restaurant for breakfast. Someone had turned on the television that hung from the rafters. As a result, everyone's eyes were drawn to it as I revelled at how people gave their attention to it so easily. People's attention seemed to be automatically drawn to it. I could see an innate desire to look at the moving images as part of our being, so that we would be drawn to watching the images in our natural surroundings. I wondered about the influence and role of our own television, how it took the place of connecting with nature.

Back at the bungalow, Mark and I began discussing the power of our attention when Damian came over and sat on the floor, leaning back against my open door. Mark was on the floor with him, and I was perched on pillows against my headboard.

"The power of our attention cannot be underestimated. It is the only power we have. I don't understand why people don't use it – they give it away too easily."

"We're all programmed to be worker bees," Damian blurted.

"But why do we follow that?" We silenced at the thought then someone changed the subject.

"I have a question for you. I heard a strange sound under the bungalow last night, moving from side to side, like a crocodile."

"I hear strange sounds every night," Mark said, laughing.

"It was probably a sea turtle, laying eggs," Damian offered.

"How wonderful," I said, grateful that I could be near such a wondrous event.

A few days before the full moon party, we decided to rent a scooter to check out the beach venue. The roads we had seen on Koh Phangan seemed relatively easy to traverse so we rented one, feeling confident after riding a scooter in Korea for a year. Mark hopped on the back and went on a tour of the island. Travelling east to Haadrin along the south side of the island, we enjoyed the lush surroundings and waved to the occasional passer-by.

We buzzed along on the scooter without incident until we veered around a bend and saw a definitive menace to scooter riders ahead. The hill was ridiculously steep, covered in sand and gravel, descending into a hairpin turn which continued up another steep hill. All this was surrounded by think jungle. There was no other way.

"Uh, Mark? What now?" I ventured.

"Go for it, Kid. I trust you." I laughed and slowly released the brake. We coasted down, gaining momentum as we approached the hairpin turn. Then as we began to ascend the next hill, the scooter ground to a halt. We were too heavy and going too slow. We had rented the less costly jump start clutch version of scooter and now realized the drawback. I tried to jump start it on the incline while wobbling from side to side. The tires spun, shooting gravel and dust into the air. We got off to assess the situation. Ahead, other tourists were littered along the incline with knee scrapes and bent fenders. Finally, Mark pushed it to the top of the hill where we could see that this hill was only the first in a series of others. We stood uneasily weighing our options.

"You should take a truck taxi to town, Kid. I'll ride the scooter and meet you there."

Moments later a truck taxi stopped for me and I hopped in. We travelled over seven more hills along rugged coastline, gravel the whole way. Truck taxi drivers along the road had amazing skill and knew how to work the truck over the hills with the changing weight of the cargo.

The beautiful view from this vantage point overlooked jungle foliage and out to the teal water. I couldn't wait to see what was waiting.

After Mark caught up with me in Haadrin we meandered through narrow street side shops with beautiful things, along to the most beautiful swimming beach I had ever seen. Embraced by hillsides, the teal shiny water was laced by pristine white beach, glowing against blue sky. Abundant shaggy palms waved while vibrant greenery pulsed as the buzz of insects pealed from within the exotic foliage. The sparkling water held bobbing tourists while Mark and I shuffled along the beach, smiling, eyes wide at the intense beauty. Restaurants sat back from the beach fronting bungalow operations, nestled in the shade of palm tress.

"Okay, now that we know the scene, let's head back. I'm covered with dust and would like a shower. Those hills were blazing hot, but I made it without any scrapes. Some guys were bleeding and pushing their bikes the whole way."

"Be careful driving back. I'll meet you there for dinner." Since we had signed a three day agreement, Mark drove the scooter back to our beach.

The day of the party arrived. Everyone was buzzing with excitement. The bungalows were full and many people were wandering about in sandals and shorts talking with others in the restaurant. We all smiled in anticipation of the big event. Mark and I went off to our bungalows to shower and prepare for a night away from our home base.

Word spread quickly to hide valuables because with everyone at the party, abodes were a target for thieves. I stashed my stuff in various places, gathered my things, and asked that my tiny lock hold any intruders at bay.

When Mark came over, he brought a cup of mushroom tea. We sipped it, excited about another night of new awareness. Our perceptions became enhanced as we laughed, reminiscing about our previous excursion into the unknown the week before. Then, it was time to go as we heeded a call from someone loading the truck

Sitting in the back of the truck taxi packed with tourists for the 9 p.m. ride to the party, Mark and I awaited our departure, squirming in our seats. I knew our time was so valuable, our most precious gift in life, so I tried to distract myself from the delay.

"Hey, where's the moon?" someone joked because the moon was no where to be seen. Others swigged beer and passed it around, but I declined because I didn't think mixing beer and mushroom tea would help me in understanding. I liked the clarity of the effects of the tea and had no desire to get drunk. Mark took a healthy swig.

Finally the driver put the packed truck in gear and we ambled through the palm grove in a calm evening breeze, leaning into each other and enjoying our journey to what we knew would be an incredible night. The truck radio blared Bon Jovi as we rode along dusty roads where small homes with rattan platforms were tucked beneath palm trees in the jungle. Thai families gathered outside beside campfires celebrating their ancient custom as everyone enjoyed the night of the full moon. We zoomed along worn jungle paths under sleepy palm trees, then onto the rugged part of the island. We approached the hill Mark and I had encountered with the scooter. I took a deep breath. A line up of other trucks were waiting their turn to jostle loads of tourists down and up the gravely hills, throttles choking, air thick with exhaust and dust clouds rising behind the tires.

When it was our turn, our sputtering truck rolled down then up, down then up, then back to the edge of a cliff to get a run at the next hill. I imagined the truck launching backward off the jungle decline, deep into the ravine below and I panicked. I had to stop the ride. I grabbed Mark's arm then hopped out the back. Mark tapped the side of the truck and followed me. We stood beside the red brake lights, dust clouds in the air, as I tried to catch my breath.

"This ride is nuts," I said, not sure I wanted to get back in.

"I know. But you'll be okay. Come on, let's get back in."

I twisted my foot uneasily as the others moaned for us to carry on. I inhaled deeply, trying to steady myself, holding the side of the truck. I knew I needed to ride on as I couldn't spend the evening there on the side of the road and I felt I needed to trust the others who were calling us back to the truck.

"Come on," Mark said, encouragingly, holding my arm. I took a deep breath.

"Okay," I said. The others cheered as we climbed aboard and I continued to look forward as the truck backed up dangerously close to the edge of the steep decline. Our driver was laughing at the trial to get the full truck up the steep gravel hill, as other trucks slid braking, causing dust to rise in the air. We held our breath as the truck lunged upward, finally cresting the top of the hill, then over a few more until we jostled into a grassy field filled with tourists, lights and pumping music.

"That way to beach," our driver shouted out, pointing toward the lights. At once, Mark and I entered the moving scene and were swept along in a river of people heading toward the beach. In the thick of the party, a knowing came over me like a wave and I stopped in my tracks.

"Mark, I need to be on my own tonight," I said, blurting out my truth.

"Are you sure?" he asked, incredulously.

"Yes," I said, knowing I had to make a break.

"Just remember this was your decision," he affirmed, walking off in another direction.

I watched him for a brief moment, surprised at my own request, then headed forward into the beach scene immediately spotting David. He was alone and greeted me with a smile. "I've lost them already," he said, referring to his friends from our bungalows.

"Let's find a place to sit in the sand and figure this out," I said.

We moved through throngs of people to an open spot on the sand in a sea of partying people, the brilliant moon now visible, rising from the hills behind us. I pulled my purple sarong from my bag and laid it out, settling onto the feeling of velvety sand beneath me. I sighed relief at the peacefulness of it.

"Is your boyfriend going to come back drunk and pound me?"

I laughed. "No. Mark's not my boyfriend."

"He won't be mad?"

"No," I answered, the question running through my mind. "He's a friend."

I took some deep breaths to steady myself in my heightening sensitivity. I released a feeling of tightness in my stomach, trying not to throw up. I told David I needed a moment to relax because of the effects of the mushroom tea. He nodded then looked off into the crowd.

I tried to regain my composure, feeling I needed to start conversation, so that David and I could enjoy the evening. He zoned out while I tried to calm myself. Finally, I felt better and turned in to begin conversation.

"I'm feeling better now," I said, wiping the hair back from my face, happy that I didn't throw up in the sand right in front of us.

"I'm feeling a little unusual too," he confided. "I tried something a guy recommended. I don't feel very much but its nice to just sit here and relax."

"Oh, good," I said. "Its nice to know I'm not alone. I tried these mushrooms last week for the first time and it was one of the most amazing experiences of my life."

"I heard with mushrooms the more you take the lesser the effect," he said. His tone was chipper and his bright blue eyes appeared friendly.

"Yes, its not as strong as last time but my perceptions are enhanced. Its perfect to sit here and watch the scene."

The waves ebbed and flowed ahead of us as we gazed onto people dancing with their hands up in the air. Pumping reggae music vibrated from clubs that lined the beach with flashing disco lights that pulsed to the beat. Some people packed onto open air dance floors while others danced barefoot in the sand. Some Thai families brought their children to picnic on blankets, smiling at the revellers around them. Our eyes wandered over the throngs of people clothed in vibrant hand dyed pieces from the local shops, wrapped around others similarly dressed. It was a party in full swing. Utopian mutual acceptance permeated the scene. Everyone enjoyed the night together under the full moon as it slowly moved moving across the sky.

"Did you know the moon is a satellite?" I asked him.

"So, it's reflecting?" he asked.

"Exactly," I said, feeling the truth of the observation.

"Cool," he replied, looking up. "This is the craziest party I have ever been to."

"Me, too," I said, laughing and taking in the wild sights.

"Wait til the boys in Jersey hear about this. They'll be on the next plane," he said, proudly mentioning his friends.

"Look at the stars. I wonder if they're watching us, peering into our little party in this lost paradise."

"If they could, this would be the party to peer in on," he laughed.

Within a few moments, the nausea had passed and David repositioned himself in the sand, turning in toward me. My focus became more acute and I focussed on the behaviours of those around us.

"Look at those people over there, laughing and having fun. And just a few feet away a girl is crying with her head in her hands. We're all in the same place but having totally different experiences."

"Yeah, its true," he said, considering the thought.

"It tells me that any experience is available and we just have to choose the ones we want."

"We can choose our experiences?"

"Yes, you can choose what you want to feel, what you want to experience."

"I thought we just lived the life we were given." His eyes were wide at this new information.

"We can live the life we want. If we don't like something, we can change it."

He started to laugh. "That's a new one! I've never heard anyone talk like that before. Where did you say you're from?" he asked.

"I'm from London, Canada."

"You mean, there's another London?"

"Yes. We have Richmond Road and Piccadilly Street, Thames River and Hyde Park. It's modelled after London, England," I blushed.

"I never knew that," he said. "Another London."

"It's not nearly as big, but it's a nice city. I grew up with my older brother and sister and parents in a nice house in the suburbs."

"My Dad owns a pub in Jersey and I grew up inside listening to stories of the men there. It was a great place to grow up. I learned so much. But now, I am here with you on this beautiful beach at a wild party. It's a trip!"

"This is paradise! We're alive, so alive!" I exclaimed, my feelings expanding. I wanted everyone to hear. "Love is all around us!"

"Where did you get that idea? I've never heard anyone talk like that before."

"Life has shown me many secrets. They are there if you look for them and want to know. Life is a beautiful tapestry of magic if you want to see it that way. It's your choice."

I noticed others listening to us, leaning back on one elbow or with an ear turned in. It reaffirmed for me that what I speaking was good. I knew it to be an incredible truth.

"Life becomes great when we choose to see it that way. We can be anything we dream, anything we want. Seeing life as it is and revelling in its beauty, life takes on new forms of beauty. Life and all its majesty is there for us, as if it is dancing from our attention on it. We just need to see ourselves and clear our own minds of negative experiences to become aware of it."

David stared ahead, his eyes wide as the party pulsed around us. Revellers tore off clothing and raced into the waves ahead of us, causing everyone to laugh. Firecrackers cracked off flaming light that sped across the sand and into bushes, flaming out, somehow avoiding ankles on its pass.

This unique moment in space and time opened my senses widely, and I began to explain all that I saw in my own words and perspective, sharing the fruits of my awareness. It was as if there was only myself and the sky and my friend at my side.

I talked about what I wanted to know about people's behaviour that perplexed me. I wondered about the things we do but don't think about, and the things we think about but don't do. I wanted to know why people never thought so much about what they were doing or why, or even if that was really what they wanted to do. I listened for insights David could offer, but mostly my questions were completely new to him, so he said he had never thought of those things before.

The party unfolded interestingly and David and I talked on for hours. We laughed and enjoyed the bizarre scene, sharing our truths and our perspectives of events. The warmth of the others who sat nearby created a loving, protective cocoon from where we could speculate safely within.

After a while we became tired and decided to head back to our bungalows. We went to the grassy field and hopped into another truck taxi home.

We said goodnight and each headed into our own.

That night I didn't write anything in my journal because I knew it was already there inside me. A new addition to my being.

The next day was peaceful and stories of the party floated through the restaurant. Everyone had had a good time and my tiny lock had held strong. All was well and David began to visit me at my porch, curious about what I was beginning to understand. He talked with Mark as well, and they shared conversation over beer, but in a few days Mark came to me to talk.

"I'm heading back to Korea to get a job. I've become too absorbed in this relaxed way of life. I have to get out of here." The words struck like mud on a window pane then slid down into the moment. I inhaled knowing this would alter my experience.

"I haven't considered leaving yet," I said wistfully, contemplating the fact that I had no definite future plans.

"I'll give you a couple of days to figure out what you're going to do before I leave. Deal?"

"Sure. Thanks, Mark."

"No problem, Kid."

Over the rustic telephone in the office, peering at the various yellowed maps of the area, my parents voiced their apprehension about my staying on alone.

"I've made other friends," I reassured them. "I know people here now. I'll be fine. Don't worry." I hung up the phone knowing it would be okay.

The next day, Mark and I sat silently enjoying breakfast. "Will you be alright if I leave? You need to leave too, move on and get a job somewhere. You can't stay here for the rest of your life," he said protectively, chuckling.

"Sure. Now I know David, and he'll be here for a while," I said, feeling slightly unsure about placing my trust in a new friend. I knew I needed to stay on, that I wasn't ready to go.

We enjoyed some more hours together in the days before Mark's departure, and I tried to show him that words could not express the meaning of the experience we had shared. We both seemed to understand the depth of our bond and the tremendous value of our time together.

"Thanks, Kid. I never would have done this without you," he said, on his last morning.

"You're welcome, Mark. You're a worthy travel companion. Thanks for everything. I'll miss you," I said, watching his expression.

"If you want, you can come meet up with me in Korea. You can find another teaching job, I'm sure. Keep in touch with email," he instructed.

"I will. And thanks for the offer. I'll keep it in mind."

We hugged, then I watched him walk toward the road carrying his duffle bag on his way to Bangkok. I wondered what awaited Mark on his journey, and what awaited me on this new phase of mine.

As I walked over to David's to tell him I was on my own, I passed other bungalows along the way that had previously been hidden from view. There was a whole other realm existing down the beach from my safe abode. Quiet bungalows were lying side by side in the sand in the shade of palms while visitors watched the sea from cozy hammocks as I walked past. David's bungalow lay beside the ravine, and I watched cautiously as I climbed the steps to knock on his door. It was open and he was on the bed, rolling a joint.

I laughed. "So this is your pastime here on the edge, hidden from prying eyes?"

"Thai stick is some of the best in the world," he said, jovially.

"What kind of creatures do you have living here beside the creek?" I asked.

"Mosquitoes, mostly," he replied, gazing around into the corners of the tiny room with powder blue painted floorboards. The cozy nook held a double bed with flowered sheets, a rear bathroom just like mine and two windows. It was an earlier build, more rustic than mine, but exhuded the feeling of a well loved place.

"I have two speckled geckos living behind my mirror and a few large spiders in the rafters. Mark had cockroaches and wasps. And Debra had a green snake. Just keep an eye open, okay?"

"Right," he said, completing his joint, then sparking it up. Smoke swirled as he handed it to me.

After a few puffs, we rose to go for a swim.

"Come on, I've got something to show you." I said.

"There's more on this mystery train of yours, Cassandra?" he said, putting away his things and tidying the space as I stood at the door, the sun warming my legs.

We walked to where we could sit down on the sandy bottom. "Its shallow! We can just sit here in the water and relax!"

"This is fantastic! Its a natural bathtub!"

"It's divine. And so relaxing."

As I got to know David more during the hours shared in the water, on his porch and on mine, I found him to be very mature for his innocent look. We found a lot to talk about sharing stories of life in our respective worlds.

"I can see it changing and becoming more of a dream, if we can let it happen and let in the love I feel is waiting for us. Life can be anything I want," I said.

"Why do you think that? I thought that life is already laid out, and we just live it," he said, as if the work had already been done.

"I'm exploring my mind and finding that my thoughts relate to my experience somehow, which means that, I am affecting it by thinking."

"That's a new one for me. What are your plans now that Mark has gone?"

"I don't know. Its hard to think about it. I'm wondering about getting a job somewhere, but I haven't decided."

"A lot of people talk about Australia. Have you thought of going there?"

"Yes, I've been hearing the other guests buzz about it, some on their way back and others yet to go. Bangkok is close and easy to get to on my own. I could teach English there and still come down to the islands."

"You could find work in Bangkok, rent an apartment, then travel down to this island for vacations."

I stretched my vision to the horizon that echoed the steadiness in my being. "I want to make the right choice. I believe so much in the greater force in my life that I want to surrender to its suggestions. Something is interplaying in my life, and maybe the synchronicity will uncover the path."

"I hope it works out."

"I have some days to decide before I need to think about money. I've been here more than a month, but its hard to think about leaving such a beautiful place. There aren't any jobs around here, so I guess I have to think about moving on. I'm going to listen to the signs, and see what comes up."

During the next few days I explored this pinball approach, gathering signs as I saw them, such as in the words of another or images that jumped out at me. Because of the self contained nature of my living conditions, the controlled environment helped me avoid distractions. I listened and watched for clues around me, hoping something would be revealed that I could interpret as definite.

As the days went by, the messages surrounding Australia were mixed, and I was uncertain of which way to go. There was something I was missing in how best to handle making the decision. I thought I should remain faithful, keep listening, and then I would be shown.

Rolling back into the water, I saw my tanned skin sparkle beneath the surface. I sat up and salty water poured from my hair down my body. I looked over at David who was reclined sexily on one elbow, watching me.

There was a tall blonde man walking down the beach, strolling along the shore looking down at the sand. He was alone and my focus was drawn to him. "My eyes are riveted on that man every time he is around. Why do you think that is?" I asked, curious.

"I don't know," David said, lazily gazing toward the beach.

"I think I need to know why. I have to follow the signs," I affirmed.

Just as we set foot on the beach, the same man re-appeared walking toward us. David looked surprised. When he neared us, he said "Hello."

I said, "Hello".

"Do you know?" he asked me, his eyes boring into mine. "Do you know what will happen?" I looked at David who was looking at me, then back to the man.

"No, I don't know what you are talking about," I said, trying to relax and go with the flow.

"I'm looking for someone who knows," he said. I just listened, waiting for what he had to offer. We agreed to sit together on the sand because the connection was intense.

"I'm Robin, from Holland," he said, offering his hand.

"I'm Cassandra, from Canada," I said, shaking it.

"I'm David, from Jersey." David and Robin conversed about the exact whereabouts of Jersey. We moved under the palm trees and David and I sat in the sand while Robin sat in the hammock. I watched as his gaze focussed upon the people on the beach.

"They're just being lived," he said. "People: they're here, and they're just being lived." I looked at David, my wide eyes meeting his.

Robin looked at me and said, "Teach me what you know."

I was overwhelmed by his directness as if I had been called to the stage without having rehearsed. I mumbled a few words of encouragement, and he turned to stare out to the sea.

"You're onto a good thing. Keep going," he said, looking directly at me. I rolled back in the sand to absorb the alternate reality of direct personal messages to me through the words of another person.

We sat there for a long while mostly in silence. I was speechless, and I wanted to hear what Robin had to say.

Finally, I looked up at him and asked, "What are you saying?"

Then, he said simply, "Choose where you want to go."

Then it dawned on me and I remembered what I had said myself: choice, the assertion of my choice was the missing piece. I needed to participate in my destiny! Robin's words jolted me into remembrance.

"Yes!" I said, in exuberance. David smiled at me. My mind went on in question, then I asked Robin a question.

"Where does your information come from?" He just looked at me, then out to the sea. I wondered about the journey he was on. We sat in silence for a long while. Finally David spoke.

"Where are you staying?"

"Just over there, but I'm leaving the island tonight."

I was surprised. I didn't know how much I had been able to help him, maybe not enough. It had been so overwhelming.

"Thanks, for the message," I said to Robin.

"Thank you," he replied, then he left us to catch the night ferry.

I went back to my bungalow to think. I made my decision to stay in Thailand and find work in Bangkok because living there would allow me to visit this island in a matter of hours. Once I decided, I felt great relief like a release of energy to the task which proved to me that my energy went out to my goals. I wrote about choice in my notebook so I would never forget it again. 'Choose for yourself, know what you want and let the rest work itself out.' I just needed to start the momentum by choosing direction, and then I would be shown the way. It was all coming back to me now: Ask and you shall receive.

I came to see that life acted as a mirror, reflecting back to me what I was sending out. It was like I could dream up possibilities, sending out thoughts, and if it came back, it was like, 'Yes, you can have that.' So I realised that I did indeed have choice - everything wasn't already decided.

I learned to maintain momentum and allow that momentum to be directed into the choices that became available. It was a dance between my desire and my destiny. They walked hand in hand and one would not shoulder the weight of the other.

David and I settled onto the beach near my porch in the seats that Mark and I used to share, sitting on the beach looking at the sky. "In my opinion, life's goal is to enjoy myself as Cassandra and to make choices, becoming myself unique from all others. We are not here to be passive 'livers'. To me that is 'just being lived' as Robin said. I want adventure and enlightenment, and I sense that desire is the biggest part of me, so I will make that huge and be the best I can be and use the help that is offered."

"There are always people willing to help," he began, somewhat stiffly turning his reddened skin from the direct sunlight. "The guys at my Dad's pub were always willing to help me. They told me to go for anything I want. Now, you're saying the same thing." David leaned back to absorb the coincidence.

I gazed back to the peaceful view and continued, shaping the understanding in a way I could remember. "I want to live and feel my reality, created from the realities available. I can be great in my unique presentation, and that is what I need to do. And in the meantime, I can experience absolute happiness and a life of accomplishments. I can love others along the way and help them, too. It's a glorious way to live and it will do life justice."

"It's interesting that you think life cares about you. I never met someone like you before," he said, turning toward me on his towel. His narrow limbs bespoke his youthfulness and his freckles revealed his innocence.

"I never knew before. I just realised it here staring into this beauty every day, that something is loving me back," I said.

"It sure is beautiful here," he said, gazing about, the light reflecting off his baby blue eyes.

"I'm beginning to see that in some way I am creating my reality with my thinking. That is why my experiences confirm my ideas. What I believe truly exists as my reality. But my thoughts can change, my beliefs can change, and that is the beauty of it."

"You always talk about beauty."

"Life can be anything I want, depending on what I choose to see in it. How can I expect it to be any different when I am the one living it?"

"So it can be anything?" he asked.

"Anything you want. I want to cultivate happiness, so I make a conscious effort to aim my thoughts in a positive direction, catching any negative ones and turning them around into something positive."

"That sounds like a good idea," he said, grinning at me.

A few days later, I noticed the results of my efforts multiplying. Gradually, I began to see the positive elements first. It started to happen naturally as if my mind preferred the pursuit of positive thinking. This changed things within me, allowing me to experience my life in a new and beautiful way. I didn't have to resist the negative and talk myself out from the limited feeling I felt while judging or making something wrong. It was easy to do, like letting go.

Waking up from the heat of the bungalow, I opened my window to the sea. The fresh air swelled in and I praised the shiny day. I followed my morning ritual of rising and making the bed, stretching then entering a cool shower, while watching for creatures passing by the openings. After tidying up, I opened the door to sweep, enjoying the gentle palms and serene beach. Water ebbed at the shore, reflecting dappling light on the wood planks of my bungalow. I moved across the sand in bare feet just like the local family, inhaling the fresh scent of the breeze and smiling to my world.

Called by hunger pangs, I walked up to the restaurant. Seeing David, I glided up to his table, my sarong skirt fluttering with each step, and said good morning.

"Good morning," he smiled. Guests smiled with their fruit shakes and plates of banana pancakes. David was more social than I had been and each day I met someone new and exchanged information with other visitors. They were curious about my writing and asked me about my pursuits. With the breeze blowing, looking into sun kissed faces, I shared with others my experience of opening.

"It just started happening here, I think because I have time for reflection without any demands or schedule. I wanted to know that life could be beautiful."

Some were familiar with my kind of journey and were on their own pilgrimage into knowing more. I loved to hear their stories. Others gaped wide - eyed in awe, wanting to know more about what I was doing but knowing their short stay here would soon be up. I could see the desire for more in their eyes, but nonetheless, they still packed up and moved on. David sat quietly watching their reactions. The energy we created in conversation was palpable and peaceful: the Thais smiled over as if to say, 'Now you see what we see.'

"I'm going to move to Bangkok and find a job, so that I can come back here," I explained to a couple who had recently arrived.

"Blimey! That's the way. We'll have to be back in the U.K. in three months."

"That's a good trip," I offered.

"Yeah, but it means junketing along, not staying anywhere too long. The nature of the trip is different for you and us." After that we parted, knowing the journey would carry us to different places. A moment shared and a glimpse into another lifetime gained.

After enjoying delicious pancakes and a fruit shake I went out onto the beach to take in the wondrous beauty. Sitting on the sand, I thought of all I had been shown in such a short time. It was a lot to handle. I knew I was seeing into something incredible in the way that life was opening up to me, or more correctly that I was opening up to it. Still, I couldn't help doubting what I was being shown. I wanted to believe as if life and I had become friends, but getting past my limits took some effort.

I was afraid at times, fearing the possibility of a trapdoor beneath me. I could go somewhere wonderful with my mind and be shown something new and beautiful. Then I would come down into me and feel fear. I was afraid to believe in my own unlimited possibility, being more accustomed to fear feelings deep inside.

Something seemed to witness my struggle. It was as if I inched out further and further onto the branch of a tree when everything I had ever been taught told me that the branch would snap from my weight. But the twig at the end of the branch was calling me, pleading with me to move forward and trust that it would hold me. I was hearing something new, something different than what I had been taught, something wonderful that encouraged me to believe in what I couldn't see but could only feel.

I encouraged myself in my notebook. 'Choose it; it's yours!' 'Take it to the top, sister!' 'Life's a trip, ride it out.' 'Have no fear!' 'Get the info and run with it!' I considered how great I was feeling. 'It's incredible!' I wrote. 'Give your energy to it. Let it out! Nothing is going to stop me,' I wrote. 'Believe it. Why do you doubt? Have faith, all is intended that is good.'

Chapter 4 – White Linen

I was enjoying quiet time with David on my porch in the mid afternoon sun, when two travellers moved across the sand with packs on their backs into a bungalow facing the shore. She had long dark hair, and he had dreadlocks. Once they settled in, they came over to us dressed in swimsuits and we began to converse.

"Hey, how's it going?"

"It's divine," I answered, smiling.

David stood to shake hands. "And you?"

"Great. I'm Huey. This is Samantha," he added. Within moments Huey was in my hammock lighting a cigarette from the candles perched on my window frame. He had long curly brown hair and reminded me of Lenny Kravitz. Samantha sat on the porch swinging her legs over the side. Her long black hair framed a bright face, with pretty brown eyes.

"We're from Toronto. We are you guys from?" he asked, puffing on his cigarette.

"I'm from London," I smiled. "Nice to see some Ontarians here."

"Cool," Huey nodded. Samantha smiled.

"How long are you here?" David asked.

"Two weeks in the region. But only about five days here. We're going to the Philippines to meet up with some of Sam's family, then I'll be coming back down to meet some other friends for the full moon party," he explained.

Samantha added, "We'll be doing some island hopping in the Philippines. My family is spread out. It will be the first time to meet many of them." She smiled, excited by the prospect. Samantha was sultry and beautiful, and seemed very natural.

"So you lived in Korea, too?" he asked, after hearing more of my story.

"Yes, I loved it."

"I just came from Seoul. I live there now. I make children's books, create the English language text and the artwork. Some of them are published."

David and I were impressed. We liked being together and felt instantly comfortable.

Spending our afternoons as a foursome, changing my experience into something more social, writing took a backseat as I enjoyed their company and conversation. I jotted down only a sentence or two of insights in my notebook - 'Faith. Have faith in what you know or don't know.'

A few days later I was inspired to write more details in my notebook, withdrawing from my new social experience to do so. Sam, Huey and David were out for a walk in the water. I could see them from my porch. A feeling of jealously had reared its head inside of me. I had been so involved in my private companionship with David prior to their arrival that I found myself reacting to Samantha's attention to him. I questioned myself endlessly as I was certain my feelings for David were not romantic. I liked Sam too, and in pondering the situation some new insights became apparent for me.

Relax and use the power of negative emotions in another way. Channel jealous energy effectively elsewhere and deal with the emotion separately. Loving many people is important, so deal effectively with the energy of destructive emotions. Time will lend an answer.

The next afternoon David sat at the end of my bed, reclining just as Mark had done, facing the doorway. I sat at my headboard, intrigued. Mysterious yet mature, his short blond curly hair, blue eyes, thick Jersey accent and sense of humour kept me laughing. I knew our friendship must have appeared intimate to others, after all the hours we shared in private. But our friendship centred on the exploration of our individual perspectives.

I had never had a companion so much my junior and took the opportunity to ask many questions. David was six years younger. I reflected on my past when I had allowed cultural norms to curb my behaviour, but now I realized I didn't want arbitrary limitations placed on me by society. I knew that in order to understand my theories I needed to implement them, however uncomfortable or against the norm. So I reminded myself to stay conscious of my true feelings knowing that my friendship with David was an important learning environment.

Late in March I sat on the beach, staring out at the sea which had been calm the duration of my stay. The gentle warm weather had been the perfect backdrop for personal change. I had lived on the island for a month and felt it was time for something different. I was curious to see what life would be like in Bangkok, trying to maintain peace of mind in the middle of a giant Asian metropolis.

"You're going to Bangkok?" Huey said, sitting down beside me on the sand.

"Yes," I replied, pulling my attention from the horizon to look at his dreadlocks falling over his shoulders. They were such joyous dreadlocks, neatly tied at the back of his head. His soft, smooth voice entered my realm of awareness, and I nodded.

"Sam and I are going back in a few days. Why don't you come with us, that way you'll have someone to travel with."

It seemed like a great idea so I agreed at once.

"Okay, I'll leave you to your pursuits. I know you were busy enjoying the scenery."

He padded of as a smile took form on my face. The understanding was appreciated as I now began to see that life heard my experience, and others who also listened, knew as well. I still had many questions about life, about what was beneath it all, how it worked, and how it fit together. I knew I had some work to do on becoming more and believing more, but I had discovered that love and guidance was always within me.

The days passed quickly until it was my last morning. David brought over his things and created a pile on my porch. He wanted to take over my abode. A wave of reality engulfed me, as I knew my life would be changing forever. I wasn't sure I wanted to let go.

"You'll be back soon," David said. "I'll be here for a while and you're welcome to stay with me when you return."

"Thank you. I hope so." We hugged.

And then I was leaving the beach.

Sam, Huey and I took a truck taxi to the pier, then travelled to the mainland by ferry and boarded a night bus. We settled in and closed our eyes in hope of sleep for the 12 hour trip. We arrived in Bangkok at 6 a.m. and were directed off the bus at a downtown location. We hopped into a taxi to my hotel. My father had booked me a room at the Landmark Hotel, a luxury four star hotel, to help ease my transition into life in Bangkok.

With a key to a room on the 32nd floor, we were let in by a smiling bellboy, who accepted my tip then left. A large picture window pulled us through the room to an expansive eastward view over the vast horizon. Low rise buildings stretched out for miles and a light layer of smog coated the city. We lounged in the plush high back chairs, chatting and catching our breath after the long ride. After some coffee and cookies in the room, Sam and Huey collected themselves for their flight to the Philippines.

"I'll be back in a week to meet my friends from Korea," said Huey. If you want to go back down to the island with me let me know by email. I'll be passing through Bangkok and staying for one night. Maybe I can sleep on your sofa?"

"I'm sure that would be fine. I hope to have my own place by then. I don't know about going back down in a week, but I'll think about it."

"I'll email you. So think about it," he said, then hugged me.

"It's quite a change to be back in real life isn't it, Cassandra?" smiled Sam.

"Yes," I smiled back, and we hugged goodbye.

"Be good. And look for my email," said Huey, heading toward the elevator.

"Sure thing." I waved out my door as they entered the elevator. When the elevator doors closed, I closed my door, locked and leaned against it. I took a deep breath. I was on my own now. I returned to the view trying to relax as I sipped coffee and let the moment sink in. I picked up the English language Bangkok Post newspaper from the coffee table and began to flip through the pages. The glaring city news overwhelmed me. I put it down to take a shower.

Hot water began to steam up the clean, shining bathroom as cool, ceramic tile greeted my sand scuffed feet. A soft white cotton robe hung on the back of the door and the spotless mirror beamed with my reflection. It was a refreshing change and I pushed back the curtain to the focussed shower spray. Stepping into the flow, I luxuriated in scented soaps and shampoo.

Towelling off in plush white cotton, I wrapped myself in the robe and flipped my hair into a turban. Returning to the view, I stood above

Bangkok, sipping the last of my coffee and wondered what the city had in store.

Piling onto the soft bed stacked high with pillows, I turned to the employment section of the newspaper. A few English language schools had ads for part time work. I reviewed them knowing this was my avenue for work in the city.

Rental suites were abundant, scattered all over the city in various unusually named districts. Narrowing the search down to a few central addresses, I changed into city clothes and collected my transit map of Bangkok. My route seemed easy to navigate so I planned to view three apartments.

As I exited the hotel the heat enveloped me and I began to perspire. Immediately, I went into a corner store for some A/C relief and a bottle of water. After downing half of it, I put it into my bag and went looking for the bus stop. The map said the first apartment was only two stops away. I found the bus stop and hopped onto the next bus, thinking how easy it was.

As the congested bus sidled down the busy road, the air was thick with exhaust. I quickly lost track of my directions as the street signs in Thai characters were impossible to decipher at the speed we were travelling. The sounds of the bus were loud as it jammed and surged, spinning me onto other passengers as we clung to the handrails. The Thai passengers seemed resolute with my tossing about, eyes closed as if in meditation. I got off at the next stop. My frustration was made worse by the heat and I crossed the street of blaring traffic to wait for the bus running in the opposite direction, thinking it would lead me back to my starting point. Choking on exhaust particles I boarded the next bus then watched as it turned and twisted through traffic. I was so lost that my map useless.

Hours later I returned to my hotel almost in tears and ordered room service. Thankful for the cool, quiet room, I reviewed my map and set out a new plan for the next day. Then I settled into the bed to watch TV. Clicking through the channels I tried to learn more Thai and decided on a movie with Thai subtitles. Sunset fell over the dusty city as I watched from my plush bed, grateful to be high above the chaos.

The next morning I awoke at dawn and pulled open the curtains to watch the sun rise over the horizon. An orange sky became hot with light as the city began to wake. Thai style developments stretched out for miles as the exotic flavour of the land peeled from its pulse.

I dressed lightly and packed my bag with a map and water bottle, then headed out. April was the hottest month in Bangkok, I was told, made immeasurably hotter by the walls of concrete buildings and sidewalks. Somehow in the heat and bustle I was soon lost again and frustrated. Buzzing scooters accosted my ears and thick smog filled my lungs. I was tearful and jumped into a taxi for my hotel. Then, I called my father.

"You can come home if you want," he said, trying to comfort me.

"I can't. I have to do this on my own," I was holding back tears, realising the stark toll this was taking on my serenity. I took a breath trying not to cry.

"Well, see if you can find yourself an apartment. Then you'll feel more comfortable having your own home."

"Thanks, Dad. I'll try."

"You're welcome. We love you."

"I can do this. I have to do this. I'm going to keep trying," I said, my throat tightening.

"Okay. I'm here if you need me, just a phone call away."

"Thanks Dad." I hung up the phone and a gush of tears flooded from me. I was surprised at my own reaction and tried to pull myself together. I decided I needed a simple excursion to take my mind off the stress of trying to create a new life in a writhing foreign metropolis. I decided to take myself out for dinner.

I changed into a dress, freshened up and went to the elevator. The doors opened. After entering, I rode down only a few floors when the doors opened and a smiling, pear shaped woman with dark shoulder length hair got on.

"I like your dress," I said, admiring the lively, colourful flowers.

"Thank you," she smiled. "I like yours, too. To where might you be wearing it?"

"I'm taking myself out for dinner," I replied.

"Me too! Why don't we go together?" she asked, surprising me.

"Sure! That sounds great!" I felt better at once.

"I'm Luisa," she said, offering her hand.

"I'm Cassandra," I said, shaking it.

"Are you here on business?" she asked, perking up.

"No, I'm here looking for an apartment and a job. I'm going to live here."

"Oh, how exciting. I'm here on business, for a conference. I'm from Melbourne, Australia."

"Oh, that's wonderful. It must be exciting to travel all this way for work. I'm Canadian."

"Oh, wow! You're a long way from home."

"Yes, I am. It's been a little stressful lately because I've just come from a very relaxing month on the island of Phangan."

"That sounds fascinating! You can tell me all about it over dinner."

Luisa and I hopped into a tuk-tuk and rode to a restaurant she recommended with bamboo decor and colourful paper lanterns. The enchanting ambiance greeted us in delightful melodies, Buddha sculptures, and beautifully dressed Thai women with hands together at their hearts making the traditional 'wai' gesture in greeting.

We were led to a small table with candlelight beside a bubbling fountain with orange Koi fish swimming just beneath the surface of a small pond. Jungle foliage wrapped around us as we nestled into two chairs and were handed tall menus. Tiny umbrellas with pineapple skewers topped our daiquiri glasses that arrived at our table at once. We enjoyed the evening while serene Thai music played as we shared stories over delicious curry, coconut rice and pad thai.

After dinner we hopped into another tuk tuk and rode back to our hotel, laughing about our chance intersection and knowing our life paths would take us in different directions. We wished each other well as the elevator doors closed and I returned to my room. Behind the door I sighed with relief, enjoying the glimmering city from my quiet room. Bangkok did indeed have something to offer me!

The next morning after French toast and coffee in my room I scanned the Bangkok Post more determined to find an apartment. Setting out in the swelter of heat, smiling and listening within, I found my first address. I chatted with an English speaking uniformed Thai woman who led me to a darkened, stuffy apartment with one window that opened onto a concrete parking lot where a gaggle of youngsters played basketball. She seemed to think it was a great place and tried to sell me on the room size and easy access to shops as we moved through the sparsely furnished space. I hurried out after thanking her. She had provided the first step.

I felt satisfaction and a sense of achievement at having viewed my first apartment and I went on to view others with similar zeal. I was curious about the life lived by each landlord, how they worked throughout the day providing housing, while so many of their compatriots lived on the street under bridges and in makeshift homes built from cardboard.

Back at the hotel hours later, more familiar with the city map, I sent off my resume to an English language school in a good district. Then I headed to an Internet café beside the hotel where I received an email from Huey. It said he would be back in three days and asked it he could stay with me for one night. He reminded me of his invitation to join him. I wanted to escape the city but would I be ready?

I got a call from one of the schools for an interview the next day. I dressed accordingly and presented myself professionally, laughing to myself that I was fresh out of utopia trying to be serious and seem interested in working. I left the interview feeling confident and went back to my hotel room to scour the newspapers.

The next day I got a call from the school. I had been hired! I was ecstatic. My journey would continue in Thailand. I joyfully called my father, who was happy it had worked out for me.

"Any word on an apartment?"

"Dad, I just got a job! I'm happy to have one success!" I was overwhelmed easily as my serenity receded into memory.

"You're doing great. You'll find one soon, I'm sure. Good luck, honey. Call me if you need me."

"Thanks, Dad," I said tearfully and hung up. The experience of Bangkok was testing my resolve to the extreme. I knew I needed to go to the island with Huey. Just then, the phone rang.

"Hi Cass, this is Andre from the school calling you again. Because Thai Thanksgiving, called Song Kran, is coming this weekend, we're going to start you after the holiday rather than put you in for one or two classes this week. We'll see you Wednesday next week."

Thank God! I thought to myself. Now if I can only find an apartment, I can go to the island with Huey with my work done. I went to bed asking for the help I had on the island to reach me through the din of the city. I had faith I would find an apartment.

The next day I ventured out for my sixth day of apartment hunting and stood in front of another disappointing property that didn't reflect the image in the advertisement. The taxi driver sped off leaving me in a cloud of dust. I stood frustrated and hot in the middle of the road on the verge of tears. Thais looked me over from plastic lawn chairs in fenced yards nearby, leaning forward to gaze upon my situation. I felt the energy closing in.

Out of nowhere a taxicab sped along side of me and stopped. I could think of nothing better to do than to hop in. To my surprise the Arabic driver spoke English and smiled at me in the rear view mirror. As we drove, he told me a little about his life and how he learned to speak English while living in Saudi Arabia. When I told him about my situation he took it upon himself to help me find an apartment. My mood lifted as he darted back along the narrow streets into the district I wanted to explore.

He paused as we passed apartment buildings asking if they looked suitable. It wasn't long before he pulled into one with a large controlled entryway that was well lit and populated by Thai businessmen. Two female watch-keepers that inside a windowed office smiled as I approached and told me of a vacancy on the top floor. The taxi driver waited in the lobby while I was shown to the vacant flat.

"The rate is 6000 baht a month," she said, while escorting me to the elevator. I smiled as it was well within my budget at 200 dollars. On the sixteenth floor, she led me down a wide, well-lit hallway. She unlocked a solid wood door to a beautifully furnished open plan living room with high ceilings and a lovely leather sofa set. There was one hot plate beside a small fridge and I walked through another wood door to an adjoining master bedroom with a large double bed and built in wardrobe with a full-length mirror. There was a full ensuite linking both rooms. Doors led out to two separate balconies where I could wash my clothes and hang them to dry. "It's perfect. I'll take it." The woman smiled, saying nothing, then locked the door and returned with me to the office to sign the papers. I paid the deposit and collected my key.

I smiled at my taxi driver, waving the key and almost hugged him.

He smiled. "Now, back to your hotel for your things?"

"Yes! Thank you!" I happily hopped in the backseat and we drove to the hotel. He helped me carry my bags and then drove me back to the apartment. I tipped him generously.

"Thank you so much. You have no idea how much you have helped me."

"It's good to help," he said smiling, and putting the cash in his pocket without checking it.

"Have a nice life," he said.

"Thank you. And you, too," I smiled.

While unpacking my things I considered the arrival of Huey from the Philippines the next evening. After a week in Bangkok the shocking change had taken a toll on me. I had accomplished my goal of finding work and an apartment. I told myself I deserved a reward.

Huey showed up late the next night in time for only a quick meal and then sleep on my sofa. We got up early for breakfast then rode to the airport for our flight to Surat Thani, the port on the mainland where we would catch the night boat to Koh Phangan. We shared the evening at the pier munching on fresh fruit and delicious snacks from street stalls.

When the ferry was ready to board at 10 p.m., Thais were ushered upstairs to the top floor and all the backpackers to the second floor where we chose places on mats lined up along the open windows. It was like being at a big sleepover with 50 of us settled onto narrow beds with tiny pillows, lying side by side wrapped in whatever we had brought as blankets. I covered myself with my sarongs as the low hum of the engine slowly powered away from shore, cruising us through the night to Koh Phangan.

During the eight hour sail to the port of Thong Sala the windows were kept open and a warm breeze caressed us as we lay in our beds side by side. Looking out the window from my mat on the floor I could see the bright stars in the black sky as I inhaled the fresh sea air with a sigh of relief. It was good to leave the chaos of the city.

After a peaceful night's sleep, lulled by the gentle rocking of the boat, we arrived at the pier on Koh Phangan. It was early dawn and the island was just beginning to wake. We were directed toward a truck taxi and enjoyed the sunrise and cool morning air as it rushed into our faces on the ride to the beach.

Arriving at my safe haven I exhaled as we made our way down the sandy pathway between the palms, giggling to ourselves. I hadn't written David to tell him we were coming. Expecting to wake him, we surprised each other when I found him awake, having just returned from the night before.

"Hello!" we said to each other.

"We're back!" I said. He welcomed us into the bungalow. Huey claimed the hammock at once and I sat on the bed, arranging my things as I listened to Huey and David converse on the porch. The rustic wood hut gradually returned me to my simple ways of being as I reconnected to the scents and sounds of serenity. I inhaled the tranquility as I shook the tremor of big city life from my mind. Just then, a call came from the porch.

"Hey Cass, you're missing a beautiful moment," said Huey.

"I'll be out in a bit," I replied, holding backs tears of gratitude. Appreciating the space that welcomed my return so lovingly, I looked up at the morning sky and gave thanks. Then I meandered out onto the deck to join them.

The beach was quiet before the rise of the other revellers. David leaned back on his elbows on the porch and Huey reclined in the hammock. I sat on the bench at the end, relishing the quiet moment.

"How was Bangkok?" David asked, as I opened a bottle of water and drank.

"Bangkok was a steamy, noisy contrast to here. It was really hard," I laughed.

"That bad?" he said, with his eyebrows raised, as if considering his own transition into the 'real' world after leaving this place.

"Let's just say it took a toll and I'm happy to be here again," I said, gazing back out to sea.

"It sounds like you need to remember what it was like here," he said.

"Yeah, I need to get back to that place inside me."

"I've heard of people finding something amazing in some unique place in the world, and then all they want is to get back to that place. But it's a feeling, an experience. And once it's over, it's gone for good. A few lads and I have been chatting about it the past few days."

"It's a place of feeling but also a place of being," I offered. I could feel the familiar relaxation beginning to find its way into me.

"But it may not be the same experience ever again," he said.

"I want to find peace again. I feel like it was stripped away from me in the city with all the noise and bustle and demands of society, to conform and follow along and keep up. It takes a lot of concentration to participate in that."

"Yeah, you are right," Huey interjected. Three of us, talking, listening.

"But that place you found inside, it won't be the same place because you have changed. It can be better, though," they smiled, encouraging me.

"I guess the first 'knowing' is a once in a lifetime thing," I said, staring off into the distance.

"I am experiencing it now, thanks in part to you for introducing me to such a place. You're a wise sage." David smiled.

"Wow, you think so?" I blushed. David smiled at me and turned to gaze at the ocean. Its calmness entered our hearts and minds. I spread my arms wide, wanting to draw in the serenity and peacefulness. Feeling it envelop me, I was moved to tears and turned aside discreetly to wipe them.

The next day I relaxed at the bungalow all day until night, my candles flickering in the window frame in the twilight, Tracy Chapman singing from my small speakers on the ledge. I had barely moved all day, wanting only to recline and enjoy the view. Huey's three friends arrived from South Korea and we chatted for a bit: Craig from Calgary, Ken from Edmonton, and Sunny from South Korea.

"The full moon party is tomorrow night," said Huey.

"I want to wear something new," I said, wanting to shed my skin and transform myself. "Who wants to go shopping tomorrow?"

"I'd like to buy some body paint for tattoos," said Craig, sitting on the bench under the window, a handsome blond man with cerulean blue eyes. His lithe build and sensual demeanour was intriguing but something told me to be wary.

"I'll go too," said Huey, his face only partially visible in the flickering candlelight.

It was time to sleep. David and I shared the double bed and Huey lay in the hammock. The windows were open all night as we slept in the warm night air. It felt nice to have companions close to me. I felt protected.

The next morning we could hear loud music playing from the restaurant speakers. The vibe was picking up. Excitement for the party was beginning to build. We taxied into the village and wandered about for over an hour collecting our revelling paraphernalia and then headed back to the bungalows.

After dinner, we excitedly prepared for the party. Craig moved his things into the communal bungalow and began to paint tattoos on the arms of people who wanted extra appeal in the florescent lights. We pondered what insignia would best suit our moods and states of mind, as some of us indulged in mushroom tea. I shared a cup with David who was trying it for the first time, each of us eagerly awaiting the beginning of night. After watching a few loads of hooting, hollering revellers leave for the party we climbed in to our truck for the hilly and treacherous ride to Haadrin beach.

When we arrived on the beach we stayed close together as we made our way through throngs of partiers to an open patch of sand. Music pumping and lights flashing, the mood was intoxicating. As soon as the six of us sat down and declared our rendezvous spot David and I looked at each other and knew we needed to be alone to share the insights of our increased perceptual awareness. We moved toward the shore, witnessing people staggering and stumbling, to those who were meditating cross-legged on large rocks. The contrast of experience drew us into observation and it was a long while before either of us spoke.

Watching people mingling around us from our safe spot in the sand I could see active energies everywhere. I could see through their behaviour, fascinated by clarity, and tried to understand what was going on with our human tribe. What motivated us to do the things we did? I shared my observations with David about the apparently strange nature of people and their self-involved ways. What was our true purpose as a race and how we were fulfilling it?

David stayed silent, his eyes wide with new awareness.

Observing behaviours more closely, I could see motivations, and saw processes playing out. Some people appeared to be enjoying their lives while others appeared in conflict with themselves. I watched a man arguing with himself over his inaction after a woman walked by and caught his attention, as if he was badgering himself for not stopping to talk. He was so self-involved that he didn't realize his antics were being witnessed. Was this real? Was all of this happening?

Indications of confidence and individual strength were easy to pick out, as people marched with certainty and acted naturally. They danced well to the music and flowed with the surroundings. How could I see so clearly into these people?

I explained to David what I could see as he sat gaping at his expanded perspective, eyebrows raised. I continued to talk out loud, exploring the situation, moving my arms across the sights surrounding us, comforting myself as I speculated in safety with my friend. Then I put my arms up to the night sky and stars and asked, "Okay, what's going on? There's something going on here. David, what is it?" I asked, hoping he might have an answer as he rolled back in the sand, laughing.

"Come on, what is it?" I jokingly pleaded with him, knowing I may find deeper meaning in any response he gave, wanting something new to bridge an understanding. The people around us carried on with their situations, completely self-absorbed in their experience, oblivious to our concentrated observation. They looked amusing to me as if they were trying to be something other than what they were, as if they were acting in a play on stage, but on their own personal stage, alone. I looked down the beach, filled with sights and scenes that seemed surreal.

"This isn't real. Look at it. There's something about it," I said. David was lost in his own observations and said nothing. I put forth more ideas hoping for answers, challenging the surroundings to respond to my inquisition. "We're animals but were acting like we're not."

And then it happened. A brilliant dawning came over me like a huge light into my consciousness, engulfing me in an incredible sense of awareness. All at once I felt everything that burdened my mind disappear as I was filled with euphoric lightness and a sense of understanding of all life. In that moment I knew what I was, I saw what I was - a magnificent being of light. In that instant, I knew humans weren't the limited beings we thought we were. I awakened to the reality that I was not just my body or my body just me. My eyes opened wide to the expansiveness I felt within.

And for the first time I understood that the essence of my being was a combination of immense love and intense energy and that I had friends in the universe, and they were all around me, and it seemed that all of them were smiling. Something was witnessing my awareness and I sensed that I now understood more of what 'they' already knew, as if 'they' were my teachers.

Instantly I released the seriousness within me and the part of me that looked at the ground before each step. Feeling peace in every part of my being I saw the entirety of what I had become, as if I were a ball of yarn that held lessons of my experience, making me unique to all others.

In that moment I knew life as easy and carefree. I saw clearly that nothing really mattered, because the experience wasn't unforgiving or final in the way I had previously believed. It was an 'experience', one that was unique to my wishes and expectations and in that it was surreal, not predetermined. The moment was huge and thrilling for me. I was speechless. All I could do was drink in this new feeling, this immense awareness and understanding.

I became aware that my being was a manifestation of energy and that in essence I was joy, bliss, love, and all the wonderful things, and that as the nature of my being and experience, I need not worry over anything. I already had everything I needed as part of myself. I could live, breathe, move and think for myself, and that was all I needed, truly.

In that moment, I felt so much relief that I wondered if I was glowing to anyone around me. But even David didn't notice this awakening I was experiencing at his side, as I sat with my mouth agape and my eyes open wide. I had a strong desire to just laugh and laugh as if I had just been let in on life's biggest joke.

I looked around me at people moving in front of my eyes and I wanted to stand up and shout, "Hey, it's okay! Life is truer than we have imagined! It's more different than we have believed! It is so much bigger than what we have thought! Love it! This is joy down to your soul!"

In that moment I realised my words meant something - they weren't just empty sounds. They were energy forms that I created and expelled, heard by all of life, like the sound of a beating drum. I knew then I must choose my words well.

I looked around me at all the people who were where I had just come from and I wanted them all to see what I was seeing, to know what I was knowing, to share with me in this new awareness. I wanted them to understand the power and energy we possess and that we're not just powerless beings moving through life. I knew that if we knew our own power, really knew it, we would use it wisely.

I saw how it was all connected and wondered what life would be like from this perspective, after the secret was revealed. How could life intrigue me now that I knew its secret? Then I thought about the potential enjoyment of showing others and I settled back into the sand to take in all that my visual field had to offer. It was amazing.

David and I returned to the group. Everyone was enjoying themselves, and having a good time. Craig sat down beside me unexpectedly and asked me to go for a little walk.

I agreed, and we walked toward the sand, sitting down near the shore.

"You have been having a good time here, I can tell," he said, matter of factly.

"How can you tell?" I laughed, wondering about his intentions. His face was illuminated by the moon, handsome, but I felt no romantic connection.

"You look beautiful and peaceful. I would really like to talk with you more."

"Oh," I said, not finding the words to continue. I watched a man walk past us to the shore and before I realized what was happening, I saw him urinating into a discoloured pond – the outdoor bathroom. I immediately stood up.

"Let's go back to the group." I felt finished with our exchange, as Craig obliged, seeming kind and respectful.

David, Huey, Craig and I returned to the bungalows about 3 a.m. to quiet surroundings. Ken and Sunny were in their bungalow and Huey climbed into their hammock to sleep. I didn't want the night to end.

"Let's sit down on the sand and watch the stars," I suggested, going inside to get my sarong. I spread it on the sand in front of the bungalow and Craig sat down on it beside me. David sat on the porch. I lay back to look up at the sky and watch the moon high above us. Everything was silent, except for the gentle lapping of the waves. Serenity filled me and the moment beyond words. For a long while we basked silently under the night sky.

A chill crept along the ground so Craig went inside to get a sweater. David went inside too and they chatted quietly as I sat smiling, looking up, feeling joyful thinking of the beautiful experience that had opened me to so much.

Just then I saw shadows of two men walking past me toward the beach. In a foreign accent, one asked, "What is this? Ein creep?" The other snickered as they lumbered on. In that moment, my feeling plummeted as I felt judged and criticized by their name calling. I wanted to swear at them, to make them wrong, but nothing came to mind. Then I caught myself, and heard from within: *Do not give others power over your feeling. Do not give in and condemn others. They know not what they do.*

Trying to regain my sense of inner balance, exhaling with force, I realized that life would still confront me with challenges. How could I look like a creep to someone when I was feeling so grand, and so full of love on the inside? The insult had a lingering effect on me. I knew I had more work to do.

When Craig returned, I told him what had happened.

"Don't even worry about it," he said. "They don't even know you. It doesn't mean anything. Just forget about it." He lay down on the sarong beside me for a few moments, but then I felt it was time to finish for the night.

The weight of the negative feeling subsided and I went into the bungalow and took out my notebook. How could I put into words what I had learned that night? I chuckled to myself as I sat back on David's bed. Words were so limited. I felt like it was trying to describe a kaleidoscope, explaining it in one colour.

Still, I felt inspired to try. 'Life takes you through certain experiences for the things you need to learn.' 'We are acting as if somehow we are above the other animals and life with whom we share this planet.' 'Everything I say means something; words are not just empty sounds. Does this apply to everyone?' Then, I wrote, 'Yes, I think so.' 'Everything has been necessary, in an indirect way sometimes, but needed to make a point. When does this system end? Does it?'

I tucked my notebook under the mattress as David, Craig and I piled into the bed. It was too cold for anyone to sleep in the hammock so we closed the windows and shut the door. Between them, I was happy to hear David and Craig fall asleep, as I stared up at the black ceiling, loving my life.

The next morning I felt the familiar stillness inside. Words were unnecessary and breaking the silence hardly seemed worthwhile. I padded gently across the sand for breakfast, moving to my favourite table and smiling easily at everyone around me. I felt special that such an incredible experience had happened to me. I knew others would love an awakening like mine but few made it a priority, probably thinking it would be too hard to find. I wanted to share with them what I was experiencing and give them a taste of how easy it was, with dedication, the right time and place.

I finished my pancake breakfast and coconut shake and walked to the beach, watching seabirds soaring through the air. Gazing at the horizon, relishing the moment with my peaceful surroundings, it dawned on me that 'enlightenment' was not unattainable. It was simply a knowledgeable state of being, achievable in much shorter periods of time than I had believed. Whenever I had ever heard the term, I had imagined lifelong solitude and contemplation climaxing only late in life. But I was seeing for myself that enlightenment was a process, with very powerful stages of development that was available to anyone who believed in their abilities to bring it forth on their own terms. Everything was orchestrated wonderfully, like a symphony. I just needed to realize it and see it the way it was.

Huey, Craig and their friends left for Korea the following day and I felt my awareness fading as I busied myself with conversations and travel between places, planning my next move. I realized that my mind needed to entertain itself as I pondered and postulated the intricacies of daily life. As a result my clarity seemed to come and go. It was like getting close to a pirate's treasure map then losing sight of it and falling back it into blindness again. I latched onto something, but I just couldn't figure out what.

As the days passed in warm, telling breezes, caressing me on the beach, new and more powerful beliefs poured through me. Silky, soft sand lay white and glowing beneath my feet, as I reclined to view the sea, drifting into it. I heard things I wanted to hear inside, about my life, about my family, releasing things that had trapped me along the way, feeling more freedom with each release.

Cascading energy cleansed me as new insight poured in, enriching my experience to where it was only the awareness of my self and nature that existed. Tears rolled down my face as I released ideas I had held onto about the meaning behind events. Blue hues imbued my vision, the tinkle of waves soothed my hearing and the soft sand warmed and cooled me at the same time, gently coaxing me into the present moment. Rocked back and forth by the experience, I let go of pain I had held onto, the hurt that I had identified as wrong, saying goodbye to blame. Oh, the tears, how they exited my eyes. Then with release, exhaling, I felt buoyant, reaching a new surface inside myself.

Joy filled me, as I reached upward within, to the next rung on the ladder calling me forward, daring me to believe there could be another way.

Let in the energy so greatly that it is constant guidance. Use it to better your life and world, not against it. Like the sun's rays, energy is available to you.

Kind, loving, gentle words were whispered to me from within, comforting me, teaching me not to fear. My mother wasn't so wrong, if I took her point of view and examined it. I could see how she saw things that way; and myself, maybe I didn't understand at the time it could be different. I didn't understand I could be myself beyond the scope of her actions. Memories of unrest broke like a series of waves, searing me as they crashed until fresh air kissed my face and lungs, all negativity disappearing on the wind. The sorrow passed. I was me again, loving life.

Revelations caused my body to jolt upright, a culmination of my wishes, an alarm clock was going off inside me. I tossed and turned on the sand at times as I moved through thoughts I had carried, releasing them, not bothered by the glance of strangers who had no idea what I was doing. I smiled and sent them love with a promise that I would one day tell.

The nature of my thoughts changed in a profound way as the realizations created a lasting effect. They slowed down, and the amount of thoughts decreased as the quality increased, as if my ability to think and reason became more magnified.

I spent a great deal of time correlating my new understanding with a review of my past, looking at my life with new eyes. It was like taking a large wrinkled sheet and shaking it in one big wave like motion and watching the wrinkles disappear. I had to readjust my perspective of life because I was seeing things from a different viewpoint: a conscious perspective.

Scanning the pages of previous writings, I felt ahead of them, easily answering some of the questions that had plagued me. I was not sure what I was glimpsing, whether I was entering into a realm of thought or into something bigger. I was building foundations for understanding. I still had many questions about what I was facing.

The day of my departure came. I hugged David and we promised to keep in touch. Our paths diverged as I boarded a truck taxi to the pier. I was excited about my new life in the city. I felt responsible and capable.

I boarded the ferry with the bustling crowd and busy tourists. It appeared that many had jammed a lengthy journey into a few weeks or less. Some seemed stressed out just to be there, as if they couldn't shut off their minds. We settled onto seats in rows, then later after reaching land, I boarded a night bus to Bangkok. I gathered on the sidewalk with a Thai man named Chalart who was travelling with his sisters. We greeted each other and exchanged a few words in English, then in Thai, about our lives. They were kind people who asked if I travelled alone. I said yes, and they took it upon themselves to sit with me at the back of the bus and watch over me for the trip.

The next day in Bangkok, we waved goodbye and exchanged Thai-style smiles.

I arrived home at my building and rode the elevator to the top floor. Turning the key in my lock, the door clicked then pushed heavily on its hinges inward. The room was stuffy so I opened the doors to the balconies and lay my bags on the bed to unpack. The breeze swept through the room bringing fresh air and the scent of a busy city. Stepping out onto the concrete porch in barefeet I inhaled the scents and sensations of Bangkok. It had missed me, and I had missed it. Life was taking place here. How would I uphold my serenity in its fervent grasp? The view over the city went on for miles and I gazed out upon it: lights, dust and sounds; wondering about the lives being lived by the millions of people who inhabited the densely populated plateau.

The doors of the bookcase creaked when I opened them to place my small stack of books back on the shelf. Otherwise empty, the mahogany built-ins were elegant as well as regal, lending a sophisticated charm to the white walls that stretched ten feet up. The comfortable leather sofa cushioned me perfectly while I read the Bangkok Post. Stories and pictures of excitement in the city drew me out to explore.

The Klong River ran north and south through the middle of the metropolis, dividing Bangkok into east and west portions. My building was on the east side where tourist blocks were only a ten minute cab ride. As I walked along the thoroughfare I watched a mass of motorcycles zip through traffic as if on their own highway, weaving between the cars at close proximity. Horns occasionally honked in a friendly manner as the mass sped along.

I got on a bus and rode to the shopping district, hopping off as the bus quickly sped on. Moving among tourists and locals, the city pulse swept me along, hot and steamy, almost dreamlike. People forged onward while respecting each others' space, moving gracefully from side to side on passing. The flow was evident and I knew I had better find it because Bangkok moved fast.

I bought a few things, some fruit, a bracelet. I allowed the mood to envelope me until it began to get dark and lights came on. It was time to go. Back inside my apartment I brushed my teeth and went to bed.

On my first day of work I rode in a taxi to be sure to arrive on time. Hopping out at the office I was met with air conditioned rooms and smiling teachers. Eunice, one of the school's directors, took me aside.

"I'll be preparing you today. We have some options for you and you have some forms to fill out." Her British accent jolted me into an alert state. She was a professional expat who had been teaching English abroad for many years. Her bronzed hair and blue eyes sparkled from olive-sun skin. Her dignified but jovial manner made me feel comfortable and she seemed to enjoy that I was Canadian.

"You're Canadian so you speak French as well as English, correct?"

"Yes, I studied French in school for eight years."

"Terrific. You will have more choice then. There's work here on a regular basis; morning businessmen, housewives, students preparing for tests. There is also a full time opportunity as a Kindergarten teacher at an elementary school."

"I like the idea of being a Kindergarten teacher. I love children and I taught Kindergarten classes in South Korea. Where is the school located?" She helped me find it on the map. It was ten minutes from home, on the same road. I would have a short commute.

"You have some choices regarding transit. I'll get Andre to explain it to you." She called into the other room.

Andre came bounding into the room showering his grin on us.

"Sure, Cassandra, let's have a look here." We leaned over the map as I considered Andre. He was South African, handsome and his enthusiasm was infectious. I could tell Eunice was smitten. I listened as he instructed me on modes of transport.

"You will have your choice of bus or canal taxi, which is a long boat that picks up at platforms along the Klong river."

"It sounds exciting!"

"Oh, don't be too excited. It's rustic so be sure to hang on tight. You don't want to fall into the Klong." He made a face. "I take the motorcycle taxis – they're fast, affordable and fun! But wear a helmet."

"Cassandra, we have a student who wants to learn French. She is going on a trip and may attend university. She wants to prepare," Eunice said, entering the room.

"Thanks, Andre," I said, and he bounded out of the room.

"That sounds interesting, Eunice. If its elementary French I would be interested," I said, knowing my Canadian French was packaged in the classroom.

"She's a delightful girl, hard working and kind. I know you'll like her. It's Wednesday evenings for an hour or two. We keep it very flexible because of her studies. Do you think you could take her on?"

"Okay, I'll give it a try."

"Just do your best. Here's a textbook to brush up on and her phone number. You two can set it up. Her name is Lani."

"Great. When do I start?"

"You can meet me at the school there at 8 a.m. Friday where you will receive training before classes start Monday."

"Okay. Thank you, Eunice."

She smiled. "You'll be great. Thanks for joining us. I'll see you at the school at 8 a.m."

"I'll see you there," I smiled and left the building. Walking down the sidewalk with the textbook pressed against my chest I considered my life in Bangkok. I was a true resident. It was a wonderful feeling and I walked for a while in the direction of my home, along street side shops and through various districts, until I was tired and hopped onto a bus.

When I arrived at my building I went into the restaurant on the main floor, realizing it served as a kind of cafeteria for the whole place. I ordered something new from the menu and stared out the window contemplating the life changes that had happened in rapid succession. I sighed in satisfaction then ate my delicious meal.

I entered my apartment and opened the balcony doors for the breeze. I picked up the receiver to call Lani and set up our first appointment. She agreed to come to my apartment the next evening to begin the first class. After I hung up the phone I went to the bathroom where something on the floor caught my attention.

At the threshold to the bathroom lay a stick figure of a person. The body was made from sticks from the broom that rested against the wall nearby. The head was made from a dust ball. The shape was obvious and unmistakable. It looked a person at the edge of a threshold. I shook my head in disbelief then picked it up and threw it off my balcony.

"Be free," I called out as it blew away in the wind.

The strange occurrence stayed with me but I carried on with my tasks and soon forgot about it.

The next evening Lani arrived at my door. She had a strange look on her face when I opened the door, but soon smiled as I welcomed her inside. We got along easily and I taught her some French. She told me about her plans to live in Paris for six weeks. She was studying to enter university. I could tell she was a serious student.

At the end of the lesson, I walked her out to the parking lot where she climbed into her BMW and waved as she drove away. I admired her take-charge manner and smiled at her luck in driving such a beautiful car.

On my first Saturday in the city I picked up the Bangkok Post to read the tourist section. I found a lengthy list of art galleries with a map of locations. I decided I would work my way through the list each weekend.

After hand-washing my clothes and hanging them to dry on my porch, I boarded an early afternoon bus in front of my building that travelled into a residential area. The bus came to a stop in a neighbourhood unlike any I had ever seen. It was an eclectic mix of industrial buildings and family homes.

Nestled back from the road at the end of a pathway lying beneath a few trees sat a rustic looking red barn. A large, tilted wooden door was pinned back with a rock as a couple of smiling foreigners stepped over the threshold and onto the path. We exchanged hellos as they exited the gallery, similarly enchanted by the unusual scene.

Inside the rustic entrance soft music played and incense floated through the air. I overheard a British accent while I strolled with hands clasped behind my back, appreciating beautiful colourful artwork depicting realistic tropical scenes of waterfalls, jungles and nature. The resident British artist had fallen in love with Thailand and stayed on, he explained to a foreign couple as they laughed candidly and spoke of amazing Thailand. Smiling to one another we made our way from painting to painting, feeling the joy in the artists' delight of a tropical paradise in the middle of an Asian metropolis.

Stepping out of this illusory setting I floated to the bus stop for the journey another beautiful gallery and several more afterward. Delighted by the vibrant art I toured on throughout the afternoon, strolling along a tented street side market with colourful clothing, handicrafts and metal bins of hot, tempting Thai food. Then I headed home for a meal at my home restaurant which had quickly become like my own personal kitchen.

Gentle, smiling Thai women put warm, delicious plates of noodles and vegetables in front of me, wanting to communicate with me. I used my dictionary and tried out words with them that often brought laughter. The pronunciations had to be just right. If they understood me they would repeat the word several times, pleased that I was learning. I enjoyed our time together and I always left a good tip.

On my way to the elevator I returned the smiles of two women in the booth who tracked my arrival and departure with interest. I felt comforted and loved as I entered the elevator, happy and humbled as the doors closed.

On the 16th floor, the hallway stretched out empty before me. As I approached my room a pretty, young Thai woman in a dress came out of the apartment beside mine. We greeted each other.

"Hello. We are neighbours," I said, putting my key in the door.

"Yes," she smiled. "Hello."

After I closed my door I pondered the quality of her life as I pulled an iced tea from the small fridge. Opportunities for young women were normally only in offices, schools and shopping centres or else in clandestine establishments. Her polished outfit told me she had ambition and I wondered how she envisioned her future.

From my bookshelf that held books I had picked up along my journey I chose an anthology of Buddhist authors, looking for another perspective on the unknown. I settled onto my sofa and was taken to another time and place, into the thoughts of a monk in a monastery. Peace emanated from the words but where were the thoughts going? What was knowable in an 'unknowable' world? There must be something to find, something within that we can know and teach, I wondered. There must be a way to understand how to perform at our best. Suffering the translation, I closed the paperback, desiring an easier form of spirituality that would be more accessible to modern people.

Chapter 5 – Chalkboard Pictures

On Friday morning I walked three blocks to the canal taxi platform, passing the bevy of young motorcycle drivers leaning against red and white sport bikes. A popular pick up area, they gathered chatting while waiting for fares, decked out in motorcycle gear and sport helmets. I smiled as I passed by, hopping onto the sidewalk that lined a road jammed with cars. The cement wall in front of my building blocked much of the noise and smog of the street. I lived on a busy thoroughfare. Smog and dust filled my nostrils with scents of a ruddy river as I walked toward the canal.

I followed Andre's directions down a side street and found a collection of business people in suits of conservative cut and colour waiting on a dock. The murky grey water sloshed under the wooden platform that filled with more people as we waited. Soon I saw a rushing boat approaching from the left, already packed with passengers. We stealthily piled in, as the boat paused only briefly before veering off and accelerating. I handed coins to a red aproned attendant and received a chit in return. I smiled and made my way to the centre of the packed vessel. Crammed together we fell forward then back with the force of the boat at each stop. Speeding along the surface of the water we passed many boats from the other direction. This river was a busy two-way thoroughfare. Having never seen anything like it I gazed in awe at the sights and the serene faces of passengers. Quiet and seemingly contemplative, they sat with their eyes closed. The breeze flowed through at a cooler temperature than the heated fray of the street and I felt much more relaxed to be on the water.

Speeding along, I saw makeshift homes positioned right up against the fence that lined the canal. There were even some abodes under bridges, complete with television lights flickering within. A woman wearing an apron was hanging cleaned pots on a fence as we motored past. I was amazed at how they had adapted to every condition.

The boat finally pulled up to the fifth platform and I hopped off to navigate my way to work. The building was a large cement structure with decorative architecture and Thai flags in front. I mounted the steps and entered through grand doors. Just being out of the heat refreshed me even though I could feel small particles of smog on my face.

After my meeting with Eunice, and a few hours of preparation in the English department and meeting of other foreign teachers, I left to explore the city. Walking along the sidewalk I passed many interesting sights and occurrences that demanded examination. The busy city had many stories to share and people with varying degrees of bliss showing on their faces. I wanted to share the love I had experienced on the island and looked for people to return my knowing smiles. Many smiled back to me and most seemingly enjoyed life.

When I returned to my apartment the heat inside the room was suffocating. I pushed open the balcony doors. The straw man on the floor did not reappear and I thankfully didn't see anything else until I looked in the bathtub. At the bottom was a two inch cockroach. I shrieked.

I immediately found a cup and covered it. Then I found a piece of paper and slid it underneath. I went to the balcony and threw it out but the wind caught it and returned it to my adjoining balcony. I picked it up and again launched it over the edge. This time it was swept away and its wings opened up as it coasted downward. I was happy to see it go.

Lani was scheduled to have another lesson that evening. When she arrived she looked more relaxed and our exchange began to feel more like friendship. When we finished the lesson she looked at me resolutely.

"How have you been enjoying life in Bangkok?" she asked.

"I love it here. Its very interesting. It's very hot, but there is so much to explore." As I explained what I liked about the city, I couldn't help thinking about the straw man on the floor.

"Anything unusual happening?" she asked as I stared at her.

"Well, yes," I said, not sure if my story would scare her. "Do you really want to know?"

"Yes, tell me. I'm Thai," she smiled, encouraging me to confide.

"Well, when I came home last week I found something on the floor that I thought was strange. There was a straw man made from the sticks of my broom with a dust ball head, lying at the edge of the bathroom door."

"Oh," she said. "That is strange."

"I just picked it up and threw it off the balcony hoping the straw man would find freedom," I laughed.

"Hmm. Well, the reason I asked you is because of what happened the first day I arrived here. I got into the elevator and pressed floor 16 and after the doors closed every button on the console lit up, as if someone pressed them, one at a time. But I was alone in the elevator."

My eyes were wide. "What do you think it means?"

"In Thailand we believe in spirits. That is why we have spirit houses outside in the yard. It gives the spirits someplace to live because they don't know about size."

I laughed.

"We put flowers and fruit in the spirit house so they don't live in the main house," she said, looking at me. I looked around. There was no spirit house in my apartment.

"Do you think a spirit is living here?" I asked, shivering.

"Maybe. Sometimes if it is hot and then cold it can be a sign. I don't know for sure. Just pay attention. If you need anything, you can call me."

"Sure. Thank you for telling me."

After she left I felt a little uncertain but brushed off the feeling. I tried not to think about it.

On Monday morning the school assembly began with the entire school population standing in neat, uniformed lines headed by teachers. I stood with the Thai Kindergarten teacher who was my new counterpart and listened as the school announcements played in a booming Thai voice over the intercom.

The students looked sharp in pressed navy uniforms and stood at silent attention until it completed with a Thai song of worship to the King. Everyone sang along word for word pledging their allegiance. Then classes were led single file to their classrooms. I walked with the Thai teacher, a plump, stern woman in her fifties. She corrected the boys for any dalliances on the way through the hallways with piercing stares. One glance was shocking enough to bring immediate compliance. I smiled at the students and held the classroom door as they filed in. Each student found their seat and assigned desk. Clearly they had visited the classroom with their families to prepare before the start of the year.

The veteran Thai teacher held a two foot switch as she droned on about conduct. Hours went by as the uniformed boys squirmed, bored and restless.

At lunch time, the children pulled bags from their desks and began to eat, chatting and giggling even as this new regime was thrust upon them. I sidled up to the teacher and pulled out my lunch to get a better read on her. She stared at me resolutely as I worked to bring a smile to her face.

"Do you mind if I do some drawing on the blackboard during my lessons?"

"Yes."

"Yes, I can't?" I frowned.

"Yes, drawing." She met my eyes and smiled a tight lipped concession.

In the afternoon, when I was introduced I wrote everything on the board and made jokes. The children seemed to enjoy my jovial manner, a contrast to their Thai mother figure. I wanted them to enjoy learning English, and after a brief intro, the Thai teacher stepped in and began teaching with me from a book. I repeated the words back to the students with her, as we smiled and began to work together.

The day ended with the sounds of other students walking in the halls, amid chatter and the sounds of locker doors being opened. I felt exhausted and I could hardly imagine how the boys made it through their first full day of school. I gave them big smiles on their way out the door, cheering them on.

Back home I went to the restaurant and dove into pad Thai noodles and a coconut shake. After dinner I walked the stairs to my apartment, enjoying the exercise past open air windows at each floor. I pulled a chair to the porch as the sun was setting and gazed out for miles across the vast horizon. Colours of the enchanting city shot out in exotic bursts: high rise buildings in the pink sunset, dust clouds rolling along at a distance, a yellow glowing ball burning bright as it descended over the sprawling metropolis. I saw a slum neighbourhood behind my building, protected and nestled from the winds in rows of corrugated metal. A shanty district right below my window! Bicycles and pedestrians buzzed everywhere along cleverly networked pathways lined with entrances and buckets to collect rain water. These were the homes of some people who earned money from tourist, working street stalls, selling market items and other forms of entrepreneurialism.

I moved inside, struck by the effects and variation in experience. I chose my life the way it was. In Canada there is a cultural expectation about living environments because winter has dire implications. We have to have homes. But the warm climate in Thailand made housing optional. People slept outside all year long.

My days at school began to brighten as my lessons developed into drawing games. I drew chalkboard pictures of animals, numbers and words as my students called out the correct answers. They learned quickly as I carried on, bringing laughter into the classroom, having fun with the language.

One morning I slept in. I approached the bike boys at the corner of our lot.

"Can I have a ride please, just 10 minutes up the road?"

"Yes," smiled a Thai rider who then handed me a helmet. I was required to wear a conservative skirt to the school everyday so my only option was to sit side saddle as Thai women did. My driver explained, "Hold here and here," he said, pointing out two remarkably small plastic grooves on the back of the bike. I hopped on and steadied myself. After a nod I found myself buzzing into traffic, weaving between cars, getting ahead and making good time.

When we arrived at school I breathed a sigh of relief. "Thank you," I said, ever so gratefully.

I entered the classroom as the Thai teacher began the lesson, with a scowl, as I quickly found my seat near the window to the hallway. I smiled back to the children who looked my way.

Days in the classroom were mostly the same. I would sit for hours until my chance to teach, speaking in English if the opportunity came about. Lunch breaks were shared with other teachers who worked at the school.

One afternoon riding home from work on the '60s model bus (no AC!) we stood crowded together in the heat swaying from side to side. The hot temperature was reluctantly giving way to evening bliss where it normally dropped enough to be pleasant and bearable.

Usually I was the only foreigner among all the Thais on the bus, but this evening a tall, handsome man stood in front of me. He looked Canadian with his short blonde hair, blue eyes, preppy style and sporty sandals. I couldn't take my eyes off of him. I decided to be assertive. At his stop I followed him off the bus.

"Hello," I said.

He turned around and smiled. "Hello." We conversed naturally as he spoke with a Canadian accent. "Are you Canadian?" I asked.

"I'm German, but my Mom is Canadian. She's from Ottawa. I'm Harry," he explained.

"I'm Cassandra. I'm from Canada," I smiled. The conversation became comfortable as we chatted.

"I'm going to be meeting some friends later at a pub nearby. I could meet you here at seven. Very low-key, just hanging out."

"That sounds like fun," I answered, reviewing my inner messages. "Sure."

"Where do you live?" he asked.

"To be honest, I don't know!" I blushed and turned to orient myself.

"You don't know where you are? Then, why did you get off the bus?"

"I wanted to take some chances, you know, break down barriers. I just got off the bus to talk with you."

"Is that wise in a city such as Bangkok?"

"It worked out, didn't it?"

He smiled.

It turned out we lived within five minutes of each other. After making plans and exchanging numbers I went home to get ready, excited at beginning a new social life in Bangkok.

Harry met me in my lobby and I smiled to the desk ladies. We walked over to the canal platform and he led me to a place he said I would love, down a side street and in through the doorway that appeared out of nowhere. We were led to an outdoor patio. With a wave to his friends, we approached a handsome group seated at a small round glass top table with a candle on it. Surrounded by others enjoying a tranquil evening in a backyard setting, the evening was surreal. The noise of the city disappeared as we sipped quality wine and nibbled on spicy crackers. Couples spoke quietly in the warm and inviting ambience as Harry and I shared our histories of how and when we had arrived in Bangkok.

"So you've just arrived here after living on the beach for a month?"

"Yes, only a week or so."

"At my work, there are mostly very serious Germans who could never dream of living like you. I've only been here a little over two months on my six month contract but you make me want to run off and do the same," he said, lifting his glass to mine. "I like you," he smiled.

"Thank you, Harry. I like you, too," I said, my glass meeting his.

"I'm happy I met you. We can hang out and get to know each other but I have to tell you that I have a girlfriend in Germany. She will be coming here in a few weeks for a visit."

His eyes carefully watched mine as I exhaled. He was very handsome and the wine and candlelight was having an affect on my imagination. But I trusted that what was happening was for the best.

"Okay. Well, it will be nice to meet her, too."

"I have a swimming pool on the roof of my building so you should come and take a swim."

"Oh, that is awesome. I would love to swim on your roof!"

And so it began, that Harry and I began to share time discussing matters of the heart and mind, swimming in his rooftop pool. Some evenings we had the pool to ourselves, and he stared deeply into my eyes in the light of the moon. His mystique intrigued me and I was tempted to know his private world. Instead, we shared dappled sunsets over the city, horizons across colourful masterpieces drifted for miles. I danced along the edge of the roof, singing and enjoying my newfound freedom. So far from home but in the presence of another.

The heat was intense, the crowds thick, and staying above frustration from not understanding more than a few words in Thai and getting lost regularly, I tried to be positive about the situation. Testing myself to make changes in my behaviour and do things I wouldn't normally do, challenged my limits. Who was really enjoying the experience anyway?

Moving people and striding throngs kept me in a flow of other worldliness. With a rhythm of its own, the flow granted entrance into hidden byways and obscure environments, leading me through a hanging cloth doorway and into a room of women speaking quietly. Working with their hands they looked up, silence spoke the truth of the moment. Soft smiles echoed back. I carried on, walking into another part of the store. I was followed by one of the women.

"I know you are here. I see you."

"I see you, too. Thank you." Staring into her eyes for a reason as to why she shares these statements with me, and if she does with everyone. I think not. Soon, I am gone looking back at a woman who is watching. I wonder if I will return.

Walking onward I came to a used bookstore. Smiling at my luck, I meandered through the aisles looking over an array of English books. A purple binding caught my attention and I picked up a paperback with an interesting cover. The The Alchemist by Paulo Coelho. I knew immediately it was a good find and paid for it at once.

The bus arrived and I encountered some surprised Thais, perhaps witnessing their first blond woman. I smiled and sat down among them. My eyes moved from person to person. Politely, they did not return my glances and I studied them more closely. What kind of pants, shoes and how did they get them? Many of them seemed to be living similar lives to mine: waking, working, and travelling home each night to their families. I was told that Bangkok expanded far into the distance because many jungle villagers had found work in the city but were forced into long commutes by the high cost of metropolitan living.

Social customs and conduct seemed to be the same with strangers. Eye contact or a nod of acknowledgement was all that was needed to convey meaning. Sometimes gestures were made to one another with respect and courteousness. Often women would follow the lead of a Thai man of age or status when someone needed to take charge. Although men seemed to always take the dominant role, I saw this as tacit consent on the part of the women.

I put on my headphones and disappeared into the music. As my eyes wandered, I reverted back to the serenity of the familiar songs from the beach. Tracy Chapman's voice took me back to those moments as I remembered aspects of what I had learned while swaying in my seat. I felt appreciated by my Thai peers as I could feel their energy meld around mine, discovering new conversations with life that I hadn't been attuned to before.

The subtle messages seduced me. Life became so loving and gentle. I was entranced by the way it spoke to me and the means that were chosen. In conjunction with my thinking, as if I had just spoken my wish into a microphone, someone rushed to fulfill my request. I wondered if others knew what was happening. On one occasion, I gazed deeply into the eyes of a girl behind a sales counter after she supplied me with exactly what I had been looking. She had reached down to pick it up as if it was waiting for me.

At times, I could hardly contain my laughter and had to remove myself to regain composure after trying to explain my thoughts to straight-faced Thais. Soon I learned to keep my findings to myself. If I was distracted or frustrated my surroundings seemed to shut down disturbingly. Late buses or rude people would crawl up on my skin like a dragon, taunting me to take action. But as I expanded my perspective even amid the most intolerable moments of heat, confusion and chaos, I was able to steady myself. Then I could rise above the chaos and move between the people like a placid pinball, observing the ant like movement, letting it take me along. At times I was hesitant and passed up a concession made for me. Older Thai women especially would react negatively, impatient that I was not flowing with instinct, which then disrupted what followed. A domino effect was felt by everyone, and I saw this for myself. We needed to be conscious of the group. Staring into their eyes as they passed, it was like they didn't know my world of thought and only perceived their own, looking blindly into such a different world. We could not see the same thing.

During this time of exploration and introduction to my new understanding of life. I wanted to share what I had learned with my family. I emailed them and spoke on the phone every two weeks. One day, I spoke to my brother.

"Life is like a game we're playing blindfolded with no instructions and no one can tell us how to play, we just have to go ahead and play it."

He considered my words but scepticism shaded his voice. I wanted to give him something to help him understand the freedom I had come to know, hoping it would challenge him to take his own.

After a lesson with Lani one evening, she wanted to converse in English.

"You have everything in Canada. Why do you come to Thai?"

"Thailand is so beautiful. People listen to each other here, without speaking."

"We have very old culture in Thai. Thai know each other very well."

"Canada is a new country. We can learn more about listening."

"Did you find anything happening?" she asked, and I knew her meaning.

"No, everything has been quiet. I think its okay," I said, feeling relieved.

"Okay, good," she smiled, looking at me from behind eyes with the polished inner mirror. I wanted more time to talk with her but our time went quickly. We took the elevator down together to the entrance. She waved goodbye to me as her car rolled out of the driveway.

I had begun to develop an appreciation for Thai modern art. Colourful, natural images and brilliant impressions of historic masters spoke with dedication to craft and a rich appreciation for beauty. I imagined myself creating treasured works that I would be proud to hang on my walls as I gazed from one to the next, knowing it took years of discipline and practice. Still, the desire played on in my mind.

Harry called one evening and invited me to a party. We travelled together by taxi to the house of one of his colleagues. Weaving through dark streets in a prestigious neighbourhood we rolled up to a large home where people stood with wine glasses gathered beside a bbq on the driveway. Jungle foliage encircled the yard bringing a tight knit feeling of community to the group.

Talking in a group of people on the walkway by the side of the house, drinking wine in the warm evening air, I was introduced to several of Harry's business colleagues. It was great to meet new faces and converse with other foreigners living and working in Bangkok. I chatted with a Dutch couple from South Africa who came for the peace and safety of Thailand. I spoke with several others with different accents in the dim evening, the constant crackle of the bbq in the background as we munched on potluck food.

Inside I was lead through a palatial dark wood and crème-toned living room, through to a silent backyard, across the lawn, past a pool, to a gazebo nestled in the back corner surrounded by jungle. In it three German people including Harry sat sipping wine. A few candles flickered on the small round table showing only the outlines of faces.

"Cassandra, welcome. You've found the haven," said Harry, in a proud tone.

"This is amazing," I said, pushing back vines to enter and sit in the interesting space.

"The Klong river runs past this house. Right behind us," he said. In the pitch black I couldn't see or hear the big river flowing as I revelled in the hidden abode. Two others joined us as a couple left, padding across the dark lawn to the house. We sat in awe, appreciating a quiet night in the centre of Bangkok. After a while, music pumped from within the main house. We headed in to dance. Admiring the sensuous interior as we danced, I revelled at the ability of foreigners to make foreign lands into home. The owners of the house had returned to Germany while their son stayed on, a friend of Harry's. Thai girls milled about sipping wine, watching us dance to disco beats.

When the evening came to a close Harry collected me and we taxied to my home. He made sure I was safely inside then spun off in the yellow cab. I smiled at the door ladies and rode up in the elevator. My hallway was quiet when the elevator doors opened. I unlocked the door and went inside. The warm space greeted me and I opened my porch doors for the air. Laying in bed before sleep, I listened to the sounds of the city, honest and true, a beautiful place to live.

My days in the city were busy. I didn't have a lot of time to myself, at least not as much as I had had at the beach. I could feel that my inner self yearned to express itself again. I tried to take the time on buses to ponder life's mysteries, retreating to that place inside, but it had become more difficult to still my mind and hear the peace inside. The messages hung on, just out of reach.

After one long day at school I took the usual ride home on the bus. As we neared my building I saw smoke billowing up into the sky. When we got closer, I saw that it was very near to where I lived. When I got off the bus, I hurried down the sidewalk. Traffic had slowed to watch the smoke. Concern mounted. At my building I was shocked to see it billowing from behind it. I ran to the steps where the ladies assured me our building was fine. Some homes behind our building were on fire.

Our elevators had stopped working so I hurried up the stairs up to the 16th floor. I let myself into my suite and dashed to the balcony. From my porch I could see that directly behind us at least a third of the slum village was engulfed in flames. As I stood looking down I saw that my Thai woman neighbour was on her balcony too.

"We have to help them! Let's go!"

"No. We can't. You must stay here."

"What?" I said incredulously, thinking that she would be strong enough to join me to help douse the flames.

"We can't go. Maybe the fire was set."

"What? Who would do that?"

"These people don't pay for this land. They are just living on it. There is nothing we can do to help."

I stood there speechless, seeing the situation change entirely. I still wanted to help, but I saw that life in Thailand was very different from what I knew. I watched as people ran dousing the flames with buckets of water until I could watch no more. I was glad to be safe yet pained by the plight of others.

Harry's girlfriend Bridget arrived from Germany. Harry and I had nothing to report aside from nights spent gazing at the sky from the pool. One night the three of us went to a house party which was in full swing when we arrived. I was introduced to Harry's friends. Later on, one man approached me for conversation. He was American and struggled to find the right words as I twisted on my heel. I had spoken briefly with him during the evening but did not feel compelled to know him any better.

"I have never seen you around here before. It's hard to meet decent people in Bangkok. I'd like it if..." then his words were broken off by loud noises from the kitchen. Silenced by the ruckus, we chuckled at the moment. When the noise stopped, he started again.

"How about if," and again the loud noises drowned him out. Someone was bouncing off the walls, knocking pots and pans that hung from a rack. Laughter peeled from the kitchen full of drunken inhabitants.

By this time I understood the psychic message to mean, 'Don't bother,' and I moved through the crowd to find Harry and Bridget dancing in the living room. I joined them on the dance floor, confident in the notion that people revealed themselves in subtle ways that gave credence to their true nature. If the American stranger had been someone beneficial to have in my life at that time, life would have worked with us to facilitate our coming together. I acted upon that message trusting that life had given me an answer.

One afternoon, wandering the sight filled streets listening to sounds of the city, I thought it would be a good idea to visit a different area of the city and boarded a ferry over to west side of Bangkok. I had never crossed the river and had no destination in mind. I was looking forward to stumbling upon an array of shopping bonanzas or some uniquely Thai experience that would render me lucky for the exploration. Hopping off at a random stop I soon realised that instead of finding a plethora of tourist friendly shops I had found myself in a conservative part of the city where only a few small shops lined a street. It was an area devoid of any attractions I thought would be interesting to visit. Moving along on the sidewalk I conceded to the notion that I had chosen the wrong area in which to find excitement and I had better start heading home as the sun was nearing the horizon. It was then that I consulted my inner direction hoping it would lead me to the correct bus stop home.

I stood on the sidewalk, out of the flow of traffic, and looked in the direction of streets that I had come. But against this logic I was being pulled down the sidewalk in the opposite direction. Perplexed, I obeyed this force and wandered ahead.

I came upon a small shop full of beautiful things. The walls and tables were adorned with exquisite works of art, each canvas bursting with vibrant, exotic colours. Drawn into the shop by the allure of the paintings I was struck by their energy and vivaciousness. Depictions of a gracious sea, mesmerizing palms or the stunning silhouette of a boy running on the beach. Family bonds were exemplified on canvas as I moved along the selections and deeper into the tiny store.

Deeper into the store I saw a few artists moving about, all men who looked as serious as scholars. As I examined the art of the talented artisans an orange robed monk moved to my side. Dressed in traditional costume he surprised me with conversation.

"Do you like this art?" he asked, smiling kindly.

I inhaled. "Yes, it truly is wonderful."

"Good."

"Yes. It is good." We smiled at one another and I could feel his calmness. I was eager to ask my most pressing questions as we stood side by side in the small store.

"Do you enjoy the practice?" I asked, my voice lowered and out of hearing range of the others.

"I like the practice. But the lifestyle may not be for me."

"I understand." I knew that Thai monasteries were strictly regimented and devoid of women. I wondered how the rigour challenged this man. We gazed together at the paintings on the walls. He gestured toward it.

"Do you want to learn?"

"Oh yes, I really want to."

He walked to the counter where he called another man from the back of the store, one of three who had been milling about with brushes in their hands, glancing over at our exchange. They spoke, I don't know what about, but I could feel something good was happening.

"Then it is settled," he said, gesturing me over. "This is Sumruey. He will teach you how to paint and you will teach him English during the lesson."

I stood, dumbstruck. "Yes, yes, I will! When do we begin? This is amazing. Thank you!" I said, smiling at all of them.

The monk nodded and I saw his awareness of a full and equal exchange, not one doing a favour for someone else, but a fair trade. It was settled. I left the art store for the bus stop with a smile on my face and directions in my hand for the route home.

The first evening Sumruey came over to my apartment he brought his friend. He showed me some basic skills about preparation and made a beautiful picture for me. Lani arrived as my lesson was ending and smiled at the Thai men as they packed up their supplies to leave. We wai-ed each other and confirmed our next evening together.

After they left Lani was anxious to chat.

"He is a good man," she said.

"I know. I could feel that."

"He brought his friend to save your reputation. It is a statement to your neighbours that your meeting is one of friendship."

"Oh, that is interesting. I was wondering why he came. He said very little."

"He is a friend to Sumruey. And maybe he wants to learn English, too!"

In the weeks that followed Sumruey started me on a path of artistic expression that opened up a new world for me. I created colourful works of sailboats and grasslands on my coffee table using watercolour and charcoal.

I continued to visit art galleries and educate myself on the styles and designs of immensely talented local artists. I tried to encourage Harry to join me on my touring, but he preferred to play Ultimate Frisbee in his spare time.

I went for drinks one Friday night with Eunice at a special place called The Saxophone. It was a popular underground expat hangout and

Eunice's friends met us there. The lighting was dim and we enjoyed some great live jazz. The musicians were expats. It could have been a speakeasy club anywhere in Europe.

A few foreign men sat at a table across the room. One of them caught my attention. He kept looking over with a penetrating gaze. I was intrigued. Later on he found his way over to my table where we briefly conversed. He introduced himself as Michael and said he was from England and that he was working in Bangkok on contract. I thought he was interesting as the conversation was light and engaging. I gave him my phone number and he returned back to his friends. Eunice smiled at me and I shrugged. She laughed and cheered my glass.

The next day I got a call from Michael. I invited him to join me on my Saturday art tour. We agreed to meet at one of the galleries. He showed up on time and we went inside to an art deco space with high ceilings and glass walls. The art did not pique my interest and I finished perusing the entire collection in a few minutes. I sat down on the sunlit steps as Michael finished his review. We began conversing about the art and about life and it was soon apparent that our views were divergent. He was a reporter and told me of various awful things he had witnessed. It seemed to have shaped his whole perspective, and he couldn't begin to fathom my point of view.

"I'll be leaving here in six weeks for Indonesia. There is some fighting there and I'm meant to cover it." He swallowed, as if he feared for his life.

Going to Indonesia sounded interesting, but at what cost?

"But why focus on negativity when there are so many things happening in this world that are beautiful!" I said.

"There's a lot that's not beautiful if you look around. There are plenty of challenges that need to be told, stories that people need to know about," he said, convinced of his purpose.

I disagreed. "You can talk about so many other things in your position. You affect people's thinking with the picture you paint of the world. Why do people need to know about something negative? How does it help them?"

"It's not about helping them. It's about keeping them informed," he retorted, defending his position and his career.

"If it's not about helping them, why do it? Why even talk about it?" I responded.

A cold, empty feeling filled the space as his expression hardened and my focus was drawn away. I realized this person was not going to fit neatly into my life. We parted ways soon afterward, trodding off in opposite directions. We never spoke again.

After another long work week, I found myself staring out over the city from my top floor balcony, seeing the land stretch for miles filled with buildings, highways and construction sites. I wondered what I was doing living in this metropolis when what I really wanted was to be near the sea. Life in Bangkok was exciting but the heat and toil had taken me away from the place I most wanted to be. My social life was growing, but the stress in my job was unfortunately keeping pace. I was tiring of the structures which I felt were too strict for the children. My philosophies and those of the Thai teacher clashed. I began to feel that her energy was pushing me out of the room. I wasn't sure what to do about my situation. I closed the door and called it a night.

Lani called me after my art tour the next day and invited me downtown for lunch. I excitedly followed her directions and found her sitting in a very cool and hip restaurant. She sat proudly at the table and hugged me when I arrived. We enjoyed delicious food. She introduced me to a new meal called Som Tum with sticky rice. It was shredded green papaya doused in a spicy peanut dressing, served with sticky rice that you could dip into the sauce using your fingers. I loved it immediately and practiced the pronunciation so I could buy it again.

"You can buy this at the street stalls. Its very inexpensive," she smiled.

"I love it! Thanks for introducing me to it."

After we left the restaurant we went to a coffee shop. She told me more about Thai life and some more unusual stories she and her family had experienced, sharing some eerie renditions of her own. I was thoroughly spooked when it was time to leave.

I hurried home through the wind and sprinkling rain. When I arrived at my building the power was out. The elevator was out of operation so I climbed the 16 flights, passing many others on the way down. At my suite the wind was whistling loudly and it blew open both of my patio doors with a loud bang. After I closed them, one snapped open again, as the rain pelted in and wind blew papers onto the floor. I ran to the phone and called Lani.

"Its crazy over here! My doors flew open by themselves!"

"Okay, try to stay calm. You'll have to go to a temple. Find one in the phone book and go to tomorrow. You have to go and pray for the spirit."

"Okay," I conceded. "I'll go." After I agreed to go to the temple the wind subsided and the doors calmed down. I exhaled. Then I went to the phone book. I opened the phone book and the pages fell open to a Christian Church. I decided to go first thing in the morning.

The next day I dressed in a skirt and nice blouse. I got going early and bought a coffee en route to drink on the bus. When I arrived at the church I was surprised to see a European styled building with stain glass windows and turrets. It looked vacant. I pushed open one of the solid wood doors and went inside. The lights were out but daylight came through the yellowed glass. I made my way to a pew and sat down on the stiff wooden bench. Around me only a few people stirred. I looked toward the altar, not sure what to do next.

'Okay, I'm here,' I said to myself. 'I'm here for the spirit in my apartment, I'm here so it can find peace and leave my apartment.' A priest walked past me in the aisle with a miniscule sideways glance. I looked up into the vaulted ceiling, beautifully carved wood accentuating the stained glass windows. The space felt light as if the voices that rang in song somehow echoed there. Were there angels on the rafters? How did this church get here?

I sat there, looking around at the alters, the religious figures and deities watching over the empty pews. The darkened church echoed some kind of need around me that I didn't comprehend. I read from the books with the delicate pages then recited some personal blessings in my head hoping something would hear me and help the spirit. I gave thanks then stood up. I glided down the aisle and exited the church. I felt relief as I pushed open the heavy door into daylight. I hoped I had done enough.

I returned home later that afternoon to a sense of peace in my apartment. The temperature was comfortable and a sweet scent lifted in the breeze. I felt calmed.

After a short nap I called Harry at his apartment. He was home and invited me for a rooftop swim.

As the sun went down we talked about my situation at work.

"You don't have to stay at this job. You have been uncomfortable there for weeks and it doesn't seem as if the situation will improve anytime soon."

"Yes," I said pensively, my eyes stretching over the view of the city. "I guess there are other options for work."

"Interview for other jobs on your lunch hour. Maybe you will find a job at another school. Try some modelling agencies, too. You never know what Thailand has to offer."

"That is bold. I suppose I could take some taxis out during my lunch."

I picked up the Bangkok Post at the corner shop and I made my way up to my floor. I put my key in the lock and pressed back the heavy door. I opened the balcony doors for the fresh air to swirl around my apartment. I booked some interviews over the phone from my suite. Over the next few weeks, I bolted to interviews during my lunch hour.

I travelled home from work one afternoon, smiling back at others on the crowded bus. I stepped off at my stop outside the local grocery market, strolling in for a cold drink and to look at the people inside. There were two foreign couples struggling to read labels as I waited in line to pay for my drink. Walking home I gazed across the busy road at men playing soccer in a large grassy field. I wondered if I would ever walk over to watch and if I would meet a handsome player there.

I wanted a man in my life.

When I arrived at my building I approached the steps as the office ladies jumped up laughing, waving me in. They were abuzz with excitement as they opened the door to their office.

"You have a fax," they said, gathering around me, eyes wide with smiles.

"You are a model?" they asked, giggling.

I quickly read the printed words. It was a casting call for a job on the island of Koh Samui. I smiled and thanked them as I excitedly gathered the papers to read in my apartment.

Riding the elevator up my anticipation soared. Once inside I plopped onto the sofa to read the whole document as wheels in my mind began to turn. The job called for three days of 'work'. The first day we would drive down to the island. Day two was the shooting of an ice tea commercial on the beach. On the third we would travel back by van to Bangkok. The dates were for the following week of Wednesday through Friday. I decided to go to the casting on my lunch break the next day and see if I could get the job.

When I went to the casting I was required to try on a bathing suit. Simple. I was there only a few minutes before cabbing back to the school just in time for my afternoon sessions. A few days later I received a phone call confirming that I had been chosen for the job. I jumped up and down across my living room shrieking with excitement! What an opportunity!

I had to make up my mind what to do about work. I was filled with ambivalence. I toiled uneasily over the best way to handle the situation and decided my best option was to call in sick for three days then return for work on the Monday. It felt right to be taking this chance.

The days crept by as I awaited my departure. I was proud of myself for taking a risk to improve my life experience although my honest nature was anxious about the untruth that would be told to the school.

On the day of our departure I made the call to the school supervisor complaining about a high temperature and upset stomach. He told me to get well soon.

I hung up the phone and sighed with relief. I would have to make two more calls from a quiet place on the island to carry out the plan, but that would have to wait.

The van met me at my building parking lot. I travelled with four others for 12 hours until the van pulled into the Don Sak ferry port on the mainland. The next ferry would deliver us to Koh Samui in four hours. Stiff and sticky, I hopped out of the van and stretched while inhaling fresh sea air. Tears welled in my eyes for the love I felt to be near the water again and I headed toward a mound of large boulders by the pier overlooking the sea.

The warm sun greeted my skin like an old friend as I climbed onto a boulder to sit and gaze upon the shining water. I breathed in fresh sea air and exhaled joyfully as I recalled what accompanied that familiar sensation. I sat in exuberance, overcome with delight in anticipation of another visit to where I most wanted to be. I smiled out to the sea for a long moment then walked back to the van to continue my adventure.

After the ferry disembarked on Koh Samui we drove to the busy beach area of Cheweng where we would be staying to shoot the commercial. I settled into the bungalow I would be sharing with another model who hadn't arrived yet. I was told that the rest of the afternoon and evening was mine but to be up early and ready for the shoot at seven.

I quickly showered and put on fresh clothes then headed down to the beach, walking along until I found a place to sit down in the sand.

People were playing Frisbee and lounging in the water. My peaceful feeling began to return as I looked into the blue skies and rolling sea. I exchanged the busy bustling feeling of Bangkok for the tranquil sights of Koh Samui. The white beach urged me to lay back and absorb the calm.

The playful sea called to me as the hot sun echoed encouragement. I waded into warm water and felt soft sand under my feet. Reaching deeper water I rolled back into it to float, listening to the muffled sounds of voices on the beach and in the water around me. I stayed floating, feet frolicking, while a light rain shower passed overhead sprinkling my face. I smiled and breathed it all in.

I stood up feeling refreshed and walked toward the beach. I dried off and sat down as my eyes wandered over the scene. I met the gaze of a man walking across the sand toward me.

"Hello!" he said. "May I sit here beside you?"

"Sure," I said, tucking my sarong around my waist and sitting on the sand. He plunked down and introduced himself as Marty.

"I saw you playing Frisbee," I said.

"Yes, that was us. So what brings you to these parts?" His accent was English. His blue eyes beamed into mine and I turned to view the sea.

"I'm shooting a commercial here tomorrow. I'm a model," I said, smiling.

"Well, isn't that wonderful. You are beautiful! I saw that right away so I thought I would come over and say hello. You probably have a lot of friends on this island."

"Well, I just arrived actually. I live in Bangkok and this is a three day job. What about you?"

"We're just staying on the island, looking for business opportunities. We would like to live here full time. With the right fit, we'll get investors to back us. It's all set up really, we're just waiting for the right thing."

We shared ideas about life philosophy and talked objectively about experience. His insights were refreshing and humourous. It started to get dark and we were still sitting on the beach talking.

"Why don't you let me take you out for dinner? I know a great spot where we can watch World Cup Soccer. There's a game on tonight."

I considered his offer, and although I wasn't a big fan of soccer I thought it would be fun to check out the scene rather than while away the hours in my bungalow.

"I do have to work early tomorrow, so as long as its not too late," I said.

"It won't be late. Come on, you have to eat don't you?"

We agreed to meet at a restaurant in an hour. I returned to the bungalow to get ready and met the other model who had arrived after paying for a flight from Bangkok. She was Danish and seemed very professional. She declined to join us for dinner.

I left to meet Marty at an Italian restaurant. He was a gentleman and we continued conversation over pasta and garlic bread. It was nice to be out and get a taste of Koh Samui night life. The game was about to begin and the noise level began to rise. Then someone across the room caught my eye as he entered and sat down on a stool at the bar. It was David! I couldn't believe the coincidence and excused myself to go over and give him a warm hug. We chatted excitedly as he scribbled a map to his bungalow on a napkin, inviting me to visit the next day.

When I returned to the table the mood had changed. It appeared that Marty didn't like my rendezvous with David as his comments acquired a sharp edge to them. When the bill came he made it clear how he felt.

"I believe in women's liberation and here's your portion of the bill." I was so shocked I said nothing and paid my bill. I laughed all the way back to my bungalow.

Everything had been going well with Marty right up until I talked with David. Was it a sign that he'd had acted as a link so that I could meet up with David? I would have never been in that restaurant if Marty hadn't asked me to go there for dinner. I sat on the side of the bed inside the bungalow shaking my head at what had happened. It seemed so clear to me. 'Listen to the signs, Cassandra,' I whispered to myself in the darkness as I climbed into bed, 'and life will work out the details.'

Early the next morning I awoke to a gentle rapping at the door. It was the producer giving us a 30 minute departure call. We quickly got ready to leave. Piling into the van we were driven to the beachfront of a luxurious hotel and seated under palm trees with plates of fresh fruit. We watched them prepare the set by raking the sand and positioning the cameras. The setting was pristine: a beautiful blue sky and velvety, inviting manicured sand. A third model joined us as we waited in beautiful bikinis on the chaise-lounges. We were offered nail polish and freshly peeled mangosteens and rambutans to eat. I felt pampered. Then we scampered onto the sand for a few takes where I reclined on the chaise watching the beautiful sky. The other two models walked along the shore a couple of times and then we were finished.

"Okay," said the Japanese producer of the iced tea commercial, after reviewing the footage.

"It is complete. You are free to go," said the Thai producer. We gathered our things and were driven back to the hotel where we packed up our things. The Thai director met us on the walkway.

"We will leave at 6 a.m. tomorrow. If you are not here to meet us, you will get your own ride to Bangkok. Agree?"

"Yes," we said, nodding.

"Okay. Thanks for your work." He said, and strode away.

"Okay, then I am off," I said to the other model, hugging her. I headed up to the road to catch a truck taxi, flagging the first one headed in the direction to David's. I hopped on and travelled hillside roads with views through the jungle to the shimmering sea. The hum of the truck beneath me vibrated the seat as I looked around at bright eyed tourists riding in couples or with friends. Smiling at their eyes, we chatted about the beauty of the island. Everyone was having a marvellous time.

I jumped out of the back at Sunny Bungalows, a series of dwellings perched high on the seaside hill of the road. The restaurant was empty so I meandered down a rocky pathway. The sea breeze swept up the hill with scents of sand and salt water, enveloping me in moisture. David's numbered sport shirts hung on a line from a bungalow perched higher up on a hill overlooking the sea with a rocky path that promised a descent toward the beach. I sat down on his porch to wait.

The view was spectacular as the silence drew me in. It felt good. I knew I was at the right place. The gentle vibe, natural and pure, seemed easy. I considered the van driving me away from this the following morning. Just then David stepped down the rocky path toward me, smiling. His curly locks longer since I had seen him last. He looked very relaxed. We hugged.

"Happy to see you here. How was the commercial?"

"The shoot only lasted a couple of hours. They said we were free to spend the day anywhere and if we wanted a ride back to Bangkok they would be leaving at 6 a.m."

"Oh." He moved around me to gather the clothing from the line and fold it up.

"What do you think about the view? Not as close to the sea as Koh Phangan but not bad," he smiled.

"It's marvellous. I like that I can see far and wide." I stood up to take it in. "What's it like here?"

"There are two blokes who run the place, Champ and Chally. It's been passed down through family I think. They hang out with a group of local guys and they all watch over the place."

"Sounds nice." I stood entranced by the view.

"If you think you will be staying I can arrange for us to get a cabin with two beds," he said, catching my eye then looking down.

"I would like that," I said. "I haven't decided what to do about my job in Bangkok. I called in sick to take this job."

"You did what?"

"I know. It was crazy. I had to. This came up so suddenly and living in Bangkok has been a struggle." We were silent. The problem emerged.

"Where do you want to live?"

"On the island," my tears welled up. The heat of the city shed from my skin, weeks of smog and dust fell from my pores. The fresh air seemed to cleanse me. I inhaled. "It sure would be nice to stay here a couple of days to sort it out."

"Like I said, I'll get us another bungalow." He packed up his clothing and returned a few minutes later with a key to another abode. This one had a view directly over the jungle to the blue horizon and calm sea in the distance. The porch was wrapped in foliage and two bigs rocks making it feel cozy and private. I settled into one of the porch chairs after laying my bag on a bed. The room was painted pink with yellow floral curtains. Scents romanced me as birds chirped and leaves rustled from life within the branches.

"I have to go out now. I have plans with some of the guys to go to Cheweng to watch soccer for a few hours. Make yourself at home. The restaurant is just down the steps on the beach. Its really good."

"Okay, and thanks a lot for making this happen."

"You're welcome." He smiled and hugged me then closed the door and trotted off. I was relieved to have some peace to let go of the stress of the city. The leaves in front of me seemed to draw it out of me, as I exhaled and relaxed even further. I could feel the city vibe leaving me, replaced with joy and fervent energy.

In the distance I could hear the waves coming into shore. The clear sky was spotted with only a few clouds near the horizon as my eyes spied a few bungalows perched along the hillside. Plants and organisms surrounding the bungalow vibrated peaceful bliss and harmony. Nature opened my senses to its familiar, loving embrace. I relished in the moment for a long while.

Staring into a life experience that seemed to be staring back at me I felt an unshakable correspondence. I asked what I wanted to know, then waited for an answer. And it came. Then I laughed, and laughed, and laughed until I cried. Life was listening to me!

I picked up my pen and notebook looking for words to describe what I was feeling.

'Think of the deeper meaning. It's there, see it!' I had said this before but then glossed over it. Now, I was reminded clearly that observation was the way to understand my experience.

Now, Cassandra. Look, see!

I saw that I was using my intentions as tools for desired outcomes. I looked at my habits of speaking and thinking, then had looked further to see those thoughts manifested in my reality. I could see the pattern to my inner thoughts and beliefs. I had been casting outcomes into my future with my thoughts then experiencing the outcome. It seemed to me reasonable, from a rational perspective. I thought that it must have been the same for others. I felt that we could all benefit from becoming aware of the thoughts we were having. And we could do this by observing them. What we were thinking affected us. Now we could control our experience with much more skill.

Things that lead to growth, thus enlightenment, are easy. Find something that feels right and you will be led to growth, if that is what you want to experience. You will be guided if you choose to be. Give up your stronghold and be led along the path of least resistance. Flow with your being. What is easy is right, until it is not right anymore, and you will know when that is. Look at the signs. They are always there. It is just a matter of perceiving them. Give up your stronghold and be led by your strength. Go with your being, what's easy is right, until its not right anymore.

I wanted to shout out loud, 'Look at the wisdom and power we have inside of us. Use your powers to heal yourself correctly and wisely!'

The beautiful scene held me in a loving embrace, encouraging me through my feeling. No one was around.

I began to think of my situation in Bangkok, as one event followed another, like a symphony of events. I had made it in the city, making a life from nothing into a beautiful system that supported me. Life held me up in my choices but in the city I had not reflected on my inner voice because nature wasn't there. The voice of the city ebbed and flowed through me like the waves at the beach, but they were static and electric vibes. I was living in a concrete jungle.

The Thai people of the city were a brave pulse, alive with the light of music and the closeness of one another. They were a very tight knit group, Thais stayed close, often several living together in one abode, spanning several generations. Their connections to one another were palpable and commendable. This is where the easy flow of so many people became peaceful yet charismatic.

Conformity was taught to us, and that is culture, how to behave. But what is that? Who's rules are those?

I could witness thoughts as they entered my mind, experiencing them in the moment, and then releasing them just as easily. I wanted the pleasure and calmness of moving easily through life, taking each moment in its fullness, and releasing to fully appreciate the essence of the next.

After relaxing the whole afternoon on the porch I began to think about dinner. As the sun neared the horizon I changed into a sun dress and sandals and struck out along the rock path as it weaved down the grassy slope and onto the beach. The yellow awning over beachside tables, called me in for a meal. I ordered papaya salad.

Sipping a coconut shake with a tiny umbrella I considered this spot to be perfect for romance. Quiet and secluded, the small beach held only a few people, surrounded with jungle covered hills. While gazing over the beach and at the setting sun I decided to stay with David for the weekend then head back to Bangkok myself on Sunday. I would think about what to do for Monday and beyond in the place where my thoughts were clear. I felt it was the best I could do.

David returned to the bungalow just as I came back from dinner. We sat on the porch in the quiet night breeze.

"I have met someone here who I have been spending time with. Her name is Cathy." He blushed. It dawned on me why he had been gone all afternoon.

"Oh. What is she like?" Now, I blushed.

"She's 40. She's English," he said, catching my expression.

It was silent because I didn't want to laugh, but we both shared a chuckle anyway.

"She's a lovely woman. She's very kind. We talk about things like you and I shared on Ko Phangan. She has stayed here for seven months," he said, proud of her.

"That's great, David." I smiled. "Is it okay if I stay until Sunday? I have some thinking to do about Bangkok."

"Yeah, sure. The place is yours. I'm not here that much anyway."

We rose and headed into the bungalow because of the large mosquitoes buzzing around our ankles. He climbed into his bed as I climbed into mine and we turned out the lights. We laughed a little in the dark, then fell asleep.

The next morning we went down for breakfast under the yellow awning. We sipped coconut shakes and talked as stiff breeze ruffled the table cloth. His attention was elsewhere.

"Are you in love?" I asked.

"In love? That's a big word." Just then the waitress arrived carrying our pancakes with chunks of fresh mango, pineapple, papaya and banana. She placed them in front of us, smiling, then went back into the kitchen.

"I met her about ten days ago at the place where Champ takes me to drink beer and watch matches. She was there with her girlfriends. We started talking and talked all night. In the morning we all went back to her place and she and I ended up falling asleep in each others arms."

A pang of jealousy moved through me and I looked at my straw. Most of my smooth coconut shake remained. I exhaled.

"What is she like?"

"She's very pretty. I'm sure you would like her."

"I'm not sure if I will have time to meet her. I've got to plan Bangkok."

"You want to be on an island. Haven't you been telling me about living my dreams? Going for what I want? This is your chance to walk your talk!"

"Yes," I replied, realizing it had been my true desire. We finished the rest of our meal over small talk until our plates were cleared. David paid the bill and we walked out onto the beach. We found a spot near the waves and I pulled off my sarong as David pulled off his t-shirt. We walked toward the waves.

"Why do anything else?" he asked. "You want to be here, so just do it."

"Leaving my job in Bangkok on these terms is an uncomfortable thought. I haven't been able to find a quiet telephone to call and tell them I'm still sick." My gaze drifted over the sea.

"Sometimes these things can't be helped. They will understand. They will find a new teacher to take your spot. There are a ton of teachers in Bangkok. You know they will find a replacement."

"Yes, there are some good teachers there," I said, feeling better.

"And this is your life!" he reminded me.

"I guess I didn't believe I could have exactly what I want. But it seems life is making that a reality. I have to trust it. I'll have to go back to Bangkok, get my stuff, and find a job down here on one of the islands. I guess its settled." I exhaled, feeling my happiness with my problem solved.

We played in the water until the sun became too hot. I thanked him for reminding and reassuring me as we went back to the rock steps.

"It's nice to hear the voice of a friend when we need to make change."

"It helps. I know I asked my Dad's friends a lot of questions about life at the pub. They gave me good advice." He was quiet, wistful, missing his friends. I followed him up the steps to our porch where he unlocked our door. He went into the bathroom then closed the door. I sat on the bed considering my choices for the afternoon. The pages of my Quiet notebook were almost full. When David came out looking fresh and smelling of cologne, I smiled.

"Having an afternoon date, I see."

"Yes, so don't worry if I don't come home. I might stay the night with Cathy."

I nodded and smiled then watched him leave, excited.

Even as David left to spend time with his new friend I knew this time was precious. I needed to apply myself to the work of planning a new beginning. The weather was perfect so I sat in the porch chair in my wet bikini, warm sun on my legs as I inhaled the fresh air. The sounds of Bangkok were fading from memory and now I was tuned in to the sea. The ebb and flow lulled me into gentle contemplation as my eyes rested on bright green leaves.

Ushering in wonderful feelings of love it felt like life and I were working together to give me the best experience I could have. I was so happy that I was on the island. It was where I most wanted to be. I was happy I had listened to my feeling and followed the trail that had led here. It was the best I had felt in weeks. I sighed with relief as the pulsating surroundings rhythmically drew out my worries and trepidation. The natural environment dissipated my feelings of stress and I exhaled releasing them fully. I stared into my lush green surroundings, ever surprised that nature cared to comfort me.

I went inside to get my notebook and lay on the bed. Sitting back against the headboard, I began to write.

Look, look at the world, look at yourself. It's the only way.

I began to fill the last pages of my notebook. 'When we are true to ourselves we can help this world. Are we afraid? We have many different types of people to do it. We can share love with the world. We can love this life!'

I breathed in fresh air as it swirled through the window, fluttering the flowery curtains that hung to the side of the frame. I admired the fresh pastel pink paint job on the on the walls and shiny grey of the floor. It felt like I had been there before, like I had seen it as a child, where it once had comforted me.

My mind was soaring. I wrote as fast as I could. 'All the answers to our questions and problems on this planet are available to us. We all have the knowledge to make change. We can use all of the sciences to help us understand physical reality. We don't have to scrap the old systems, we can work through them to create new ones. We need to understand the wonders of this magnificent planet and what they mean. There is still so much beauty and brilliance to be uncovered.' Passionate surges rolled through me.

'Humans know many things but we haven't yet been able to put that knowledge together to create a larger understanding of this existence. Most people still believe that the world is governed by chance occurrences. I had believed that! Somehow I had been convinced that that is what life was: a series of unplanned events that I was to handle the best I could. Learning that I could affect my surroundings was mind blowing for me. I was having an effect of my reality!'

'We need to become more aware in our surroundings. We need to know the consequences of what we are doing and thinking. Studying social research is one valuable way to find out more about how we are creating. I have tapped into something new and powerful and others can do the same.'

Silence struck the moment. I was riveted, erect on my bed. Pictures poured through my awareness as the visual possibilities of our future ran before my eyes. All kinds of scenarios passed by my consciousness, lasting long enough to take me through years in each vision. My future was going to be incredible, and so was the future of the world. But it was a choice. One that we must choose. I realized where I wanted to be and what I wanted it to look like. And it was all love.

Chapter 6 – Lavender Haze

It was time for a new notebook. I had been writing in the margins of the Quiet Notebook so I packed a bag and went to the road to catch a taxi. I enjoyed the breeze and view from the back of the truck as it meandered over the hills before rolling into town. I was eager to see what notebook would find me. I wandered along until I found a convenience store. I made my way along a row until I found a stack of pastel coloured notebooks. The one that jumped out at me, amid pens, straws, and decks of cards, had a picture of a blond girl leaning against a United Nations flag. It read: "Too must love. I want to be a believer in the power of love. Make me a believer, baby." Laughing out loud, I brought the notebook to the Thai cashier at the counter who returned my smile with a gleam in her eye.

After completing my task I hopped into another truck taxi and rode back to the bungalows. Inside I lay back on the soft blankets and pillows as calm air drifted around me. The breeze fluttered the curtain as I turned my body on the bed. With my notebook in hand I could take my experience higher and drift in the brilliance, recording all the beautiful events I witnessed. I floated through layers of memory, from past to present. I found that a strange gravity kept me in the orbit of certain older remembrances, even as I wished to more fully embrace new ones. Maybe there would come a time when I could balance these polarities, by releasing the old energy. I wanted to move toward that time where every moment had perfect clarity, free from any sediment of the past.

Love, happiness, bliss; anything you choose. Joy comes with creating love. You are on the right quest. Truth will take you there.

I sat up in the bed momentarily then moved on the porch to take in the view. 'I chose and choose what I want and will create. I chose to be led to what I was led to. It just took time for these things to align. I got what I believed I deserve.'

Choose what you want. If you don't like your experience, change it.

When David returned the moon was almost full. The clear sky entranced me as I sat on the porch while David buzzed around inside the bungalow. His excitement was palpable. His woman awaited. I was happy to remain as my eyes wandered the night sky. The moon hung low, casting its light on the gently rippling water. I was at peace.

Forms began moving in my visual field as moonlight danced upon the water. Enchanting me with images, I saw dozens of Dalmations stacked in the shape of a pyramid. And then circus performers appeared, making me howl with laughter.

"David! You have to see this!" I shouted from the porch.

David came out and squinted at the horizon.

"All I see is water moving. What do you see?" he asked.

"A fricken circus," I laughed, surprised with my new perception. He shook his head and went back into the bungalow. The moment was transformative for me and I refocused my gaze on the water. I was stunned. It was like having my own world-sized television. It took no effort at all, just a loose focus, staring at the water and letting my mind loose. There were images of dancing ladies on unicycles. The mood of the scenes was circus-like with three rings of wonder all around. No story line, just random movement, as if the sole purpose was to entertain me.

"I'm going out now," said David, standing over my chair.

"Oh, well its too bad you don't want to stay and explore this with me. It's really amazing!"

"I can't see anything. It's only you." He turned to get his bag. "Enjoy your evening," he said, then galloped down the steps into the darkness.

High on the hill I could see across the small inlet to the other end of the beach where a lamppost cast light upon the waves. I was curious to see what effect the electrical light would have and if I could see the same kinds of images in the water. I rested my vision in the light splay and within seconds I began to see escapades. There was a woman holding a baby and when I looked closely at the baby all I saw was ripples of the water. It was bizarre and symbolic. Water is life. I noted that the visual effect of the light on the water followed me in every direction, pointing straight at me. I knew it did the same for others. Nature loves us, I thought. I visualized ancient people sitting with nature, listening to its teaching, watching water in the same way. My mind drifted to a picture I had seen of island people sitting in a group, staring into the surrounding environment, watching nature in the same way. It was an idea thought form I had never entertained before.

I sat in the bamboo porch chair in awe of what I had witnessed. I was in love with Earth and the magical mysteries it presented to me. It felt like nature was happy that I was embracing it. In return I was rewarded with experiences I would never forget. I could feel so much love. I knew there would be some who would discard what I had seen and judge me. What would I say to them? Use your imagination and loosen your hold on life. Let it love you, too. I wanted to know all the secrets and answers to life's magical mysteries.

I went inside as the light grew dim and got comfortable on the bed. I lit a candle and played soft music. How could I know more about life? I wrote, Look for the sources. They will reveal themselves to you. If it is right for you, you will know from what they say. Don't look too hard. Be shown. What's important to know will be revealed.

I put down my pen after a full and exciting night. I went outside to say goodnight to the stars, the moon and life outside my bungalow. I smiled and felt great warmth. Then I closed the door, put out the lights and went to bed.

The next morning I rose to see an empty bed across the room. David had not come back from the night before. I eased off my bed to change into my swimsuit. The yellow bathroom lit up with fashionable spherical bulbs as a spider scurried into the corner. I peered behind the mirror, ascertaining that nothing else was in residence, then showered and towelled off. I dressed in a locally made sundress then went down to eat breakfast on the beach.

In the afternoon heat, I decided to take a trip to town for a change of scene. I gathered my things and headed toward the road. As I waited for a truck taxi in the heat as clouds of dust and exhaust filtered through the air, trucks zooming by full of tourists with eager expressions. One finally stopped with an interesting array of faces. I hopped into the back with other tourists. Couples had their arms wrapped around one another with loose fitting clothing on their bodies and smiles on their faces. I sat down on the bench and listened to their conversation while the truck continued its passage over hilly terrain.

"This island is amazing," a man said to the others. "We're having the time of our lives." The woman beside him beamed, relaxed expressions on both of their faces.

"The waterfalls I saw yesterday blew my mind," someone else offered.

"We rode scooters through the jungle with breathtaking views," exclaimed a woman.

"We have a view of the ocean just steps from our door," another chimed in. "We're thinking about calling off our other plans and just staying here for the duration of our visas."

When the truck taxi rolled into Cheweng the scene became hectic as pedestrians filled the space, all going in different directions, some using maps. Street side restaurants were full of tourists. As we veered around a bend we came upon a celebratory parade of sequined women wearing large colourful hats and feather tiaras. The truck stopped and I said goodbye to the other travellers, hopping out into the frenzy. Floating along the sandy streets of Cheweng mesmerized by streetside wagons of natural jewellery, colourful clothing, handicrafts and glittering treasures, I wandered into a convenience store where I found a cache of local craftsmanship. The beautiful handmade objects were proudly displayed beside local artisans who spoke with foreigners and customers in broken English.

I came upon on another shop of authentic pieces of art. I felt drawn inside. As I walked in a gorgeous man with bronzed skin and sparkling green eyes zeroed in on me from across the shop. I looked away but felt him approach, sashaying toward me. I blushed at his directness as he moved to my side.

"Pretty interesting parade outside. Did you see it?" he asked, smiling.

"Fascinating, really," I said, smiling back.

"Are you staying in Cheweng?"

"I'm in a bungalow up the hill," I said, swallowing.

"I'm Tim. What's your name?" He asked, making me feel more at ease.

"Cassandra."

"Would you like to go for a milkshake where we can talk?" he smiled.

I agreed and we made our way toward the lively centre. His navy shorts revealed lithe, muscular legs that supported a trim torso that fit perfectly inside his light blue t-shirt, magnifying his beautiful eyes. His chocolate brown hair glistened, healthy and bright. He reminded me of Damian.

We walked through the village in conversation as motorcycles buzzed everywhere with passengers or packages. A busy Friday.

"It's nice not to have to think about work," he laughed at the sight of the rush.

"I have a job waiting for me in Bangkok," I said, wracked suddenly by the guilt and pressure of having to return.

"Why are you living there?" he chuckled rhetorically.

"It's a long story," I replied, hesitant to draw him into it.

"Sounds like you don't want to be there, anyway."

"I want to be on an island, enjoying this great space. Bangkok is too busy for me and I prefer to be closer to the beach." We walked along the uneven sidewalk, talking over the noise, enjoying the visual charms of palm trees and handmade shops. Beauty everywhere. We ambled along to an outdoor patio behind rattan doors and into a rustic saloon. Inside we were completely hidden from the street. It was as if we had entered another world. Tables were filled with serene tourists quietly observing the space, a hidden realm away from prying eyes. We were soon ushered to a table in the middle where we took our seats.

Settling into chairs across from each other I noticed that everything was made from bamboo. Above us a thatched rattan ceiling and under our feet a floor of sand. Strings of prayer flowers adorned the unique space while dappled sunlight sparkled through palm leaves.

A waitress came to take our order and coconut milkshakes were delivered in coconuts with straws and umbrellas. We sipped our drinks and smiled at one another. His green eyes fixated on mine. I shifted in my seat.

"So what have you been up to on the island," he asked, pushing back in his chair to reveal his barrel chest, the delicate fabric tracing the sculpted outline of his fine form. My eyes fell upon his silhouette.

"I've been exploring my mind and seeing where that leads. I'm here for a vacation from Bangkok while I make some changes." His eyes narrowed as he smiled at me.

"I've been exploring, too," he said, with a gleam in his eye. He appeared at least a few years older with an obvious desire that seemed palpable. My eyes wandered over the other guests as they relaxed in sultry poses, eyeing one another.

"Do you know anything about Einstein's theories?" I inquired.

He swallowed some of his shake. "Yes, I do. He was the creator of the Relativity Theory and simplified it to mean where there is good there is no evil. Where there is evil, there is an absence of good. He said that when we come to an acceptable level of evil, we will return to good."

"Ah, good. That makes sense." I said, pondering his words.

"What have you discovered in your exploration?"

I felt as if the entire room zeroed in on my next words as the sounds around me came to a full stop. My chair squeaked as I leaned forward.

"Our thoughts are creative. I have seen them create things before my eyes. I believe we use thoughts to create experience, so we need to be careful about what we think because it will manifest." As if a ripple of energy was released from me, we sat erect. "We receive the experience of our creations while in the flow until we create again with thought." As I finished, there was a pause, then the entire room exhaled and went back to its regular activity.

"That's interesting," he said, his eyes now scanning me.

"Yes. I have found something entirely worth looking for here in paradise. My mind has opened up here," I said leaning back, sipping my drink. I relaxed and met the eyes of patrons around us. Tim shifted in his chair, his body at ease yet alert.

"I've had some awakenings here as well. The beauty opens you." He twisted his straw. I felt glued to the table and hung on as it seemed to spin.

"Einstein wanted to know about the nature of reality, the fabric that made it so. He questioned its principles and wanted to record the conditions of it." My jaw dropped because I had asked these very same questions. Then, I knew what I sought was real. My experience had been corroborated! I sighed with relief, elated that I was on the right track. Faith had led me here. Tim recited more theories on the discourse of the Universe as I listened.

"Einstein said time and space were made of the same material, merely concepts in our minds."

"That's interesting to fathom." I said.

"He said it was the fabric of time that convinced us our illusions were real."

"Wow," I reclined.

"I'm not sure I'll ever understand it," he said, as he exhaled.

"Sure you will, if you want to." I looked into his eyes to see if the desire was there.

"I have some beautiful photos from the beach and of the sunsets here," he said. I began to squirm, feeling restless.

"Nice," I smiled. The light began fading from his eyes. Other patrons turned back to their counterparts, as if a meeting had come to a close.

We reclined in our chairs, looking about for the waitress, both of us feeling the energy drop. He shifted position in his seat and paid our bill. Our time together had come to a close as we walked outside. The sun had shifted toward the horizon.

"Thanks for the shake. I think I'll go back to my bungalow and watch the sunset."

"I'll be here having dinner if you want to come back to the village later on."

I pictured myself on a bed with him: and considered the end result of such an entanglement.

"I've got a lot to think about, thanks to you," I smiled. "I may not join you but I really enjoyed our conversation. If I don't see you, enjoy your journey." We embraced and I felt the sinews of his back under the soft T-shirt. And the hint of feral cologne.

"Okay. I'll be here from about eight at that restaurant," he said, pointing to one on the street.

I imagined trying to find it alone in the dark as I hopped into a taxi truck and waved goodbye. His scent lingered. I smiled out at the passing view and the colours that led me back home.

Back at my bungalow I lit candles and wrapped my shoulders in a purple sarong and padded onto the porch, feeling enriched by our conversation. I wondered what I would choose as the sun set. I pondered whether to stay at the abode or venture out to see Tim. There was no mistaking what he wanted. A hot, sexy man was waiting to take me to bed. How would that be? Would I say yes in a situation like that?

I pushed back in my chair and wondering about his warm, loving hands on my body and waking up in his place. What would I find there? What other women were in his life? I twisted in my chair, wondering what his love could bring.

Inside my cozy abode the atmosphere seemed to reach out, offering comfort and peace. I felt fulfilled in my presence. I would spend the night at home.

The experience is happening only where you are, not somewhere else. Turn away from something and turn toward something else. You will be offered two ways.

Life was offering two choices: an old one and something new. It was just a matter of choosing which one and continuing to build momentum towards new opportunities.

'We live in a dream world where all of our dreams are coming true.' The question is then, 'What dreams are coming true?' My ideas and wishes seem to be establishing themselves in my reality. 'I create. Something is guiding me but nothing is leading me. I lead myself into situations I choose because of the nature of my intention. Choose what you want. If you don't get it, it's not something you truly want.'

Anything you want to experience in this lifetime, you can have it. If you don't get it, its because you don't truly want it. It doesn't have to be love that you choose, but every action has consequences and that's how Life can become anything. You get what you believe you deserve. Choose what you want instead. Perfection comes with choosing love.

I lay back on the bed and felt the relaxed state of my being. Light and lucid energy seemed to flow through me, bringing gifts of insight.

The first light of Sunday morning came with the occasional voice of a passerby. I opened the window and lay back on the pillows, inhaling the scent of a new day. I smiled, wondering what this day could bring that would better the last. I opened the door. David was talking to someone nearby. I heard them laughing, enjoying life. Then I heard the clomp of a heavy flip flop on the porch. David appeared in the doorway.

"Did you have a good night?" he asked, a bright smile on his face.

"It was divine. I stayed in and watched the stars."

"It was beautiful last night. We stayed up quite late," he said, placing some things in the bungalow. We were sitting on the porch when Champ invited us to join him and some friends for a get together. I followed them down the hill through some foliage and onto a platform over the sea. Several people had a seat perched above the water. We were all hidden from above. I moved to get comfortable and view the reflective sea. The uniqueness of the situation drew me into reverence and I sat quietly. The Thai boys smiled at me with knowing looks. Words were unnecessary and they understood, as I did. Lifted by the sweet rhythmic melody of their voices, I was caressed by a soft breeze and the feeling of harmony.

From the precipice we moved up the hill to Champ's bungalow, jungle vines enveloping his abode which was perched high on the hillside. Benches made from palm trees comforted us and again I turned toward the jungle to witness its buzzing. New music was playing, pumping reggae beats with inspirational and poignant words infused into spiritually politicized lyrics. The music lent charm to the moment and I enquired about the artist.

"This is Finley Quaye. He's a hit is England." The musical vibration lifted my feeling even higher. My body yearned to dance, compelled to join him in the 'higher planes'.

"I have to borrow this."

"It's mine. You can hear it whenever you want."

Back at our bungalow David moved around out of sight as my thoughts danced to the rhythms, flowing from one into the next, bringing an orderly line of splendid results. Calmness radiated through my entire being, affecting all of my experience. I was able to still my active mind and just be, happy that the changes were lasting.

I lay on the pillows, smiling deeply and relishing the standstill in my thoughts. Then David was beside me on his back. We looked up at the ceiling and breathed in the fresh air, felt the quiet calmness of our surroundings and snuggled alongside one another. It felt nice to have someone near, and we lay for a while, just breathing and being close. Then he got up and without a word continued to carry out his duties, preparing for a night out.

After he left I felt my overall feeling mellow. I was more certain and more comfortable with moments of stillness in my mind and felt less perplexed by silent nothingness. With a still mind and clear thoughts new ideas found easy, unfettered access. By stopping the output of my energy, I experienced a reversal with fresh ideas pouring forth in my thoughts.

I sat up. It made so much sense. Like the pendulum theory I witnessed my thoughts swing back and forth in duality. When stilled, I became a magnetic rod for the input of brilliance all around me. What I was being shown by Life was immense and I knew that I had to stay strong to assimilate the grand ideas and not become overwhelmed. Almost overwhelmed, the sensation of awareness poured through me as if I stood arms outstretched trying to hold a mass of light particles piled high. The feeling was wonderful and beautiful and I had to work at keeping myself centred and balanced. I knew I was capable of fortifying it, but I did have to work at it.

It was as if I was being handed the maximum limit of information that I could handle. I knew I had to continue to fortify the foundations of understanding to further my learning. My reward was all around. I wanted to become competent and confident enough to teach others even though my learning was incomplete. Most of all I wanted others to know that these beautiful, empowering experiences were available to everyone.

You have to be doing exactly what you want in life. That is how your soul communicates with you, by representing itself in your truest desires, and these are your ways to fulfillment and happiness in your life. To be truly happy, you must know what truly makes you, thus your soul, happy. You can be who you are and who you want to be. You can be both!

The new lesson plunged me into a bath of knowingness. The lessons of life were free, available to an open mind. With each step, my vision sharpened, literally and figuratively. Life became clearer in my mind's eye. I witnessed the image of a change in which all people could wake from limited illusions and grasp the fullness of life in all its wonder. I was certain that seeing life more clearly and wondrous would encourage people to join together and find true happiness in themselves, their lives permeated with joy and love. What a gift to share with humanity! I imagined what was happening inside me, happening inside others and the thought excited me. I knew it was possible to demonstrate an awakened true love, and incredible fantasy land available in each of us.

Together we could seek out others to fulfill a shared experience, shaping the path with like-minded individuals. Everything collective, nothing dictated. I believed most certainly that our true nature was goodness, after all, our true nature was the brilliant essence of life. I could see this in myself, after peeling away the layers, finding purity and love inside. I became less fearful of what else might exist within me.

I continued to search for my truest self, in each moment of the day, reliving various experiences. Society had taught me how to conform. I decided I had become tired of playing mind games and was ready to move forward. It was time to break down the barriers of the ego and begin to feel comfortable exposing the nature of my true self, with all of its brilliant innocence and naivety. I wasn't afraid of what lay beneath the surface, but would I be strong enough, in every moment, to present my truest self?

In moments like those, filled with exuberance towards another new understanding and awakening, I felt a strong sense of oneness with life around me. The feeling brought hopefulness for a new future, as if humanity was at the cusp of a new awakening. A state where we would all begin to throw off the chains of disillusionment in increasingly rapid succession and grow into the grandness and glory of the experiences that awaited us. In response to this vision, I could see that cultural traditions were needed in the past in order to place ourselves among others as individual parts of the whole, like children who instinctively fall into roles in playgrounds.

Now we were at the beginning of something new. We were beginning to understand that we are here for our own joyful development and we needed to concern ourselves with that. Loving the self was the first step because then we could accept that we could be our true selves despite what others thought. I knew we could begin to throw down the shackles of what held us and rise into this newness together. Uncovering the secrets we held within our hearts would be the fuel to fire the flame. Once the door was opened it could never be shut again.

The faith inside me seemed to be getting bigger and stronger and it was an incredible feeling. Life talked to me in so many ways that I was only beginning to see.

Choose to let it lead you into what is beautiful. Allow your wonderful ideas to manifest. See where they take you. You may choose the experiences and your soul will take you there physically and mentally. Ask and you shall receive. If you choose to love yourself as a high being, equal to all others, people will also begin to truly love themselves. This is a truth. They will see the way. Demonstrate.

i was ecstatic stepping into this new role. How could I show them? What would I demonstrate? What needed to be done?

I grabbed my sarong and joyfully ambled down the hill. I found a comfortable place to sit in the soft sand and let my thoughts wander back to my life in Bangkok. Living in the city seemed right in one way, but there was a shadow of restlessness. It was like I was living there only temporarily until I could be down at the beach again. I thought about the incredibly intense heat and congestion, and the feeling that I was living under a cloud. Many things about city life did not compare favourably to the serenity of beach living.

Shuffling future plans while sifting sand between my toes, I considered changes I needed to make. I would have to give up my apartment, say goodbye to my new friends, and forget about life in the big city. But how could I make enough money to pursue life on the beach? I needed to trust in life, have faith in what I knew or did't know, and believe that I would be led to another job on one of the islands. I just had to give it time.

Sitting in the sand, I heard my inner voice say, 'I don't like teaching in that classroom!' There it was, the dawning moment.

Listen to yourself! You tell yourself to.

Many thoughts swam through my head while I was in Bangkok and I hadn't listened to what they were saying. Perhaps that was why they remained. I reminded myself to embrace what I was feeling as I realized that those feelings held the keys to so much of my life. I knew that if I listened more closely to what I was feeling, I could know myself better and live life how I wanted to live it.

I walked into tiny ocean waves, then stood thigh-high in water. The shimmering blue waves reflected deep beauty, enticing me deeper. I fell forward and into the water as if falling into a hug. I embraced myself in the water and played lovingly as if the water was responding to the feeling of my body. Sunlight shone down, christening the moment, lighting up my skin like a beacon, sparkling before my eyes. It was splendid and divine at the same time. The water loved me, and I could feel it.

I splashed about sprinkling warm water on my skin, enjoying the feeling of intense purpose, throwing my arms open wide and smiling at the sky. I lowered my body and pushed back upon the sun-dappled surface and lay back to float.

After a few moments, my body overturned in the water. I quickly stood up, dripping.

"What was that?" I asked out loud, wondering what had happened. I reclined back into the water again and floated there, thinking of another question. The most natural question I could think of was, 'Did something actually turn me in the water?' As soon as it passed through my mind, I overturned again face first into the water.

I stood up, mouth hanging open, and I looked to the beach. Had anyone seen this? What was happening? Was something responding to me?

I tested again to see if this could be the interpretation of the response and again I was overturned in the water.

Determined to understand what was happening, I lay back in the water and asked several questions, ones requiring a Yes or a No answer. After I asked a question in my mind there was a brief hesitation, then I was flipped over. I discovered that Yes was to the left and No was to the right. I experimented, floating, testing all kinds of questions, including questions about the past and in the future. The answers to questions in the past were answered in a way that was unrelated to time, as if I had asked a question about the present. Answers regarding the future were non-committal and unclear.

You haven't chosen your future yet. It doesn't exist for you now.

I asked the sun to love my skin and keep it from burning as I asked for more answers. Was it my soul communicating with me? Were these answers inside of me, as part of knowing my true self?

As I continued, communication became more explicit as I was tipped to the left, perpendicular to the water and suspended there with the water line along the centre of my face. Then I was flipped back to starting position, then to the right, perpendicular, then returned to my back. Life was having fun with me.

When my skin began to cry out from the beaming sun I retreated from the water and gathered my things from the beach and headed up to the porch. I refreshed myself with a bottle of water and sat in the shade wrapped in my sarong. Revelling in the beauty and calm my imagination spun outward as my mind and soul opened up to each other. My heart filled with love as secrets of the Universe poured forth with beautiful simplicity.

I sat on the bed with a view through the window as a powerful connection expanded my awareness. My questions became more complex and I was provided with answers of perfect clarity and brilliance. fell to the floor in near-hysterics. I could barely comprehend the brilliance of what I was being shown, as if I had stepped into a wind tunnel of eternal knowledge. I had to catch my breath so I moved outside onto the porch.

I knew my environment loved me, so I trusted that I would know my limits. I relaxed even more as I embraced the pulsing beauty around me, insects flying and landing within sight. I was living a symphonic, harmonious moment that radiated pure positive energy. I was engulfed in a timeless embrace.

I felt heavenly, imbued with the beauty around me, but my skin needed a rest. I went inside to my bed beside the open window and propped my back up on the pillows at the headboard. I could see the porch and green foliage beaming in. My body felt loved and I noticed a slight difference inside four walls. My experience became contained, even as I opened more. I wanted to feel solid ground so I moved onto the floor.

Insights came in waves, more and more profound, as my feelings became deeper and more intense. I was rooted to the spot like iron against a magnet. I listened as inner wisdom poured through me, new comprehension blasting any previous shorelines in powerful waves: scientific balances, mathematic synchronicity, sacred geometry and cosmic resolutions. I was lit up, mind and body. I placed my hands flat down beside me. I needed to feel solid ground.

Energy poured into me, insights flooded my mind. Answers at the farthest edge of my understanding. I moved forward to make sense of my surroundings and how I fit into everything. I lifted my eyes and asked, 'Show me more.' And more came, pouring in, rushing through me, until I overflowed, tears streaming down my face. I gagged from this overwhelming onslaught, laughing and crying at the same time.

I needed fresh air. I peeled myself from the floor and moved slowly onto the porch and into a bamboo chair. The whole natural world was bright with vibrant energy and I listened to the hum of the scene, watching bees buzzing from flower to flower and birds fluttering from tree to tree. Perched on this hillside with this view I felt grateful to experience such beauty. Nature comforted me and made me feel safe as I reached beyond what I had known.

Life seemed to be leading me along that I might discover its inner workings. Life was talking to me, in subtle ways that I was beginning to understand. Tears filled my eyes as I sat overwhelmed by the brilliance. Even in the middle of such clarity I still doubted what I was being shown and questioned my interpretation. I wondered if I was having this experience because I was choosing my perceptions, making it up as I went along. It seemed too good to be true, and part of me was hesitantly unsure. But it kept coming, relentless and reassuring. There could be no mistake.

I wanted to know if others could experience these sensations as well. Why not? Everything I was learning was both logical and reasonable. But I was tripped up on occasion when encountering moments that I couldn't explain by using my sense of logic, even as the logic I was shown illuminated my own. I was getting a one on one lesson from something speaking to me through my mind and reflected back to me in my experience. I knew whatever it was that I was affecting it with my thinking.

The day shifted as light moved across the wall of the bungalow bringing with it waves of melting heat while I remained consumed in my experience. There were so many ways life talked to me that I stared into my surroundings wondering what was really there. I was aware of its faintly buzzing presence and an energy so strong that seemed to turn on like a light switch. I tried to remain receptive to the ongoing phenomenon making an effort to stay positive and alert to what my senses took in.

The learning operated like a laser. My attention was contained and focused then channelled through the experience to an atmosphere of answers on the other side. The teachings were personal and strangely familiar. Ideologies presented and responses sought were modern and culturally familiar. It was as if my own words were coming back to me. I became more and more aware that finding success in life wasn't about looking hard for answers or acknowledgement in one's surroundings but relaxing into the known. It was a tough task.

When asking a question I needed to remember that my senses were offering information. Life was a giant mirror reflecting partial images. Was I missing something? Was there more to see? What was available? Recognizing myself as a larger being than my own body I began to see that creatures around me were part of a conversation. They flew away when I thought it was time and gathered around me when I asked for their help. I wondered what was really involved and where this synchronicity ended or began. What roles were in play? It felt like everything beyond me was a collective consciousness while I remained painfully unconscious.

At times I found my visual attention falling onto something that I had wondered about in my thoughts. I learned that life could show me what I wanted if I asked. These messages were powerful that I struggled to embrace them. There was so much I was realizing to know about myself and my experiences that I would ofter cache revelations for future examination. It was a feast of such immense proportions that I was simply too full.

The nature of life would elude me and then appear so clearly. I wanted to stamp those moments and live in that understanding, forging forward like a man blinded by a snowstorm yet confident in the steps he was taking. I needed to be patient, but excitement overtook me because of what had been lain at my feet. In a physical world things required a force to act upon them to move. I needed to be patient and let these forces orchestrate my world.

I lay back on the bed and played Finley pumping softly on the stereo. Looking around the room I wondered what was really there, what was really going on. I knew that in a way, nothing around me was really there. Nothing was real. I picked up my pen and tried to capture the essence in words. 'It doesn't even feel like this is my body. I feel strangely light and permeable. I feel like I'm a manifestation of vibrating energy. I'm feeling very weak. This music is helping me, too. My hands have never shaken like this. They're shaking. This is magnificence. Faith led me here. I am in bliss.' I could feel intense energy pouring through me. My soul felt like an output centre of energy and I could choose the sockets into which I plugged.

I looked intently at the space around my skin, focussing to see clear energy, like a daylight silhouette. Then I turned my vision on the door, wondering about possible visual effects. A cartoon image of an alien appeared with pointy ears and small stature in relation to its head. Then it transformed into a pig wearing a strange costume. I wondered about the reason and the principles behind the vision and learned that life could entertain me in another new way. I pondered the confusion this visual experience could have caused people over the centuries. I thought of patients in mental wards who sat and stared at walls, laughing uncontrollably. What was wrong about their laughter? What was right?

I considered the subject of sleep and whether this same visual entertainment I was experiencing could carry on in one's dreams. What are the connections between what we see during the day and what we dream about at night? What had puzzled me the most was the activity that stimulated rapid eye movement. Was R.E.M. a product of visual stimulation during dreamlike images, presented by deeper levels of the subconscious mind? Something beyond my present comprehension interacted with me. The feeling reminded me of entering a closet as a small child and smelling the strange, musty scent of unknown treasures in storage, wondering where I really was, but smiling because I was there. I can remember as a three-year-old, alone in my brother's closet, looking up at shelves loaded with games and toys and unidentified objects. Gazing up at all the toys that awaited me, I felt happy to be alive.

And now as an adult I was learning to remember something powerful that existed in my experience, expressed as moments of intense clarity and heightened consciousness. It was something incredible that was very close and familiar, throwing light on experience and making day-to-day problems seem inconsequential.

I was beginning to put together the pieces of my experience. But it was a giant puzzle that seemed to know no end. That is existence - coming together, meeting the brightest first in the centre then connecting and becoming the source together. I knew what life was made of and I was excited to see what we would make of it. I knew it was in love with me because I could see that in my surroundings. It was there for a reason: it was there for us, whoever we were.

I wanted to group together concepts and principles that would help me understand how I interacted with my experience uniquely. Life was simple to live, really. There was so much we could do if only we pursued our potential. We could choose to follow our soul's path, and as individuals, enjoy life.

I wanted to believe that we were powerful tools here, tools of love and light and energy. We create our own experiences, as individuals and groups. These is no sense in blaming others. We give what we get and get what we give. There was no sense in blaming one another for anything. We all equally gave what we got. What we gave was returned to us.

You will see the answers as you go. They will come to you, remember. You don't need to go to them. You're a magnetic energy field -think about it.

I thought about the adjustments I had made in my world view. Four months into my stay I had started to become aware that my surroundings seemed to jump out to greet me. I picked up my pen. 'Pay heed to resources like the forefathers and founders.' I could see that our theories were built on theories, taking each level higher. We did the work together in order to bring the collective higher. To detract from this end would cause fear. That is how we would know the way. We would feel it.

Our individual perspective is very subjective. We were in everything. We play the staring role in our own lives. In every moment, we could see that Life is a daily creation for the making. I saw that my life could change according to my perspective of it. I was behind the steering wheel. Not the experience, but my experience. We needed to be more aware of our selves and thus our experiences.

I considered my connection to things around me. Massive rocks fantastically inspired weeds and luscious plant life. I appreciated my good fortune. Beyond the amazing scenery and blissful existence I knew my phenomenal experiences were not solely based on my surroundings. They were now of my choosing - anywhere. But for now, at least, this was my favourite location. I felt helped into feelings of true love and encouraged to bask in it.

I wondered about having more unique experiences.

Your life experiences will be where by action you choose to have them. They are never somewhere else, happening while you are absent. The experience is within you. Choose what you want. Be in the moment and let your ideas come clearly. Get everything you choose for yourself. Be aware. Don't judge. Just do.

Moments are magnified under examination. With each look the whole picture becomes bigger and clearer, until I can't take any more and have to rest. I thought about what I could write to myself as a reminder about the easiest way to go forward into experiencing more love and goodness and to make sure that I was always heading in a good direction. I asked myself. Again, my greater source answered.

Love will take you here. It will answer you in that first, initial thought. That first thought that passes through your head, in a fleeting instant is the one you need to listen to. You can train yourself to listen better, to be aware of what passes through your thoughts. What is the feeling?

Witnessing insight and wisdom, I felt amazed at the magnificence of life. I was seeing that life was a puzzle to be constructed through personal understanding. I loved the challenge of being tested, maximizing my skills, expanding my knowledge, and becoming more aware of the puzzle pieces around me. Dwelling in my internal consciousness became the highlight of my day, looking around inside. Finding treasures while walking along the beach, picking up seashells and rare stones.

Sometime later I heard movement on the porch. David was conversing with someone new. I took a deep breath and decided to join them and opened the door to say hello. I felt incredibly light, almost weightless, as I floated onto the deck beaming with energy. I sat in my familiar bamboo chair experiencing waves of illumination, as if the volume of life had been turned up. I said hello to David's friend. Then we sat in silence enjoying the natural setting in our tranquil afternoon, warm rays of sun grazing our legs, imbued by our own thoughts.

A few moments passed before a thin, elderly Thai man appeared on our deck. He stood looking at me, his eyes glazed, and began to speak English.

"You are a King. The people look at you and say pant, pant, pant. They are hungry." Then he turned and was gone.

I was stunned. David was speechless, his eyebrows raised, face smiling.

"What was that? Who was that?" I asked.

David shook his head. He didn't know. His friend said nothing and we went back to our thoughts.

But my life had changed.

I decided to go for a swim. I had taken my mind on such a long trip that I felt some physical experience would come as a welcome change. My face in the mirror looked happy. My eyes sparkled. I changed into my swimsuit, wrapped my sarong around my waist and stepped along the rock path to the beach. I waded out into the clear water to float, thinking about what questions I would ask this time. I wondered about the source and whether I was asking the universe my questions and my soul was answering me, imagining the rest of my surroundings as witnesses. I thought of all the great moments of inspirational breakthroughs I had been having and considered what great quest I could fulfil this lifetime. Wondering about some grand challenge I was being directed toward, I thought of what I hoped to accomplish. I breathed in deeply, taking my attention to the bright sky behind my closed eyes and asked, "What am I to do in this lifetime? What greatness can I contribute?"

Almost without hesitation an answer came into my head. 'Be a mother'. I was completely knocked off guard and shocked by the message of the simple yet complete answer. I rarely considered my own motherhood, content with my style of living and place in life. I was nowhere near ready to have children. But when I received that answer I felt happy and thought, 'Great, that's easy.' I was supplied with the tools to accomplish that. All I needed was intention.

It was Monday and I was still on the island paradise. I needed to get back to Bangkok but the last thing I wanted to do was leave my beachside abode. But I had to. I made arrangements to leave for the city later that afternoon.

After a nice morning on the beach, David and I headed into town to catch the afternoon ferry. Too late. We arrived as the large boat was motoring just out into the bay filled with tourists. We inquired about a night boat and were told it would leave at eleven. I had travelled by night boat before with Huey and I knew that with fellow backpackers I would be comfortable travelling alone.

David and I returned to the bungalows and to all those to whom I had said goodbye an hour earlier. They shared a good chuckle and exchanged some words in Thai. I felt as if they could see into my soul. The Thai boys who lived on the islands had a certain polished intuition and seemed to see deeply inside others. I wondered how much they recognised the tacit undercurrents building in me more and more every day.

I scampered down the stone steps to the bungalow, smiling as I said goodbye to David. He was heading out for an afternoon that would most likely turn into an evening, and maybe a night. Inside the bungalow I spread out my sarong and lit some candles and before sitting back to enjoy another nine hours of revelling in beauty, warmth and salty air.

I was surprised when much later on David arrived to give me a ride me to the ferry. I said goodbye again to everyone and hopped onto the back of David's bike. We drove to the pier in a quiet night breeze while I took the surreal sight of the sleeping palms against the star filled, midnight blue sky. Everything was just as intoxicating as it was during the day.

The only vessel on the pier was a large freighter. There were no other boats or tourists to be seen. There was no ferry coming. I refused to spend the night in a plastic deck chair, surrounded by sailors, in the middle of nowhere.

So we turned around again and headed back to the bungalows. Crazy! I slipped past a few people working at the bar as they smiled and waved, amused with my return. I descended the rocky path that led to the bungalow as a smile resumed on my face.

I took some time before bed and wondered what I would be presented with this night, if anything, as I sat staring out at the sky from my familiar deck chair on the porch. I felt the peacefulness and listened to the sound of the faint wave splashes on the shore. I gazed up into the dark sky and stars for a long time.

My mind was busy working to find answers to questions that had been puzzling me and I looked deeply into two stars near to one another in the sky. They seemed to draw my attention and I listened for sounds within. I felt a low humming of reassurance, as if I was being told that how I lived was good for me and so it was right. Something was there, in the star, corresponding within me. I was amazed how I had tapped into something incredible by seeking an alternative experience. I had been shown in so many ways to trust what I was being shown by life and during that moment the feeling inside me was priceless.

It was the uniqueness of the feeling that brought trust, I knew that something incredible expressed itself in my inner feelings and I believed it was in my best interest to trust and have faith in what I was experiencing, even though no one had mentioned these kinds of feelings to me before.

What is this? I would ask, after feeling something new and grand and yet in some way familiar. How can I be feeling this and seeing this? I was sure that there had to be others somewhere who had experienced these intense feelings, perhaps even living now or maybe long ago, in different times when we were in touch with nature. And where were these people who experienced and knew of life's secrets now? I wondered why these beautiful communications had remained a secret to the modern world.

I sat back and enjoyed my new experience with the stars. I was thankful I had taken the time to be with life. I was becoming more comfortable with the realization that I was accompanied by fresh and friendly sources that enabled me to see life in a new way, a new light. After having undergone experiences I knew that anything was possible. I had so much potential! I could create anything! Everything around me was a grand idea, showing me that anything could be made from nothing. Humans were powerful enough to live in a reality that was incredible and abundant.

Many people lived with fear and were taught to hold their truest feelings back. Some cultures were steeped in those ideologies. All of us had the potential to operate at the highest level, feeling joy and contentment as a result. My faith was a light burning brightly inside me and I would not turn off what I had been shown. I loved it with all my heart right back.

The next day I gathered up my things and said another farewell to my special spiritual centre. I didn't want to leave. I still felt I wasn't finished there. But I had no idea I could ever be finished. I had to get back to Bangkok, tie up some loose ends, pack up my apartment and look for a new job on one of the islands.

I said goodbye to the others again as they waved and smiled. They were giggling about something when the truck taxi pulled up, I heard them say something to the driver in Thai. It sounded like 'Lamai', which was one of the four main stops around the island, and at the opposite side of the island from the pier. The driver didn't understand my English when I tried to ask him where he was going first, whether to the ferry or Lamai. I didn't want to panic so I sat and watched as we drove, sure we would have enough time to reach the ferry, even if we went to Lamai first.

Forty-five minutes later, with fifteen minutes to catch the ferry, I was in Lamai, exasperated. I knew the drive to the pier at Nathon was at least a half an hour from where we were. The driver of the truck had been the slowest I had ever seen.

Another twenty-four hours on the island! I headed down the road through Lamai, not looking forward to immediately returning to the bungalows and, no doubt, an amused audience. I hadn't been to Lamai before so I walked around aimlessly still dazed by the crazy stream of occurrences.

As I walked in the heat the whole situation seemed like a dream. My movements seemed hypnogogic as I walked down the road, eyeing the scenery that seemed timeless, hanging like drapery in the heat and dust. I floated along until I came upon a truck that had just stopped with three foreigners in it. The dream-like situation continued as they asked, "Do you know a good place to stay?" I looked around, lost in the unfamiliar surroundings. "No, I don't even know where the beach is."

Still dumbfounded by the bizarre situation I took a deep breath and started to assess things as a Dutch couple and Canadian man hopped out with their bags in front of me. I stared down the street, unsure of my next move.

"Come with us. We're going for a drink," one said, as they urged me to join them. Smiling, I accepted.

Within a few moments we had located the beach and found a thatch-roofed restaurant that looked over the sea. We sat down at a table for four and ordered specialty cocktails to celebrate their arrival to the island. The Dutch couple were spirited and friendly and they laughed easily, making me see the lighter side of my day. Despite their pleasant company worry crept into my mood. I was anxious about another day passing and not getting back to Bangkok.

"Don't worry. You can go back tomorrow," she said, her words reassuring me. I thanked her for the suggestion. Everything would be fine, I realized. It was only one more day. The weight of the situation lifted from my shoulders.

"I have heard stories of people getting stuck on these islands. I wonder if there is anything to it," said Dave, the Canadian.

"These are very old islands. The people living here are tribal. The history is rich and goes back thousands of years," the Dutch man offered.

We enjoyed the view from the comfortable chairs and munched on snacks from the menu. The conversation was energetic and I connected easily with my new friends. I told them of my recent excursions, leaving out the extraordinary experiences and my book. They were quite supportive that I had chosen to abandon the hectic life in Bangkok and follow my heart instead.

"You're a pioneer," said the Dutch man who sat across the table from me. I was struck by his comment. The words resounded within me. But how could this man know?

"You are talented," he then said. I was speechless. I began to feel more certain after hearing his words, amazed at how I was receiving reassurance, from outside sources. Doubt was pushed aside and I began to relax.

After we finished our snacks I decided to strike out for the bungalow. Again, I thanked them for their good company and we said our good byes. I left the restaurant and walked toward the road. Two girls sitting on a porch looked my way as I passed by. One of them came running.

"Hi. Are you okay? You seemed a little down. Is everything alright?"

I was surprised by her intuition and action to help.

"Yes, I'm okay. I just have a situation to deal with but I am fine. Thanks for checking on me."

"Well, we saw you walking by and you didn't look so good. We thought we should make sure you were okay," she said, kindly.

"Thank you. I'm okay." We chatted for a few minutes and then I continued on my way, happy for another reminder that life loved me and was watching out for me. I walked on amazed at how it worked, so much behind the scenes.

I hopped onto a truck taxi for the long ride back to the bungalows. Lucky for me the bar was empty and I quietly made my way undetected down the familiar steps. I let myself into the empty bungalow and sat on the bed, wondering if I could ever leave. Hotel California. I made a solemn vow that I would leave the next afternoon. The was a new life to begin arranging.

I picked up my pen to record my feelings, slightly embarrassed that I hadn't been able to leave the island. I wrote two lines in my book.

Don't be embarrassed of your present 'imperfection'. There is perfection in you. Find it.

A song popped into my head, lyrics from Danny Michel, and I began to sing, "Three is the magic number. What it is, is the magic number." It was quite fitting. I had already tried three times to get off the island.

Give it that long and change will come.

I considered the prevalence of the number three throughout many religions, fairy tales, human conduct and my physical environment. I began to notice how oftentimes a triad of events would characterize a situation. How exactly did that work, and what laws applied to those cycles?

I wondered about that mysterious number three and saw ways that it permeated this existence. I also wondered about other theories and beliefs that were held and how they could be looked at differently to find new meaning. I wrote another message to remind me: 'The answers to this life are all around us. Where else would they be? It is a matter of seeing them. Just see them. Don't look past them. There are many ways to enlightenment. Explore the fields.'

I thought about the great experiences I had lived that afternoon, finding friends and people to help me so easily.

These experiences are in everything. 'Free floating' is the best way to have them; wandering and letting your soul lead you.

I spend a lot of time thinking and quieting my self in order to hear answers that came from within. My head started to ache because I was always in intense focus.

Look how needy you are for information. So is everyone else. You are a source. People offer you the information you seek. As you get more focused, you bring it to you more quickly. There are other sources.

As I became very focused I felt excitement throughout my whole body, the direct attention of my whole being. My hand had been moving into the position of the 'I love you' symbol people showed at concerts, with their thumb, forefinger and pinky raised. My hands naturally formed that position now like my hand was plugged into an electrical outlet.

Chapter 7 – The Colour of Ohm

"Everything is connected," I explained to David after he returned from the beach. I was on the edge of my bed, bursting to share what I had learned. "Keep looking at life until it means something. You find what you need." I smiled at him. "This takes effort even though you have help to do this. It is always around you. Ask for it. See it and use it."

David was dreamy as he folded clothes on his bed, head in the clouds. His scattered state surprised me. He was definitely a man in love, or lust.

"I use it. Like just today, when I needed a cool shower, I just turned on the tap."

"Yes," I said, "exactly." I wasn't sure if it was sarcasm, and I looked at him.

"Will you be a saviour David? Will you help save this world?"

"I'll be the friend of a saviour."

"Fine. I'll do it by myself. There are lots of people to help me. We will do it."

"Okay. And I'll read about it on the news."

"You will."

David scoffed at my exuberance.

"Things have always been this way," he said.

"Why do you think so?"

"Greed." He silenced us both.

"It's true," I offered. "Consider past civilizations, the Mayans and stories surrounding their disappearance. They raised their energy level so high that they ceased to exist in physical form."

He said nothing as he folded, looking down.

"I wonder if they have continued their existence in another realm, another level of experience." Had the Mayans had gone deeper into what I had experienced? It seemed like what I was glimpsing had no end.

"There is some history around Stonehenge, in England. Have you heard of it."

"Yes," I smiled.

"They say its some kind of sundial constructed by ancient Celts. Many people go there because of the energy. They say it feels good to be in that spot."

"Interesting. I wonder what that is all about."

"Some things are just undiscoverable. We can't know everything."

"Why not?"

He looked at me with wide disbelieving eyes.

"David, I'm telling you. There are physical, emotional, mental and spiritual rewards I've just begun to become aware of as I explore.

There is a physical state of bliss that flows through me, titillating my emotions with feelings of love." He smiled, his face reddened.

"It's like exploring the maximum limit of magnificent love. My mental realms feel brighter, reflecting new understanding from the knowledge I'm being shown. My entire spirit is charged by the connection." I looked him in the eye, serious and sincere in my words.

"I don't know what it is, but whatever it is, it feels right. I feel awake, energized and charged." I knew he couldn't doubt me, even if he didn't understand. He put away his clothes and made his way to the door.

"Don't wait up for me," he said, winking. He was gone.

After he left I thought about humans as energy fields with magnetic capacities mingling energy with our thoughts. What was the rule? You choose to attract energies. *You actively exchange energies. I thought about my recent experiences, new ideas and desire to see new ways.* I had often felt a sense of urgency when I had gone into these higher intensities, as if I needed to understand and process the information quickly.

My quest for connection to the grander and grander feelings exposed a lack of understanding. *Look for the deepest meaning behind everything. There you will find the answers you are seeking.* There was something to be understood and I knew I was making progress to become more enlightened and aware, even as I shifted through pieces of the puzzle that sometimes had no end. I needed to find the right level of observation to allow me to live my life happily and easily without being caught up in all the details. I just didn't know which details were important.

Thought control emerged as a lesson I needed to master. I stood witness to a continuous live screening of thoughts running through my mind. It was a new understanding that everything around me could see and hear my thoughts, as if their effect went out from me affecting everything in its path. It was impressed upon me to use my thoughts with care, as tools and not to self-destruct. Being attuned and by listening closely I learned new things previously unknown such as the vibration of my thoughts. The energy of every thought released itself to the creation of my new goal.

Now my goal was to embark upon a new life. I needed to construct a whole new existence: new job, new place, new town. As I lay in bed, I realized I had only days to make all these changes. I went to sleep with the creation of a new life on my mind.

* * *

I awoke the next morning and felt happy. I went for a breakfast, then a swim and said goodbye to my surroundings. I packed my things while appreciating my stay, smiling and feeling grateful. About an hour before I planned to catch a taxi I joined the others for a retreat to the beach platform. We scaled down the large rocks, through vines and tree branches, and seated ourselves among nature that surrounded us.

Thai men sat smiling, genuine and true, enjoying themselves thoroughly. I admired them as they sat shirtless and tanned with lithe, strong bodies. They laughed and smiled easily with each other. It's true what they say about smiles of Thailand. A friendly exchange was rewarded with the most genuine of smiles and when you got one, it made your heart melt. I wanted to know more about their ways, and shifted into my familiar standpoint of objectivity. Then I asked Champ a question.

"What's the oldest age on this island."

He gazed into my eyes and answered, "What's age?" His answer brought me to another level as our eyes met. Then his eyes glazed over and his expression changed. He seemed to reach beyond me as he spoke.

"Our lips just move, words come from out here," he said, as he waved his hand behind his head. I absorbed the depth as he continued, "I have a small voice and it comes from here," as he held his throat. He focussed on my eyes and said, "Others have a biggest voice and it comes from here," as he held his heart.

I felt bared as if he could see into my soul, as if he knew what I had been doing alone for hours in the bungalow, my innermost secrets revealed. This communion on a deep level resounded within me. Then he smiled and I smiled, silent and touched. The strange gaze faded from his eyes as he turned to join the others in conversation. I remained in a quiet moment of titillation.

I replayed his words in my head, sensing another strange message from life. I had been spoken to with love, his words seemed in the direction I was headed: sharing these astonishing, heartfelt ideas with others. I paused to consider that I was experiencing another incredible dream.

I knew my departure was near.

"I have to go," I said, "I'm sorry to break up the party." There were groans and moans as the others shifted. But I had to catch the ferry. I had to start my life. I started to unfold my legs to stand, but it was difficult to gather the energy to get up. Immediately I noticed that something very strange was happening. A strong force was pulling me down to my seated position. I managed to stand holding onto branches, and tried to move forward. I pushed myself to make my way past the others. I felt a strong pulling sensation, like the tension of a large elastic band. They looked after me, asking "You're going now?"

"I'm sorry I have to go." Astonished, I pushed on, steadying myself as I went, directing my resistant body to the bungalow. Like walking into blowing wind, I leaned forward, concentrating on my ascent as I moved through trees and over rocks at a steep angle. The whole while I felt the same sensation pulling me back to the gathering. I carefully placed on foot in front of the other along the rock path to the bungalow. I continued against the draw. I dared not turn around because the force was so strong I thought that I might be dragged back along the ground.

Finally, and with some relief I made the bungalow. I collected my bags, stunned at what I had just felt. I walked up to the road past the restaurant and waved goodbye to the others, having relocated since I had left.

"Leaving already?" one man called out.

"Yes," I croaked and turned back toward the road not wanting to take a chance that another event held me back. Within a few moments a truck taxi came and I hopped in, feeling relieved while enjoying the sights of the palm lined ride to the pier. Somewhat drained and fatigued I could still feel the subtle sensation as I looked out from the truck to enjoy my last moments on the island for a while. I thought to myself, 'All I have to do now is stay on this truck and I will get to the ferry on time.'

Rolling along the dusty road through Lamai, the town I had been in the day before, I still felt the pull, perplexed at what exactly was going on. Driving to the end of a road, leaving the tourist area we came to a junction and rolled to a stop. Just as we turned the corner the tugging ceased. Instantly it dropped and was gone. I looked around at the others in the back of the truck. With my eyes wide and mouth open in surprise I wondered how I could share the experience. But their distant faces closed that door. I kept it inside and smiled to about my unique experience with life.

We made Don Sak pier on time so I walked down the long dock to the crowded ferry ahead. A forty minute ride would deliver us to the mainland, and from there I would take a night bus to Bangkok. Backpacks were littered everywhere. Tourists sat wedged between them, all over the sun-drenched deck. I headed inside to a bench seat by a window. I needed to write.

I opened my notebook and began to pour my revelations onto the page. You can see anything in this life; just choose to see it. There are other people who want to experience it with you. Find them. *Intend to have thought control, pursue higher thought planes and you will be opened to the magnificence. Understanding and unique experiences come easier to you now because your thoughts are mingling on higher planes. You get what you want easier and faster and the people come quickly to guide you. You're on a mission of enlightenment.*

I rested my head back on a plastic blue chair, exhaling upward while attempting to digest the sophisticated information. I wondered if my experiences were 'real', in a way that meant they were available to others. I cautioned myself, considering that what I was experiencing was outside of the 'sane' realm. My need to judge the situation was eased by the realization, It's real if it's here, if it's perceivable. It's not 'insane' because nothing is.

People filled seats around me leaving a perimeter so that I could still breathe and think on my own. Some closed their eyes in a peaceful gesture. Others sat quietly. The space was comforting and soon the engine started and we coasted away from the pier.

As we sailed I looked out at the moving water. I wondered if some part of me had crossed over to some land of experience that others hadn't experienced. I wanted so much to share my experiences with everyone, certain that others could gain some unique knowledge or understanding. I wanted to pursue the boundaries of life's incredible experience but these boundaries kept giving way. I put my pen to paper, 'If we can do it, let's do it. Spiritual.'

Looking far out across the beautiful sea I saw a rainstorm on the horizon and wondered if it would reach us before we arrived at shore. I gazed at the people around me who sat in chairs resting their eyes. They were all so beautiful and unique, seemingly unaware. Every being here is having a different experience. Every being is the purpose of this experience. Wonderfully, all perceive it differently.

I pictured myself on a flower-lined pathway. I imagined the flowers that grew there as places in life that awaited me. Our destination, the Surat Thani pier, was at an industrial seaside town, yet another unique place in this experience. I remembered what I had learned and reviewed it on paper. 'The world is the experience. Everyone chooses their own experiential identity and realities derived from the thoughts of the whole. Energy creates matter. Our energy creates us. Three steps: Unaware experience, knowing, aware experience. You choose to let things stop you. You may do so or give it up and let go into experience.'

Focussing on shapes to physically explain my feeling, I toyed with symbols and figures. 'There is one alone. Two can balance. Three is the balance. If you choose duality, to live with the love you choose to live with the pain. Non-duality is balance; duality is representation. This is what Buddha talks of, fruits of his brilliant enlightenment,' I wrote. But it wasn't his; its yours, it's there, just as you are.

We have been fitted with many tools to attain glory. Lead to the light of your soul, feel it; elation, bliss, art, music, physical creation. You create what you want to love in your life; experience it. Do I see what I want to see or do I see what's there? I looked out the window and saw a floating stick in the form of an arrow, pointing back to Koh Samui. I chuckled to myself, then thought about moving up, to get some fresh air on the deck.

I walked carefully through people and packs to find an empty space to sit. I found a spot next to a handsome man with sandy blond hair, striking blue eyes, and bare chest with an interesting shoulder tattoo. I wanted to know what it meant.

"What is that symbol you're wearing?"

He turned to me and smiled. "It's 'Ohm', the sound of the earth, when every creature makes its sound at the same time." I was silenced by the beauty of it on his shoulder. We began to talk about our visits to the island as a petite tanned woman with brown hair turned away and made a face.

We arrived at the pier where our conversation continued over coffee. His girl friend, whom he had been ignoring, finally said they needed to move on. Our buses were loading. We parted with a close hug. My heart thumped as I waved goodbye, walking into bright sunshine toward my bus. I exhaled as I plopped down on a seat beside the window, an open seat beside me. I curled up in both and slept through the night covered with a blue sarong and the big yellow sun pattern.

I awoke from a strange dream in Bangkok. A Thai man was tapping on my leg. He gently informed me that we had arrived. The sounds of the city clanged around us as I gathered my bags and stepped out into the early morning haze. I smiled and thanked the bus driver for getting us there safely then climbed in a taxi to sort out my life.

The steam of the city embraced us as we zoomed along through busy streets. I exhaled and felt the steady earthy pulse of the city I was ready to leave. Where would I go from here? Once inside my apartment I shed my slept-in clothing and showered. Afterwards I opened the employment section of the Bangkok Post on my coffee table. In short order, I found a listing for a full time Kindergarten Teacher on the island of Phuket, off the southwest coast of Thailand. I rolled back on the sofa hardly believing my luck. I found my resume and headed down to the office to fax it off.

I imagined myself getting the job because it was exactly the type of job I had hoped for. I figured it was no coincidence that it had appeared to me and I had to trust such an obvious turn of events. I could hardly believe what was happening.

The next day I got a call for an interview to be held in Bangkok. I would be meeting with a German man who was a friend of the school owner. I followed the instructions to his apartment, climbing out of a canal taxi in a nice area across the river from my old school. I was so much happier to be here than there!

I smiled at the concierge in the lobby and he led me to the elevator. I thanked him and ascended to the floor he had chosen. When I knocked on the apartment door a stiff, serious looking man with wisps of straw-blond hair greeted me, inviting me into an impeccable art deco condo. Large windows displayed a view across the canal. I was immersed in a surreal experience: across the canal from my old job, interviewing for my dream job! I answered all his questions and smiled enthusiastically. Finally the man seemed to have made a decision and told me I was free to leave.

"Thank you."

"You are welcome. Good luck."

"Thanks. I really hope to get it."

"You're welcome. I'm sure you will do well." He smiled and closed the door. I felt great stepping into the elevator knowing that something good had just happened.

The next day I got a phone call for a second interview, this time on the island. I was thrilled there was a free trip to Phuket! Within days I found myself at the departure lounge at Muang airport. After a one hour flight, I arrived on the island and boarded a bus filled with yodelling tourists whose drinking antics entertained me until the bus pulled up in front of a small beachfront hotel in Karon. I settled into a nice room provided by my prospective employer.

The next day I caught a taxi to a small school nestled in a quiet setting of palm trees. It was a dream scenario.

"You will like it here," the owner said, in an American accent, while drawing from a cigarette, her wild hair and blue eyes darting over her desk. Staring down at me, demanding compliance with an uncompromising shine in her eye, I recalled the words of the interviewer who told me she was a 'passionate' person.

"I'm sure I will. I'm really looking forward to creating my curriculum."

"Just remember: academics in the morning and art in the afternoon. You can't change that. Another teacher tried to change it and the parents got upset. We had to change it back. The children need academics in the morning."

"Sure. Sounds like a good plan." I raised my eyebrows as she turned her back to me, shuffling papers on a table behind the desk.

"Do you like it here?"

"Yes," I said, wondering why she looked at me with prying eyes.

"Can you live on this island? It's not like Bangkok, with clubs and all night partying. It's a quiet place, serene, with beaches." She grinned looking for any sign of disapproval.

"I think living on an island will be perfect for me. I'm really excited."

"Okay. You may start Monday next week, eight in the morning." I had five days!

"Yes. Thank you." I smiled.

"You can stay at Beachside Bungalows until you find a place to stay on the island." She smiled at me, her strength showering upon me. I smiled.

"Yes, thank you," closing the door as I left.

"Do not shut it!" she shouted.

"Sorry," I said, opening it again. I moved through the open concept play area with classrooms off on each corner. The kitchen was in the back. I looked inside and saw three Thai women preparing food.

"You make all the lunches in here?" I asked.

"Yes and sometimes breakfast too. We do everything," one said, smiling calmly, nodding to the others.

"It looks great. I'm the new Kindergarten teacher. I'll see you all on Monday." They smiled.

After I returned to my hotel I rented a scooter to tour the area. I sped along paved roads, up and down hillsides, with magnificent views of sea and jungle. The school was on the east side of the island but I liked the feeling of the west side as I sped through different beach districts. Kata was a quiet, interesting place with all the amenities I wanted and not a lot of flashing lights and tourists. It was less populated, quieter and cleaner. The beaches were amazing. Club Med and a few other resorts had also discovered this place. I knew that I had made the right choice because everything looked good. The perfect transition from Bangkok.

The next day I flew back to Bangkok to clear out my apartment. I had signed a six month lease so I left money with the office ladies to cover the term. I wanted to have a place to stay for visits to the city. Even a short trip back into the hustle and bustle of the city made me glad to be leaving for a life on the island. Another new life was beginning to unfold and I was peaked with enthusiasm.

Over the next week I formally resigned from my job telling Eunice she could visit whenever she wanted.

"You'll have to rent a two-bedroom so you can put me up!" she encouraged, promising she would visit. I agreed that it was a great idea.

Saturday morning July 4 arrived and I climbed out of bed excited about my journey to the island. I hustled to pack up my things, leaving some behind to keep the space. My direct flight to Phuket left at 11 a.m. so I hopped into an airport taxi and rode through the streets wistfully saying goodbye to Bangkok after three months of life in the city. I smiled, reminiscing at all the discoveries I had made there.

As I sat in the hard plastic chairs of the departure lounge, eyeing the people who waited along with me, I found myself wondering what types of experience awaited us. What was the face Phuket wore? Would we all find what we were looking for there? The moment seemed to etch itself in my mind as I caught sight of a buoyant blonde man entering the room.

With a bounce in his step his determined pace immediately caught my attention. I watched him dart across the room to a chair directly in front of me. Opening a handbook with a large print title 'Phuket', my attention was stuck to him like a suction cup on glass. His short, blonde gently wavy hair looked soft enough to touch. His fair translucent skin outlined a strong jaw, and his wire framed glasses sat upon a smaller, rounded nose. His long lean arms showed well defined forearm muscles and my eyes went up and across his chest.

His attention was focussed on his book as I struggled to find words to initiate conversation. I could think of nothing to say but the obvious.

"Is that a book on Phuket?"

"Yes," he said brightly, glancing at the cover. "Have you been there before?"

"Well, yes, only briefly though. I interviewed for a job that I am flying down to start," I said, looking into the depth of his eyes.

"Oh, that's great. What kind of job?" he asked, putting aside his guidebook.

"It's a teaching position in a Kindergarten," I replied.

"Oh, wow. You are a Kindergarten teacher. That's great," he said, sounding enthused.

"Yes. Thanks," I smiled at his kind eyes.

"I'm Jo. In Norwegian, it is pronounced as 'You'. But in English it sounds like Joe."

"Okay, Joe," I said in the English version. "I'm Cassandra."

We shook hands and the grasp of his in mine went through me like a volt of electricity, instantly heightening my appreciation for him. I squirmed as the moment became more intense.

"What are your travel plans in Thailand?" I asked.

"I'm going to Phuket to learn about Muay Thai, or Thai kickboxing. There are some great dojas there that I want to see." He put his guidebook into the bag beside him.

"What is a doja?" I asked.

"It's a place where they practice martial arts. I am a martial artist," he said, confidently.

"Oh, is that violent?"

"Not if you practice well. The aim of the martial artist is to be so good that you will never enter battle. You learn mind control and special techniques to make your opponent inactive without any real harm. Restraining and reversals are common techniques. You end up using the force of the other person against them."

"Sounds like you need a strong mind for that," I said, my eyes wandering over the well defined muscles beneath his t-shirt.

A voice on the overhead speakers called out the flight to Phuket. We got up and walked over to a line that was forming as our conversation continued in easy rhythms.

"Let's see if we can sit together on the plane," he said, boldly. His captivating presence focussed me so strongly that I almost couldn't speak. I let him do most of the talking as we made our way over the warming tarmac in the hot sun toward the stairs of the plane with others who were boarding.

As we approached the steps, he offered to take my bag. I turned to hand it to him, speechless.

Onboard the plane Joe spoke with a flight attendant and arranged to sit beside me. As he sat down on my left I noticed that everything about this felt natural.

"So, tell me about where you are from," I asked.

"I am from Hemsedal, Norway," he said proudly. It was well-practiced Oxford English.

"Where is that exactly?"

"Hemsedal is a village in the middle of Norway, in Scandinavia, next to Sweden. It is in Northern Europe." I tried to picture the geography but couldn't place it in my mind.

"I'm sure it's beautiful," I said.

"Norway is a beautiful country. We have many mountains, valleys and fjords. You have heard of fjords?" He spoke with a strong assertive voice, but his hand moved with tenderness.

"What are they exactly?"

"Fjords are mountains that come down steeply into the ocean, making a beautiful view. Norway is famous for fjords." He had many statistics about his homeland at the ready but I still could not imagine the location. We began to talk about other things and I told him about my journey through Thailand. We buckled in for takeoff.

He noticed my trepidation as the plane jostled on ascent.

"Are you okay?" he asked, compassionately.

"Yes." I stared out the window during the steep incline. I felt him move closer to comfort me.

After the plane gained altitude we were served lunch. My orange juice sat untouched.

"Do you want my orange juice?" I asked.

"Sure. You can have my apple juice," he said, trading me without a second thought, just like old friends. The heat between us began to rise as we smiled and laughed together, enjoying our new connection.

Again, upon landing, I stared uneasily out the window. Joe reached over and held my hand.

When we arrived safely at the Phuket airport we went inside the terminal to collect our bags. When ours appeared he lifted them onto his cart and began pushing. We headed to the doorway side by side and I looked at this beautiful man on my left who had already amazed me with caring and kindness. Just then I heard my inner voice say: You will marry him.

Dumbstruck, I pushed the thought aside. I remained at a loss for words as he chatted easily with me about the things he wished to see on Phuket. We boarded a bus headed into the beach area of Karon, toward my hotel, crammed among others as we continued our intimate conversation while staring at each other more resolutely.

"Do you recommend a hotel? I don't have a reservation." I tried to hide my smile and excitement as I casually replied, "Why don't you stay at mine?"

He agreed and when we arrived we got off together amid the gilded gazes of other passengers who had overheard our conversation and knew we had just met. We checked in and chose two rooms side by side at the top of a gently sloping hill that led down to a breezy restaurant beside the road. The beach lay just beyond.

His northern features: wavy flaxen blonde hair, focussed slate blue eyes and milky translucent skin became entrancing as he enlightened me about his life in Norway. We spoke over a meal in the warm restaurant with fresh breezes blowing and birds chirping. Stories of his experience as a slalom racer in his home village of Hemsedal enchanted me as the sound of his voice gently thumped at my heart's door.

"I have plans to attend college in September," he said, eating heartily. "I will study at computer technology." He explained that mandatory military service in Norway had demanded a year and a half of his life. Afterwards he had served for six months as a United Nations soldier in Lebanon. I watched him intently. What was he was about to bring into my life?

"How long will you be staying in Phuket?"

"I have planned to stay three weeks," he said, as he chewed voraciously. I smiled to hear we had so much time.

After lunch we moved up to our bungalows, admiring the setting from our open doors. We sat on the lawn to survey the view of the calm blue sea peeking between buildings and swaying palms. Talking comfortably about our homes and lives, I felt at ease with him, and we moved closer together. My hand brushed his and he stroked my back to remove some grass. We were like two magnets separated by diminishing degrees as we laughed and played in the sunshine.

We rented a scooter and took off for a romantic drive along the beach areas on the south-west side of the island. I held his firm abdomen as we drove, admiring the gentle slope of his neck beside my cheek, intoxicated by his scent. The beach area was filled with scuba divers and resort visitors while the local Thai population melded with the foreign influence basking at their beachside hotspot.

We cruised the winding hillside roads, enjoying the sunshine, while looking for houses with 'For Rent' signs out front. I needed to find a new home and Joe was eager to help. We stopped at some vacancies along the way, learning that each village was a unique microcosm, separated from the last by dense jungle and breathtaking beaches. The warm breeze welcomed us as we drove along the seaside. I leaned into Joe as he placed his strong hand on my thigh.

The sun began sinking to the horizon in a beautiful tapestry of colours as we pulled into a beachside restaurant in Karon for dinner. During our meal I learned that Joe was four years my junior. A smile emerged on my face as I realized a lesson in David.

After driving back to our hotel we walked down to the beach for the sunset, and sat together in the sand for the final dance of colours across the sky. The beautiful, surreal night became deeper and deeper blue, drawing us into a brilliant sea of stars. Powder soft sand held us as we snuggled under the sky.

Joe rubbed my shoulders as we stood at the bubbling shore, staring up at the bright moon and stars, gently easing my muscles into surrender. Basking in the joy of the moment we caught ourselves in a tender embrace at the edge of the calm sea. I felt as if I had known this man for a very long time.

We walked entwined to our hotel, knowing we didn't want to be apart.

"Can I sleep with you?"

I burst out laughing at his forward approach.

"What do you mean by that?" I asked, giggling.

"Well, I mean, can I share the bed with you?"

"Yes, I guess so," I said shyly.

"Don't you want me?"

My face reddened. "Yes, I do. We can 'sleep' in my bed if you want," I said, trying to clarify my intentions, wanting to be on firmer ground before getting intimate with him.

"Sure," he smiled, then went into his room where I heard some noises. Then he entered my room with his overnight bag making himself very comfortable. I had to laugh.

"Why are you laughing?" he asked.

Smiling at him, I could hardly stop laughing.

"I'm not used to your manner, so bold,"

"Oh. Usually Canadian men play games about what they want?"

I laughed out loud. "Yes, I guess maybe that's it. We are not so obvious about it. Perhaps we linger in mystery."

"There is some mystery here? I thought just that we like each other."

"Yes, it's true," I squirmed. "I like it. I'm just not used to your level of honesty, I guess. It's refreshing." I smiled.

I was laughing because I was nervous, and I climbed into bed wearing a tank top and pajama bottoms. He hopped in wearing shorts and we embraced under the covers. He kissed me sweetly and softly stroked my back. I breathed in his breath. We nuzzled and lay close together, listening to each other breathing until we fell asleep.

When we awoke in the morning Joe kissed me on the nose.

"It's going to be a beautiful day!" he said, and went into the bathroom. I lay in bed, hearing the waves in the distance and feeling the heat rising. I wondered what was happening and if I was falling in love with Joe. Somehow, I felt it was necessary to be with him, to know him in this way. I couldn't understand why I felt that way.

Then I got up and opened the door, letting in a fresh morning breeze, feeling as if a new start in my life had begun.

When Joe came out of the bathroom he had an idea.

"Let's move into one bungalow because we can save our money." I just looked at him. His enthusiastic grin waited for my affirmative response.

"Sure. Why not?" I said laughing. What else could I do?

We began the morning with fresh pancakes, shakes and a large plate of fruit. Joe was very health-conscious and we talked about the ways he kept his body fit. Later on, we hopped on a scooter and cruised around the island, stopping to take photos at vistas and enjoying spending the time getting to know each other. Our relationship felt so natural. I appreciated the way he protected me, waiting for me at the door of public washrooms, taking the outside place walking on sidewalks. He was a gentleman and treated me graciously. I felt like a princess.

When the evening came we found a romantic restaurant high on a hilltop with views of the sea. Lit with candles and caressed by gentle breezes we dined on delicious Thai food. Joe wasn't reserved about making sure we had the best experience possible and always asked me if I had everything I wanted. He catered to my needs more than anyone ever had before.

When we returned to our bungalows I giggled to myself because we were now living together. Just like that I had my relationship. I had love.

"Do you want something?" he asked, as we readied for bed.

"I would love a water."

"Okay. Anything else?"

"No, that's fine. Thank you," I said, as he closed the door behind him and went to the restaurant to get some water.

When he returned with the water, I just looked at him. He was amazingly kind and considerate. I smiled and took the glass from his hand, drinking some then setting it on the bedside table.

"Come on, let's get in bed." There he held me, and kissed me and stroked my skin. He wanted to be closer to me and I wanted to be closer to him.

At seven in the morning he gently woke me. "It's your first day at your new job."

"Yeah," I said, stretching and just waking up. We kissed on the lips then he went to the shower. I sat in bed, shaking my head, wondering just what I had found in Joe. When he came out of the shower I was still sitting there on the bed, dazed as to the beauty of my real life dream.

"Is everything okay?" he asked, coming to me.

"Yes, its more than okay. It's amazing. Thank you so much," I said, meaning it deeply.

"You are welcome. I have never met anyone like you. Something makes me want to do everything for you, like you are a princess and I have to take care of you."

I softened, taking in the compliment. Tears came to my eyes. I wiped them.

"Are you okay?"

"I'm okay. It's just a little overwhelming. You are so kind to me, so gentle and giving. I am very lucky to have met you."

"I'm lucky to have met you too." He held me then, and I held back my tears of gratitude even as some spilled onto his shoulder.

After a beautiful breakfast together where we talked quietly about our plans for the day, I hopped on my scooter at 8:15.

"What time will you be home? I want to make sure I'm here when you come home from work," he said, surprising me with his level of commitment.

"I think around four but maybe earlier. It should be a full day."

We kissed goodbye.

"Have a good day," he said. It felt so comfortable and I waved goodbye as I motored off in the direction of the school, daydreaming.

When I arrived at the school the children were playing in the yard. I went into my classroom and began to set up my morning routine. My schedule at the school was light. The schedule had already been made for the summer months so I started to learn the routine which would take some time.

My classroom was a long, windowed room, divided in half by two large windows that looked out onto the covered lunch area and play equipment further out in the yard. Gail introduced herself to me with a firm handshake and a strong British accent. She was platinum blond, hair in a tight bun, with big blue eyes that shone. She stood almost six feet and her towering presence was amplified by her stature.

"I'm pleased to meet you. It will be nice to have a Canadian working here."

"Thanks, Gail. It's nice to meet you too. I look forward to working together."

"I'm teaching the pre primary, the children just below your class. Nadine is Australian and she has the toddlers. They nap a lot of the time. But you can come to me with any questions. I've been here for nine months and have it pretty well worked out. Or ask the Thai ladies in the kitchen. They will help you."

"Sure thing," I said, turning back to my desk where I was planning my curriculum. I was eager to create a beautiful plan for the children who would begin in September.

The morning sun filled the room as I sat at my desk preparing for the day. My summer students were five and six years old and spoke German, French, or Thai and in the process of learning English as well. I was instructed to cover the primary subjects of math, spelling, English grammar, and art in any way I chose. I began to develop ideas about how to incorporate my perspective of life into useful material digestible for my young students.

When I returned home, Joe was there waiting for me, smiling, fresh from a long run, showered and glistening. We talked about our days. After dinner we sat on a grassy patch under the palm trees in front of our bungalow. I spread out my sarong and we sat while I enlightened Joe on my pursuit to understand life.

"But how do you know these things are really happening?" he asked, trying to understand my point of view.

"Because I've been paying attention. I can't say they are really 'happening,' but they are happening in my experience. And if that is so, then they can happen in everyone's experience. They can happen in yours, too." He looked pensive, and slightly frightened to consider that he was having an affect on his experience. The responsibility of the concept was daunting to him and he wanted more information.

"Why do you think its responding to your wishes for it?"

"Because I ask for things to happen and they do. For example, I wished for you."

"But was it exactly me, or someone close?"

"Someone just like you, with the insides of you. Someone gentle and supportive." I tried to give him bite-sized pieces without overwhelming him, but I wanted to understand more in my own life and he witnessed my exploration, testing the boundaries of his own understanding.

He reclined on the grass twisting a blade between his fingers. He was considering a new perspective, different from what Norwegians believed, and it clearly challenged him. He sat up.

"But who believes this? Who do you know that thinks this way?"

"I don't know anyone. Maybe its only me. But that doesn't matter. I don't need approval to believe what I believe."

"I like that you want to try something new. I like that you want to believe good things are happening to you. I think it's a good idea. But many people have studied this life. Why do you think you can find something new about it?"

"Life continues to grow to evolve to change. There will always be new ideas." He was taken aback by my pioneering enthusiasm, as I was by his structured dogmatic perspective.

"Let's take a break and walk on the beach. Maybe I can understand more if we go into nature." We walked on the beach holding hands, enjoying our closeness. We kissed naturally and he put his arm around my shoulders.

Each evening after dinner Joe and I searched for a house for rent. We both had scooters by now and looked for rentals together and individually. I especially liked the road I took to work. We went to check out one with a sign hanging by the road. We parked our bikes just off the driveway and strode up the gravel hill to see a deserted free standing abode surrounded by jungle with a screened in porch. The screen door slammed when I walked in, echoing into the distance. In the rustic bedroom dead bugs lay on the floor and dust hung in the air.

"I don't think this is a good one," Joe said, showing his protective nature, and dismissed it as an option.

One day when I was driving home from work I saw a For Rent sign hanging in front of a cute cement house with a yellow ceramic tiled front porch surrounded by a large yard with a few palm trees. I had seen the house before and loved it. The sign was new.

I sped home to get Joe. He was moist and reddened from a long run on the beach. He quickly showered while I waited out front on the bench, watching palm leaves sway and listening to the sounds of his preparation. We motored over to the house and pulled into the store next door. A straight faced twenty-something Thai woman introduced herself as Dao and got the key. She led us over to the house. She eyed us suspiciously as we smiled and raved about the house. The covered porch with yellow tile was wiped clean, with two chairs perfect for viewing the surrounding flowering bushes, coconut palm trees and green grassy yard. As she put the key in the lock, I saw a sticker on the front door that read, 'I love Koh Samui.'

The front door opened into a spacious soft green living room with white ceramic tiles, high ceilings and a sculpted black wood sofa with blue flowered cushion covers. An ornate spirit house hung on the wall. Two bedrooms led off of the living room and at the back was a large kitchen with a high ceiling and a bathroom. Walking through the house with only a few pieces of necessary furniture, we looked out the sturdy wooden windows to the grassy yard, with a long washing line hanging out the side. In the backyard, where chickens and roosters were penned, a slight incline rose toward the jungle. A few small abodes lay just under the palm trees.

"How many?"

"One. Or Two. He's my friend. I am the renter," we smiled awkwardly.

"My father-in-law, owner. My husband, son of owner," she said. "You come back later. You talk to him."

"Okay, perfect. Please hold it for me. We'll be back in two hours," I said, excitedly.

I hopped onto the back of Joe's scooter and waved back at her as we pulled out onto the paved road, swerving as a car approached. We regained balance, then burst into laughter.

"I guess you are moving in," I asked, as we whirred along. I squeezed him from behind.

"Yeah, I guess so," he said, turning his head to the side. I inhaled the scents in the breeze. The light of the sun shone in my eyes.

We drove down to the beach and parked then walked hand in hand to the shore. Beautiful waves glistened in the sun, bathing the brown sugar beach where couple walked and children played.

We walked into the cooling waves then strolled into a beautiful scene of palm trees, endless teal sea and powdery sand.

"I'm thinking about staying longer on this island."

"That would be great! If I get this house, you can just stay with me. That would be wonderful!"

"Yeah, I like the idea of staying here and working out on the beach."

"The rooms need painting. Do you think you could help me paint it?"

"Of course! That would be my pleasure, especially if I stay with you. I would love to help out."

"Ah, this is shaping up perfectly! It's going to be so much fun!"

"It is!" He picked me up in his embrace and we kissed. It felt good to join the others on the beach in love with one another. We sat in the sand and spoke about our wishes and dreams for the future.

"I want to become very strong in martial arts. I want to learn martial arts then teach others what I know."

"I understand wanting to be strong. But the violence?"

"It's not if you use it well. It doesn't have to be."

"That's a relief," I sighed, trying to understand how our individual visions fit together. I listened to him talk and felt swept into his vision of love and the way he wanted life to be. We left the beach further enthralled with each other

Driving back we pulled in to the store to meet the landlord. He was waiting for us and smiled easily, rising from his chair. He told me the price of 6000 baht per month (about $200), payable on the first day of each month. He said I could paint it, but at my cost. I agreed and paid for one month's rent. He gave me the key and I jumped for joy. He smiled and laughed with his daughter-in-law. We waved goodbye and raced back to the hotel to collect our things.

"We did it! I have a home!"

"Let's go get your stuff so we can move in right away."

After gathering our possessions at the hotel we drove back to my new home where I lit a candle as we unpacked our things in the master bedroom at the front of the house. The walls needed some tender loving care because they had not been painted in years.

"I will help you paint. I am staying here with you, so it is only fair that I contribute to your home," said Joe.

"Thanks! That would be amazing!" He hugged me, just as happy as I was about the new home.

On my next day off we went to the paint store and got enough paint for the whole house. When we returned to prepare the house for painting I carefully took down the spirit house from the wall saying aloud that I hoped the spirits didn't mind the movement and would be returned soon to the same spot.

We painted the living room light blue to match the sofa cushions and the master bedroom yellow. We slept in the second bedroom that had not been painted to avoid the smell of paint. Late that night Joe awoke in the middle of the night soaked with sweat.

"I had a nightmare that someone was chasing me. It was really scary!"

I jumped up and ran to find the spirit house and put it back in its place on the wall, over the damp paint.

"Do you think its from that?" he asked, incredulously, having seen it only as decoration.

"I'm not sure, but it could be. Anyway, its back in its place now. Go back to sleep." I consoled him and we fell asleep in an embrace.

The next morning, I asked him how he slept.

"I slept fine, but that was a crazy dream!" he said.

I shook my head, realizing the importance of ancient traditions and behaviours unknown in my part of the world. Joe and I worked until sunset the next day finishing the kitchen and second bedroom in pink. It was just like new!

We reclined on the porch chairs in the evening calm and sipped cold iced tea from the can. I felt blessed. Joe reached over to hold my hand.

"And now you have a real home," he said, smiling.

"Thanks to you it is a beautiful home." I was elated and jumped into his lap. He embraced me and covered me with kisses.

It was mid-July and I had been in Thailand for four months. My experiences had kept me glued to the surface of an incredible experience, waiting for any bubbles, knowing that within them was a truth I needed. And now I was falling in love with a strong, handsome Norwegian whose love was tender and true.

Joe's spiritual world was unformed. He had shrugged off conventional religion preferring to believe in the wisdom and power of nature. For a long time he had wanted to look more closely at his experience, examining the inner part of it more closely.

Growing up in a small mountain valley village, Joe had learned about survival in the most extreme conditions. The way of life in his homeland, he explained, was simple and solid. Despite a blanketing cold that hovered for many winter months, his family had learned how to be nurtured by nature. Most people were outside as much as possible, whether for a walk, recreational pursuit or a neighbourly visit, but always dressed properly for warmth. Keeping harmony with the nature was important to Norwegians, as its influence could not be ignored.

Skiing in all forms was a regular pastime in the winter months and his village was blessed with a beautiful resort called SkiHemsedal. During the short summers, women in his village ventured deep into the forests to forage for wild berries, the whereabouts a strict secret. He fascinated me with stories of life, of Farmers who released their sheep in the mountains over the summer, collecting them in the fall by listening for the bell around the flock leader. He spoke of the mountain range as a backyard playground. His mystery seduced me. I began to open to Joe about some of the more personal experiences I had been having. He sat quietly, considering my words, wondering what to believe. I ventured into a realm of feelings that I had never shared with anyone before, feeling that a circle was completed when we were together.

While I was teaching Joe toured the island by scooter and exercised on the beach, arriving home before me everyday. When I was home we shared the hours cruising, taking in the sights and sounds, stopping by various trails by the side of the road. We ventured everywhere together, Joe always willing to accompany me on whatever jungle byway I found, or philosophy I cooked up. Our friendship continued to grow and grow.

Some days we visited the markets or took trips up the north island road. We talked about wanting to help people and the world at large, so we supported the local shops and food stands buying delicious take out Thai soups and salads. Drinking all manner of tropical fruit juices, and experimenting with new foods every chance we got, we would retreat to my yard and take in the scene from my porch chairs out on the grass. Light traffic buzzed by beyond the bushy hedge that muffled motor sounds. We could people watch and keep an eye on the action.

My yard was a circus of moving creatures. One afternoon as we sat relaxing on the front porch, something moving in a tree caught my eye. A branch was wiggling and a bird was flying up and down making a lot of noise.

"Its a snake! Let's go look!" I exclaimed. Joe and I hurried over the grass to see the bright green tree snake but by the time we go there it had hidden. The bird began to calm down. We walked in the grass more aware of the ecosystem to which we belonged.

At night there were glowing insects and a cacophony of sounds. Shining stars twinkled above us as the symphony of creatures lent an ideal backdrop for our philosophical exploration. Staring up to the night sky, our faces far enough away from the candlelight, we could talk about anything. And so we did. In the darkness, in the peculiar sounds of the night, we found the truth in each other.

Feeling comfortable with Joe and understanding the scepticism that challenged me, I began to share my innermost experiences. Describing my changing perspective was my daily education as I had expanded into a perspective that allowed me to see my own place within it. I felt vulnerable by revealing my transformation to Joe, uncertain about judgements he would make.

I tried to explain how my understanding drifted back and forth between worlds, trying to compare them while looking for similarities and indicators of more meaning. I was peeling myself away from the experience to see it more clearly. With this exploration, the awareness of something beyond what my eyes could see became apparent. Exploring this 'awareness' with someone I could really love filled me with joy, as I worked to compose theories that would logically demonstrate to him what I was experiencing within this enlightened state. What was happening? Was it real? Did my experience flow from one to another? Was I doing it? Did my actions matter?

"I am wondering about the idea of a cause and effect relationship within my experience. How far does this relationship go? What about my thoughts, the movement of my body, and the awareness of something that seems like a soul?"

I could see the judgement limiting him as he struggled to understand what was making me feel so good, causing me to exclaim that life loved me, loved us both.

"Are you sure that this is true, that there are these things in life?" he asked, in trepidation, wanting to support me but afraid to leave solid ground.

"Does it matter? Is it good? Do you like it? Isn't that the question?" I had learned the same lesson and tried to hold on to all the good I knew in the face of opposition. Joe turned toward me and looked into my eyes. There was love in them and we embraced. We watched the night sky until the chill moved us inside.

Joe's feelings steadily developed for me and his love was becoming apparent. He was experiencing the same doubts I had harboured when the experience began to open to me.

"I know you are good but these ideas are completely different than anything I have heard before. I need some time to consider them."

"I can understand that. But also know that your questions help me focus on what is important in my understanding and allow me to double check my information and find new answers. You are helping me. I want to know how it sounds to someone else, how they regard this new information. I am curious to hear your response." I encouraged him to voyage with me into the unknown. My love for him deepened everyday as I saw his gentleness extend to embrace me, regardless of the 'sense' I was making to his logical mind. He trusted his feeling for me and bravely pursued my new ideas.

"You can do anything you want, be anyone you want. It's all inside. You just have to bring it out. If you have faith, you can experience anything you want."

Joe was deep within himself asking if what I was saying could be true. He was inspired by my search for meaning and my pioneering manner, but he wanted to run everything I said through his voice of reason and quiet second thought. I told him it was futile, that those mechanisms were plagued by conditioned teachings, and that he would have to seek a new way to understand what I was saying. He was hesitant, uncertain if I was putting one over on him. He was falling in love with me, but what I was saying seemed too good to be true.

One evening after a steady two weeks at the school, after a nice sunset dinner with Joe, I decided to go for a ride to a place where I could be alone. I hopped on my red scooter, revved the tiny engine and glided down the winding road, past the Thai family houses and thick jungle forests. I took a road up the hill that weaved down the other side and headed to the waterfront. Gail had told me about a long dock on that side of the island that reached out into a calm bay. I set out to find it.

I found a road with a small sign that pictured sparkling water in the distance. The moon was full in the dark sky shining out over the water with a rippling glow. I parked my bike in the gravel lot and walked toward the end of the dock, a feeling of peacefulness enveloping me as if I walked into a silent hug. I smiled up at the sky and took a seat on the end of the dock, hanging my legs over the edge. I watched for a while, feeling safe and joyful, enjoying the quiet and appreciating everything that had recently made my life pleasurable. I was relieved to find that my inner peace was still there, just waiting as always, to be invited to the forum.

After this deep connection I said goodnight to the moon and walked back down the dock. I rode back home, inhaling the night breeze as I looked deeply into the sleeping forest and felt a special vibration, as if the trees were buzzing. I smiled, part of a larger conversation as I veered around a corner feeling the handlebars turn under my hands. It was strange to feel like a passenger on my own ride, as the bike cruised along following the curve nicely. It was strange, but comforting at the same time, and I felt reminded that something existed within me, aiding me in life.

I had accepted that words were being assisted in some way, and I decided that assistance was some sort of divinity. Was it that my body and my actions were as well? I began wondering about my body as a tool of experience. Was it fully managed by 'the force'? What about free will? I questioned as I pulled into my drive and at once my eyes were drawn to the roof ornament on my neighbour's house. It was the first time I had seen it and stood staring at the upper half of a sun surrounded by rays. Yes, I thought. I was not fully managed by the force. But what was it then? How did that happen? I walked toward my house, along the path, considering the new information.

I entered the porch and looked down to see many bugs fluttering around on the tiles, congregating in the bright porch light. Looking around at them, two bugs caught my eye and I bent down to have a closer look. They were an unusual type of centipede and moved along steadily, one bug in front of the other like two railway cars. At one point the one behind stopped, let go of the other and turned to investigate something that had caught its attention. The first bug stopped, but waited patiently in place. Soon, the rear bug found the other again and they were off again in tandem.

I saw it as a perfect metaphor to help me understand the answer to my question. It was as if I was, in my physical form, the blind one in behind becoming distracted with life, and the whole while the first one, my soul, knew the way and waited patiently for me to become one with it. Then we could be off again as it guided me along the way. I smiled, perfectly understanding the moment.

I dashed inside to tell Joe what had happened. With my eyes alight, I described to him all that I had seen and finished with the metaphor of bugs. He was sceptical that my experience could be explained through the activities of insects.

"Oh Mom, Dad, brother, sister," he said teasing me. "Meet my new girlfriend, Cassandra. She has a great story about how two bugs following each other made perfect sense of her life. I can't wait for you to hear it!" he said, swooning through the room, exaggerating the performance, pretending his parents were there. "She's brilliant! And I just love her. And we love bugs," he said, grinning, making me laugh uncontrollably.

"But it's true!" I said, rolling onto the bed with laughter. "Believe me!" I exclaimed, as he jumped on top of me, smothering me in kisses.

"Tell me more about the bugs. Teach me about the bugs! Bring in the bugs!"

"I'm learning something from the experience! We have to be open-minded!"

"I am learning, too," he said, feigning seriousness. "We must have these bugs in for dinner." We kissed and played, giggling and enjoying each other until I couldn't laugh anymore because my stomach hurt.

I didn't manage to convince Joe that life revealed its secrets to an avid learner through bugs. Nonetheless he listened as I explained how I thought the answer was revealed to me. We joked about it over the next few days, but I maintained my theory that if one allowed oneself to look at one's surroundings with an open mind, one could find meaning in anything.

Chapter 8 – Mango & Papaya

The next night Joe and I enjoyed the sunset from my porch. The expansive sky offered colours in a wide display as we sipped iced teas and listened to crickets tuning up for their nightly serenade. Scooters whirred past the hedge at the perimeter of the lot revealing only the helmets flying by. The pace of activity died down as the evening set in.

"Hey, I have an idea. Are you up for a little trip?" I asked.

"Where do you want to go?"

"I want to show you the dock I discovered."

"Sure. Let's go!"

I drove us along the road, the evening breeze cooling our faces. Few people were driving so we cruised alone, over the rolling hills to the other side of the island, captive in tropical paradise. The winding road carried us down the hill to the seashore where we drove to the dock reaching out into the bay at Rawaii. The quiet night echoed our subtle intrusion as we neared the shore, passing two Thai men in conversation on the beach. We parked and walked toward the dock, as one of the men said, "Have a nice dream." Barely visible in the darkening night, we smiled back, in thanks.

We walked onto the dock, the ocean gently sloshing beneath our feet. The moonlight beamed bright and white and low in the sky, welcoming us. We walked to the end of the dock and sat near two young boys fishing, bantering in Thai about their hopeful catch.

As I sat beside Joe, I opened to the night sky, filling with exuberance. I concentrated on Joe's presence, wondering if he would feel something special in these intense surroundings. We dangled our legs and looked up at the starry sky. The sea was calm and the full moon illuminated the sparkle of water. After immersing ourselves in this typical atypical beauty we decided to head back. Walking down the dock side by side, I turned to look back at the moon.

"Thank you for Joe!" I said to the sky, in appreciation. "He is beautiful!" I exclaimed, basking in warmth.

He laughed. "Why are you thanking the sky?"

I gazed into his eyes. "Because all of this created you."

"I thought I created me. Why aren't you thanking me?" He was squeezing my waist, making me laugh. We walked down the dock with the moon beaming upon us, then stood in a spotlight of white light. The boys turned to look at us. The night was full and bright. We were lost in the beauty of the moment.

Suddenly, an image passed through my mind, and I stopped in my tracks. A vision appeared, a flashback to a time on Koh Phangan, recognizing the face as I stared into it now. It was Joe! I had seen him in my mind's eye four months before I actually met him.

"I had a vision of you while I was living on Koh Phangan. I saw a picture of your face in my mind."

Joe considered my words, joining hands we walked toward the scooter. He kissed me then we hopped on. Magic.

"I love life!" I said, pressing against his back. "And life loves me back!"

Joe smiled, getting used to my words about life's love for me. As we cruised back, I held him tightly around the waist, feeling his strong chest. My love for Joe was growing. Was the moon giving me the nudge in that direction of my thoughts? What had occurred in order to reveal that to me?

Back home, I excitedly explained the vision to Joe, pushing his acceptance of possibility even further.

"How much of my life is planned before I live it? I saw you, in my mind. So how does it work? Am I living out a dream? Is my dream? What is going on?"

"Are you sure it was me and not someone else's face?"

I gasped with surprise. How could he not know the effect he was having on me? The feeling of the mood stayed with me. It was Joe. "I knew significant feelings would be shared with this person, I could sense something coming through the face."

I squeezed his arm and went into the bedroom. He turned out the lights, locked the door, and brought water to my bedside table as I climbed into bed. The candle flickered as he made his way through our bedroom, to the curtains fluttering gently from open windows. He pulled the windows closed but left a small space for airflow. Secure decorative bars adorned the openings and a refreshing breeze swept in from the calm sea.

"My lease in Bangkok is up next week. I also need to make a visa run to Malaysia. Are you up for it?"

He hopped into bed beside me.

"Sounds like fun. When do we go?"

"We can leave Friday after work and catch the night bus to Bangkok."

"Great."

I smiled at him, enthused by his eagerness to help me. We met under the soft yellow sheets and kissed goodnight.

After work on Friday I buzzed home excitedly to meet Joe. He was ready and packed for our week away and had moved my bags to the door. We hailed a taxi from the street and rode to the train station. During the night ride to Bangkok I snuggled into Joe, quite blissfully enduring the bumps along the road. He held me gently, protectively, lovingly, so I could sleep. He sat upright with my head in his lap. I slept on and off during the night before we arrived in Bangkok in the early morning rush.

While we rode through the city I enlightened Joe on highlights of my daily route, all the way to my apartment building. I let him into the room and he immediately went the balcony door to open it to the view. Swirling breezes entered the space and we stepped out onto the white ceramic tile. The sight of the pulsing city still thrilled me.

"Wow," we echoed.

Red heat rose with highlights of yellow and orange as if steam were emanating from the city. The heat of the city stretched far into the distance to a flat horizon.

He hugged me from behind. I rested my head on his shoulder as we embraced. Joe kissed my neck and pulled me back inside the apartment. I gave him a cook's tour and we ended back in the living room. He collapsed on the sofa and smiled.

"I'm going to call the airline to see if I can stay longer," he said.

I jumped when I heard this and he smiled. After a brief interlude, his ticket was changed, adding another two weeks to our time together. We embraced and kissed.

When we were ready to hit the street we grabbed a map of a few art studios and ventured out into the heat. I showed Joe as much of Bangkok as I could, by bus and canal taxi to sights I hadn't seen. We snacked along the way, strolling through markets, seeing live animals for sale. Joe and I weaved through throngs of people selling fabric and handicrafts, appreciating a new experience. The vibrant colours and earthy products enchanted our senses as we held hands and walked through staying close to one another.

We sat down at a roadside restaurant enclosed with an open tarp, filled with business people eating lunch. As we ate he began to share his future plans. "I will be starting school in a town called Halden, near the border to Sweden." His gentle voice and norse accent captured my attention.

"I will be living in a four bedroom flat with three others. It is near the city centre and everything is within walking distance." I wanted to see the world from his eyes. He hadn't explored much outside of Norway, other than ski trips to a few neighbouring European countries. His honest, genuine nature beckoned me to follow. I was deeply in love with him, more than anything I had known. Our lives began to intertwine as we laughed and experienced new things.

When we returned home Joe ran me a bath as I lit candles around the house. He flopped on the bed, relaxing, while I soaked in the tub. Long moments passed in silence.

After some time he arrived at the bathroom door holding a large bath towel. I stood up as he enveloped me in softness before leading me off to bed.

Early morning came and Joe was up making coffee. He opened the doors to the golden rays, urging me to join him on the balcony. The red sun had just crested the horizon, spreading glowing yellow orange hues across the sky. A morning dawn unlike anything we had seen greeted us on the day of our journey.

After turning in the keys to my apartment we headed to the train station by taxi. Standing together on the platform, watching the sights, we listened to a Thai voice bellowing over the speakerphone. People echoed around us, our arms were wrapped around each other's waist. Finally we were instructed to board the night train to Malaysia, a 14 hour ride that would deliver us to the island of Penang, a popular destination for visa renewal.

Joe gestured for me to board then hauled our bags up the steps. I led the way down the narrow aisle looking for an open four- seater. It was a tidy, modern train, bunks packed away overhead. I plopped down into a four-seater on the right side of the southbound train and Joe settled in beside me. The cosy spot was quiet with curtains to enclose us for privacy. In a few moments the train chugged up to a steady pace. Once outside Bangkok the magnificent view of lush green fields was captivating. We sat fixated, holding hands and sipping water. The enchanting land was mostly undisturbed by modernity, pristine and undeveloped. Rice paddies layered over vast areas, glistening under the sun, the occasional vaulted hat of an Asian farmer. The peaceful stillness captivated us, warming our hearts, drawing us closer.

Carts filled with goodies came down the aisle, offering everything we needed to enjoy the afternoon. Joe generously suggested everything to satisfy our cravings and we shared food while gazing out, huddled together, commenting on the beauty of our incredible afternoon. The bunks were pulled out before sunset by uniformed staff who made their way through the car preparing for night travel. Behind the closed curtain, with the overhead lamp on, we laughed playing cards.

"I have feelings for you, deep within my heart. I don't want this to end when I return to Norway," he said, laying down his cards.

I stirred to hear his romantic confession.

"Don't go back to Norway. Stay here with me."

"I have to get an education," he said, looking deep into my eyes.

My feeling sweetened even more and I looked into my hands.

"My classes begin in a month," he said.

"We'll have to think of something. I don't want this to end either." I squeezed his hand, then moved into his embrace. We held each other as the orange sun sunk beneath the horizon and the sky darkened until we were alone in the world, two reflections in the window.

We arranged our individual bunks and then climbed into one together, our bodies side by side, our warmth shared. We kissed.

"We can't sleep like this, you know," I said, nudging him.

"Why not?" he asked.

"Because we'll be thrown off the train in the middle of the jungle in the middle of the night! This is Thailand, soon to be Malaysia. They are very strict here." He began to move his hand along my skin.

"Stop! You can't. Not now. You have to go back to your bed," I laughed, kissing his lips.

"I do not," he said, defiantly.

"This is Asia and we are tourists," I laughed, appreciating his boldness.

He held me closer and I snuggled into his shoulder, admiring his bravery. Then, we heard the guard's voice at the end of the hall. "You have to go!" I pushed.

Finally, he hopped down and leapt up to his bed with one arm. His training showed in his adept physique and I sighed watching him crawl into his bed. We closed the curtains around us.

"Goodnight Sweetheart," I said.

"Goodnight Honey."

He had adopted my endearing terms. I smiled, "Sleep well."

"Sovt godt," he repeated.

I slept comfortably through the night until lights came on in the early morning. A guard walked along, knocking on the bunks, rousing us from our slumber. When I swung down from my bunk with Joe's help it was still dark outside. Yellow light was kissing the horizon. Our bunks were snapped back into place and a breakfast cart soon arrived.

We sat cosily with coffee, munching fruit and morning snacks, watching light come over the land. A few hours more and were at the border with Malaysia, preparing our passports for inspection. Tension grew as guards walked down the aisle with German Sheppard dogs. Soon we were off again and in a few more hours we arrived at our stop in Malaysia.

After leaving the train we boarded a bus en route to the island of Penang. Travelling into the downtown of the small island we found an interesting looking hotel with many foreign flags out front. The desk staff smiled to us and spoke excellent English, welcoming us to Malaysia. We checked into a double room on the third floor and walked up the steps in the heat. In a long hallway with several closed doors we found our number and inserted the key. Upon entering we laughed at the sight of two single beds awaiting us.

"I think they noticed we aren't married," I blushed.

"Oh, yeah," Joe laughed. "Well, they can't stop us from sleeping together."

I smiled at the thought, romantic images dancing in the orange glow that descended on the walls with high ceilings. Two narrow windows opened with a view to the side street, a riot of strange scents and sounds.

Joe and I napped in each others arms on the single bed until the booming echo of a man's voice reciting Islamic prayers over a loud speaker reached our room. I sat up, entranced by the soundwaves, speculating on the meaning of the words. I moved to the window to look for the source.

"When I was in Lebanon, these prayers rang out three times a day," Joe reminisced, laying on his back, his head propped to watch me.

"Its kind of eerie," I said, looking back at him as the haunting voice dominated the space. The city's pulse calmed under the spell of the voice. I escaped within and tried to connect with something deeper, to understand the meaning of the words. As it went on I realised the words were not of my bidding. I felt unsettled until the sound of the man's voice sounded squeaky. Ten minutes later it was finished. Slowly, the normal sounds of life returned.

After a short nap it was time for dinner and a bit of exploration. We walked down to the main street of town and noticed the strong

Chinese influence on the culture. Peking BBQ ducks hung in crowded windows, the interior filled with plastic tables and chairs and people eating soup of all kinds with 'lotus petal' spoons. Businessmen ate alone, shovelling back food, their noses buried in newspapers. We joined the mob at a large restaurant with fluorescent lighting. Guessing at menu selections, we were served delicious bowls of soup. We finished it all, Joe urging me to eat more while getting his fill. After finishing we walked hand in hand along the street side shops that we beginning to close for the evening. We returned to our hotel, onto the red carpet with the two beds. Joe slept alongside me, comforting me with his loving embrace.

The prayers rang out again the next morning. We saw many people walking on without listening to the words, as if they had learned to ignore, or it was not their religion.

We walked for half and hour to the immigration office, enjoying the sightseeing and conversing with strangers about directions. After arriving at the white, specialized building, we found a crowd of others sitting on curbs and nearby benches. There was a sign on the door. Closed for lunch.

When we returned after a leisurely stroll we submitted my application and were told it would be ready in two days. We took off again to enjoy the day, admiring the broad mix of heritages: Indian, Chinese and Malaysian. There was a magical charm to the city.

We came upon a Buddhist temple. Relaxing incense swirled out to the street and we followed it into an ornate temple with a Buddha statue. Joe took some pictures of me as I walked within the bamboo and teakwood hand carved walls. We entered a large room with a golden Buddha making the mudra hand gesture, the altar covered with flower lays and fresh fruit platters. Many people kneeled on the floor in a peaceful appreciative gesture with soft instrumental music playing in the background. Joe's eyes widened to see this type of prayer to an idol that he had only read about in books. I had experienced Buddhism in Korea and knew the sanctuary of the Buddhist temple.

We had a lot to talk about when we walked through another door and found ourselves unexpectedly on the street. We agreed and found solace in the peaceful tenets of religion and shared our open-mindedness, to my delight. We continued through the streets, admiring the unique styles of architecture and then the Islam prayers began to echo over the city. It was two in the afternoon.

We followed the sounds of Islamic prayer to a lovely white spherically shaped roof at the top of an Islamic mosque. Joe took my picture with one of the towers behind me. In the entryway there were small signs about appropriate dress. Joe pulled on a white gown, and I pulled on a black one. We smiled as we walked inside, meeting eyes with as many people who would return our gaze. I wanted to know the inner workings of this belief system and understand its teachings. The space felt very peaceful and sacred. Men on their knees filled the prayer room in silence, facing the altar. Rounded magnificent archways allowed a breeze to waft through the white open space while exotic spirituality filled our souls.

We walked over the gleaming ceramic tile, between large white pillars, then quietly through a doorway into a grassy yard. A shallow square pool of water glistened in the sun with a small fountain in the middle. Several people dunked their feet and we joined them, enjoying the pool of cleansing water. Afterwards we walked around in the divinely induced silence before returning to the entryway where we hung up our robes. Newcomers kept their eyes down and quickly moved into the temple.

After taking many pictures of life in the city we went for dinner in a place near our hotel. As the day came to a close we walked down to the seaside to enjoy the warm, moist air. Snacking on freshly picked mangoes and papayas from a street cart, the juice dripped down my skin and Joe licked the trickle from my arm.

We listened to a man playing guitar and singing in Malaysian as the sun set. The scene was so romantic as couples held one another while listening to the music. The water flowed gently in the background, boats moored in the bay. The sea sparkled a reflection of yellow hues as our gazes met. The moment was beyond words. I could feel our love deepening.

"What is it like in Norway?" I asked, softly.

"Norway is a mountainous country but there are many villages in valleys throughout the region. There are about four million Norwegians and the capital is Oslo."

"I've heard of Oslo."

"Oslo is a great city, founded by King Harald in 1048. Oslo is two hours from Halden, where I will be studying. There is a lot of history to our country. You have heard of the Vikings?"

I nodded.

"There were many Norwegian Vikings. Viking churches called staves dot the countryside. You would love to see our country. Many things from the Vikings are preserved in our museums." He was excited to teach me about his country's history and I was interested to hear him speak of his homeland. He knew I was considering visiting him in Norway.

Touring the town over the next two days we studied Malaysian culture and discussed its history, strolling from place to place. When my visa was ready we prepared to board a van to take us overland to Surat Thani for the night ferry to Koh Samui. We were sad to leave.

We shared the ride with a Canadian man named Dave, a few Europeans and several chickens in cages. They squawked most of the time, but we only laughed at our unusual passengers. We conversed with Dave for most of the trip, sharing memorable experiences and topics of fascination. With his wavy brown hair and animated expressions his riveting stories us made us think.

"My friends and I were walking through a forest once. Everything was normal until we heard some huge crashing sounds coming from just up ahead. We ran to see what it was but the forest appeared still and undisturbed. We searched around for something that could have made the commotion but found nothing. To this day we have no idea what it was." He looked into our wide eyes and the conversation continued about more of our most unusual experiences. I told him some of my stories from the islands and the concept of a soul in its relation to our conscious experience.

"My Dad is a physician," he began, enthralling us, "and there is a phenomenon that only happens at the moment of death. He and his colleagues have wondered about this for years, but none can come up with an explanation, other than the presence of a soul existing within the body."

"What is it?" we questioned, thrilled to be hearing inside information.

"At the exact moment of death, the body loses exactly 0.07 grams of mass. My father and his colleagues have argued about this for years, but they do not speak about it widely."

"It could be the weight of the soul leaving the body," Joe suggested.

"It cannot be proven," Dave surmised. We agreed and sat quietly to consider the words of our intriguing exchange. Then we arrived at the pier and said goodbye to Dave, wishing him well on his journey as we headed toward our night ferry.

Joe and I were ushered to the 'tourist' level and found our place at two beds lining the wall. There were many tourists onboard the boat and it was abuzz with excited voices. Narrow mats with small pillows lined the wall on the floor under the windows. I decided to keep my wallet on me and tucked it inside the waistband of my pants. We fell asleep easily with the gently rocking of the boat.

Awoken early by the gentle voice over the loudspeaker announcing our imminent arrival to the Koh Samui port, the sun was just dawning. In the morning chill we stepped off the boat and moved toward bellowing voices and pointing fingers of the touts directing the herd of tourists to truck taxis. We rode in the back of a Samui truck, headed for my favourite spot on the island.

Later in the morning we were dropped off at the familiar locale of the Sunny Bungalows I had visited the month before. I chuckled to myself as we descended the familiar steps to the cabins, wondering if I would experience the same difficulties getting off the island as I had previously. The bungalow I wanted, the one I had stayed at before, was vacant. A sleepy-eyed Champ told us that David had left the island just a few days before our arrival. He unlocked the door for us with a smile, welcoming me back. I thanked him and Joe and I stepped in to unpack.

Inside our abode as I was preparing to shower, I took out my wallet that had stayed in the waistband of my pants since the night before. I noticed a strange mark on my skin and called Joe over to see it.

"What is THAT?" I asked, surprised and perplexed, pointing to an unfamiliar mark on my stomach: a thin red line in the shape of an eye.

"What does it look like to you?"

"It's an eye," he said, as we inspected it closely. Tugging at my skin, I could see the mark was within the blood vessels under my skin, and would not rub off. Joe picked up my wallet to examine it for any shapes that may have imprinted on my skin, but found nothing.

Amazed by the unusual symbol, I was pushed forward by another unique expression of life and I questioned the meaning behind the marking. There was so much we could know and I was certain there was more to be uncovered about the intricacies of our visual reality. Something seemed to beckon me.

Joe was interested in exploring my discovery of flipping in the water. He waited for me to change into my swimsuit so we could go to the water together.

"What should I ask a question about?" he asked, standing waist deep in the water.

"Ask a personal question that has meaning for you."

He lay back in the water and floated with a look of determination on his face. As he floated, I lay back in the water too, but my mind was thinking about what he was experiencing and I couldn't concentrate. I felt a few pulls, but it was as if my superficial focus was giving me a superficial reaction. I stood up to look at him. He appeared to be fully participating in the experience, sincerely wanting to feel a reaction. Finally, he stood up.

"I definitely felt something tugging on me, but I don't know if it was just the water or what it was."

"Are you doubting that it can happen?"

"Maybe."

"Hmm. Well, try to be lucid and don't try to hard. Stay neutral and relax."

He lay back in the water again and I gazed along the shore dazzled by the beautiful moment of sharing this divine place with my love.

Then, I heard a splash as he flipped in the water. He stood up, surprise registering on his face.

"You did it!" I burst forward through the water and embraced him. He was shocked, and kissed me, then lay back in the water to try again. I played around in the clear sea, happy he could experience something I had discovered.

Later as we walked to shore I listened to him explain his experience.

"When I stopped expecting something to happen, that is when the water pushed me over, as if it needed me to stand down and receive it. The whole time before that I was trying to make something happen, and nothing did." He contemplated his new learning, and then wrapped his arms around me and swung me in a circle.

"Thank you, Cass," he said. "I learned something new today, because of you." He held me close and our eyes met. I stared deeply into his blue eyes, my hands stroking his strong wet back. I inhaled everything about the moment as we clung to each other on the shore. He pushed the wet hair from my shoulder and kissed it, then moved his lips along the droplets on my skin, until he whispered in my ear, "Let's go up." We gathered our things dreamily, and walked hand in hand up to the bungalow and closed the door behind us. I stood with my back to him and he embraced me from behind, kissing my shoulders, his hand holding my stomach possessively. He began to untie my swim top and threw it on the bed. He turned me around and slid my wet suit down my legs. I moved onto the bed to watch him untie his bottoms and slide them down. His beautiful white skin beamed brightly, showing his muscular masculine form. He gently lay on the bed, our bodies pressing together, damp skin sizzling. I inhaled deeply. My body began to melt as he kissed me and traced his fingers along the curves of my body.

"You are so beautiful," he said, as I lay back pushing the wet hair from my face. The warm breeze blew over us from the open window and we lay together, whispering sweet nothings as the sun dipped in the western sky.

Some time later we wrapped ourselves in dry clothes and I waited on the porch while Joe went down to get us some food. He brought back sandwiches, fruit and juice and we ate our meal watching the sun go down.

After nightfall we stargazed and talked about navigation by stars. Joe shared his knowledge of history that he had learned from his historian father. At bedtime we went inside and snuggled together in the single bed, falling asleep in each other's arms.

The next morning we awoke to the sound of birds. Joe hopped up to get us some coffee as I got dressed and tidied the bungalow. By the time he returned all was in order with the windows open, welcoming the day. We enjoyed our coffee on the porch, embracing a beautiful day. With the heat rising, we changed into our swimsuits and headed down to the beach. No one else was there. We spread our towels out and relaxed in the sun.

The beautiful horizon caught my attention as I gazed out along the straight line.

"I want to change but I have been thinking the same thoughts for many years. It is hard to drop them," he said, inspiring me to reach for insight.

"It's all perspective, Joe. Choose your behaviour, words and thoughts, knowing they are a part of the experience. Be more conscious of yourself and alter your perspective to suit your needs. With increased attention your awareness will increase accordingly. Make a shift from your habitual perspective, and just look at your situation from a wider angle, look at things from a different standpoint."

Sometimes the ideas came out in words that sounded more complicated than I hoped. I found myself getting wrapped up in semantics as I pushed forward looking for the perfect combination of words to convey my meaning easily, rendering it timeless and simple to understand. This was my ongoing goal. I shifted my position on the sand, sitting up to allow energy to come through me in a straight line.

"We experience our mental creations. Take thought higher and drift among the brilliance that resides there. Creation keeps you here. Experience lets you go. That's why, once you stop thinking and creating and just be, you experience fully in every second. Use creation, then move into experience." Each time I understood the meaning and reflected magnitude, I was in love. I stopped to allow my words to steep, wanting to learn from my teaching as well. I was student of my own observations and this I explained to Joe.

"I think living in different countries has helped me broaden my perspective from which I approach life, because so many tacit rules are different from place to place. The experience has helped me to extract my hand from the cultural glove of rules I was brought up believing in. Places are different; not better, not worse, just different." I thought of all the beliefs I had come across, in people who held firmly to them. Old thoughts can keep you in fear. Choose from what you are offered, in any way, shape or form.

"It's like pulling the wool off my eyes. If the real message had been rude, I would have seen it right away. But because it is kindness and truth, I looked right past it." He sat quietly streaming sand through his fingers.

"Think of the third eye, another visual perspective." Thinking of the mysteries that I had explored and the ones that seemed elusive, I could see how my vision and the third eye went hand in hand.

"Maybe the third eye is the vision of the subconscious," he offered, lucidly.

"That makes sense. I think we can experiment with that. Ancient mystics talk about the third eye, and it has been known in Indian culture for thousands of years."

We had talked about wanting to go to India, to explore the culture there. It was on our list of countries we wanted to explore together. I watched Joe walk to the water and immerse himself, swimming and frolicking, trying to flip in the water again. I saw some splashing and laughed to myself on the shore, delighted with my companion who was so willing to explore my creations. I stared at him, knowing I would never find such a wonderful friend as Joe, who was so open minded and trusting. I revelled in the feeling of our love and tears came again to my eyes. I was so grateful. This love was overtaking me, and it was all I could do to keep up with the feeling as I felt myself changing and opening more to life. I went out to join him, wading slowly into the water, my skin hot from the sun, the water cool. I submersed my shoulders with a gasp, peering into the clear water looking for fish.

"Hey, I have an idea," I said, surfacing. "Let's get snorkels and go snorkelling. I think we can rent them over there," I said, nodding to the beachside restaurant as I swam toward him.

"That's a great idea!"

Joe and I rented two snorkels and shared the afternoon slathering sunscreen on one another and snorkelling until we were salty and waterlogged. We saw only small fish darting about but I enjoyed the meditative sound of my breathing from underwater, watching the ebb and flow of the waves and Joe's beautiful body. Joe bravely swam out into deeper water, searching for something to see. I remained closer to shore, wanting to be sure nothing large swam close to me, still tethered to my fear.

We returned the snorkels at the end of the afternoon and showered in the yellow bathroom, talking over the running water. We never ran out of things to discuss and enjoyed each others perspective. I loved Joe's steady and determined outlook, his sure way of proceeding through life. His confidence made me feel secure even as he evaluated ideas that would surely change his point of view. It was our last night on the island.

"I want to take you for a nice dinner," he said. I could see this was an important invitation for him.

"That would be lovely," I said, feeling courted with chivalry. We dressed in our best clothing and I wore perfume and eye makeup. We walked hand in hand down to the beachside restaurant, where we ordered fresh seafood and sat among other couples enjoying a romantic dinner. We filled ourselves with fish and fruit, waited on by a smiling Thai woman who respected our private time together. When we were done we walked over the sand barefoot and giggled with each other all the way back to the bungalow.

Basking in our last night together in this peaceful place we sat cosily on the porch watching the sunset when Joe became serious.

"I want to ask you something," he said, matter-of-factly.

I turned toward him to see the pinkish light casting a beautiful glow on his skin. I smiled. His lithe, muscular arms seduced me in their grasp and his kisses made me float. He could not know the effect he was having on me, his mere presence in my life.

"What is it, honey?" I said with sweetness, and I listened.

"I want you to come to Norway."

"Really?" I was elated and jumped into his lap. "But it's so cold there," I said playfully, "and Thailand is so hot. We can run away together and stay here!"

His reasoning mind took charge. "I must study, for the future." He looked out at the sunset and I knew what he was thinking. I reclined in his arms, relieved, because the question had finally been spoken. Now we would be able to talk about our future. Now we could speak our minds.

I knew that our feelings for each other were special and our bond was strong. He was beautiful to me in so many ways, more ways than I had ever known. We had visited many places: jungles, temples and beaches and travelled perfectly together always having so much fun. In each place, we shared interesting and intoxicating conversation, learning from each other and growing, while our eyes drank in the magical beauty of each other's souls.

I pressed my palm against his palm, and I said, "I know this can work."

"I know, too," he replied.

"Our love can see us through."

"We should be together. You have to come to Norway."

"Okay. Let's try to make this work."

"Okay. I want to be with you. You're the only one for me."

I stretched my arms around his neck and held him tight as the sun dipped below the horizon. Our love overflowed and there was no stopping the feeling that roared inside me. We needed to find a way to be together, even if it meant leaving the tropical heat of Thailand for the snow topped hills of Norway.

We travelled back to Phuket the next day, to the home we had made together. Pushing open the door the fresh walls greeted us, reaching up high. We unpacked our things, playfully teasing each other and rolling together on the bed. Happiness made my heart sing as I skipped from room to room. Joe was a dream come true!

The next morning I rose to shower and prepare for my day. Joe had brought coffees from next door and was sipping his drink on the sofa, making plans for the day.

"I think I'll go to Phuket town today to see if the dojo is open. I want to train there today."

"Okay, sweetie."

"I'll be home before you are though and we can go get something to eat."

"It sounds perfect!" I hugged him goodbye and headed to my scooter as he stood in the doorway ready to wave goodbye. It was a beautiful moment and tears came to my eyes as I pulled away in gratitude for having such a wonderful boyfriend.

Buzzing along the road that led over the hill to the other side of the island, the journey filled my sights with wondrous things. The vibrant greenery hung close to the road and embraced me with verdant life as I rode past. This morning I sang, my blond hair flowing in the breeze, and felt that the trees appreciated my voice. From high on the hill, I could see over the treetops to the turquoise sea and the tiny boats in the distance. This was my favourite moment, being so high above the sea, but seeing it clearly on my ride to the school.

As every morning, I was thrilled to welcome my young students to class. I sat on a chair while they piled into a circle in front of me. I asked them how they were doing and if anyone had something they wanted to say. I asked each person an introductory question so they could use their English in casual conversation. Then I read them a story. For the first little while they were usually quiet and withdrawn, taking some time to wake up to the day. The sunshine shone through our big windows and added a joyful element to our mornings. I was so pleased to be there. Sometimes I would just look at them and smile.

At lunch the children would be gathered by the Thai staff and we teachers could have a break and chat over our meals. Gail and I often found ourselves a spot on a bench and I listened to many trials. She seemed to have a lot to work through. I looked at her, seeing the glory of her life, living on the island with a Thai man on his family's land, a few English friends in her circle, and a red Honda Prelude to drive everyday. In my eyes, she had it made.

This morning she had a bee in her bonnet. "I just don't understand why they bother," she said of some students who had irked her.

"I give them all the time in the world to complete their assignment, and they still jack around like they have all day. I warned them they would have to sit on a chair outside the classroom, and they still didn't stop." She was shaking her head at the situation with five chairs outside the classroom, and five squirming children on the verge of tears.

After lunch I went into my classroom and quietly closed the door to our learning sanctuary. I put on some children's songs and went from student to student, praising them for their work. I wanted them to feel comfortable so they could build their confidence and find school a welcoming, nurturing environment.

When I had first arrived I found them to be agitated. The British teacher I had taken over from had labelled some children openly, causing separation between the children. I had cringed at her methods. As soon as she had been dismissed my target had been the boy she had shamelessly ostracised. I worked to bring him back into the fold, focussing on his innate leadership abilities. He needed direction and a firm guiding hand to find his path. Soon he began to thrive. In mere days his expression had changed from frown and strain to smiles and relief. Now he often stood beside my chair, not having the words to thank me. His beaming face told me the story.

I wanted harmony and equality in my classroom and praised each student for the contributions they made. They enjoyed our classes and looked up in surprise when the day was done with the arrival of their parents.

Driving home at the end of the day I knew Joe would be waiting for me and every time, without fail, he was there. I hopped off my scooter and almost skipped toward the open door to greet him. He was on the sofa reading a book and got up to embrace me when I arrived.

After holding him for a while, wanting to know just how he fit me so well, I jokingly asked, "Where did you come from?"

"Norway," he smiled at me with probing eyes, waiting to see if I had a better answer. I just laughed and stroked his face.

"I had a great day today. How was yours?"

"I went up island to the dojo then I took a tour around and found a sign for a waterfall. I think we should go check it out."

"Sure! How about now? I would love a drive."

"Excellent."

We hopped up and prepared for the journey. Soon we were on our scooters motoring. Traffic on the paved single lane highways moved at about 60 kilometres an hour. It was frequented by scooters, some small trucks and the occasional tractor or cart. Joe led the way as I cruised behind him, the wind in my hair, a smile on my lips. The whirring of the motor and beautiful, changing scenery lulled me into a silent meditation. I stared at his back and considered our future. Would we be strong enough to hold onto our love while we were apart? Joe would have to leave first and wait for me in Norway until I felt ready to leave Thailand. I didn't know when that would be, or if it would happen, but I wanted to believe that we belonged together. I wanted to hold onto our love.

Joe turned off the highway down a small road and we buzzed along as I speculated what was within the dense foliage we passed. There was no one else on the road as we whirred alongside the cooling jungle, darkening and closing in. The sun streamed through the canopy and cast light on the road ahead, reminding me to focus on the light and the way.

Parking our bikes at the side of the road we were met with the moist air from the waterfall, cooling us and inviting us into the jungle. We walked along a path, hearing the sounds of birds as they swooped from tree to tree, and the buzz of creatures enjoying the end of day. Joe and I moved toward the sounds of thundering water, feeling the rhythm in our chests, as he reached back to hold my hand along the path. Together we scrambled along the trail as I watched for creatures at the side. I stopped him when I saw the web of a beautiful spider. In silence I tugged on his hand and pulled him toward the sight. We gazed upon a yellow and black spider resting on its web in sunlight, hovering over the ground in anticipation of catching one of the many insects in the air. It stilled as we gazed upon it. Such unexpected beauty was all around us!

We carried on until the moisture from the spray wet our faces. A waterfall three times Joe's height poured into a small deep basin that trickled into a stream leading down an incline into a narrow river. Joe embraced me as we stood beside it, alone in the jungle. Without words we took in the splendour of nature. His strong hand stroked my back until he squeezed my shoulder.

"I don't want this to end," he said, matter-of-factly while gazing into the flow, pulling me closer. I knew he was talking about our relationship, as if he had heard my thoughts on the way. I smiled, feeling his presence deeply, breathing it into my soul. It felt right.

"I don't either," I replied, knowing my feelings were taking over. I had to surrender. The feeling was too strong. I knew we had to do whatever it would take to keep our relationship alive, no matter what the obstacles. We must be together. My logical side struggled to get a foothold on the distances involved and our different places in life. But this wasn't logic, it was love. It was love was calling me in a way I had never heard before.

We scampered around the waterfall, Joe took pictures of me catching the flow.

"This water is safe to drink," he explained. I loved that he knew so much about the natural world. I reached for a handful of water and enjoyed the taste as it refreshed my body. We continued exploring the periphery until the air began to cool as the sun headed toward the horizon.

"Come on, it's getting cold. Let's go to the market," I suggested.

"Okay. One last picture."

Joe held the camera in front of us as we leaned together smiling. The flash of the bulb etched the moment in my mind and I knew I could face Joe's leaving with a strong heart. His departure was only days away but this journey to the waterfall had frozen our intentions in time. I had to have faith in what we established by the waterfall and I was 100% certain I could hold up my end of the commitment. I exhaled with a last look at the waterfall before making our way through the jungle to our scooters, where we ignited our engines and began the journey home.

Mid trip, we pulled alongside a line of many scooters at the side of the road. There was a night market underway with plenty of fresh food and local produce. Joe and I made our way from stand to stand, our eyes exploring the array of choices. We purchased one large orange papaya, two mangos and a few bananas. Then we headed to some other shopkeepers where we stopped at my favourite cart: the one that sold green papaya salad with sticky rice, called som tum and gao neow. I became accustomed to ordering the entire meal in Thai, asking for medium spice and without cilantro. I had been taught by instructive Thai vendors and could now order everything with a perfect Thai accent. I ordered two meals and watched, Joe's arm around my waist, as the salad was made from scratch with mortar and pestle.

I was enchanted by the sight of our salads being prepared, and the way a chef would plunge his or her hand into the pot of sticky rice, stuffing it into a small plastic bag. I smiled inside, revelling in the difference of sanitation. I had never once been sick from this food. Joe chose to look the other way while our food was handled with bare hands. We paid for our dinners, about a dollar each, then hopped on the scooters for home.

Driving home in the breeze I thought about my amazing life and I gave thanks to the trees and sky as I buzzed along. Surely they were listening and appreciating.

After a few more glorious evenings together, basking for hours under the stars and clinging to each other under the blankets, it was time for Joe to head back to Norway. He would be starting college in a couple of weeks and needed to prepare. Our time together had changed us both. I had shown him new and objective ways to look at life and he had shown me new and beautiful ways to experience love. We planned to keep in touch via email.

"How much time do you think you need?" He was asking me about leaving Thailand.

"I don't know." The idea of leaving the school and the children weighed heavily on me. I didn't feel ready to go. "Let's talk over email."

"Don't wait too long," he encouraged. I didn't like the sound of that comment, as if there would be a point of no return. But I couldn't commit to a date. I wanted to be sure my journey had come to a close and I couldn't foresee the end just yet.

"No longer than two months," I said, and listened intently for the words to sink in. He shifted position then seemed to adjust to that timing. I was relieved.

The evening finally came. Joe was packed and ready to go. Tears filled my eyes as I realised not only was my sweetheart leaving, but my best friend too. I would be on my own, again.

The drive to the airport was quiet and the sun was setting beautifully. I lay my head in his lap while he stroked my hair, snuggled together in silence. We arrived at the airport and I asked for the taxi to wait while I said goodbye to Joe. I was emotional but reminded myself to think of the good times yet to come.

"Be happy, okay? I'll see you soon." I looked into his eyes, not sure if I would ever see them again. I pushed that idea out of my mind and held on tightly. Tears flooded our eyes and we wiped them, surrounded by onlookers. He was just as emotional as I. This reassured me.

"I'll see you soon," I said, with certainty.

"I'll be waiting for you in Norway." He waved and I watched him walk away. He turned and waved again, until he was at the last viewing point. I stood and waved, smiling but crying too. With his arm stretched, he waved a final goodbye, entering onto the tarmac to board his plane back to Bangkok. From there he would catch a night flight to London, then onto Oslo. His Dad would be picking him up from the train at the other end.

After returning to my house I felt Joe's absence strongly. We had been almost inseparable and I knew I needed to focus on something to distract the memory. I had two months before I saw him again and I decided to get busy developing my skills at drawing and painting, working on my curriculum, and continuing to write down nuggets from my philosophical pursuit. I had all but put aside my writing while Joe was visiting in order to experience our contact, to fully appreciate what Joe and I had to share. Now I was ready to return to my concentrated pursuits.

With each new day I rose up to inhale the beautiful breeze and tropical scents, throwing back my sheets and feeling the benefits of love. I rode to school, hair in the wind, cruising over hills and winding roads in the clear, bright, shining sunlight. Glancing across treetops to a crystalline sea dotted with sailboats brought a smile to my face. My surroundings smiled back as I sang my favourite song, 'Leaving on a jet plane' as I drove. Despite my amateur vocals I felt that the passing trees enjoyed my voice.

Driving home from work on the first day of Joe's absence, I smiled and thought about how Joe gave me a wonderful place to release my great feeling of love and shower him with it, just as he loved to shower me. It seemed that with him, my best self came out. Always seek the truest love and the rewards are immense. You have to love yourself, and then you can love others.

On the first Saturday, I was happy in my solitude, enjoying the time to reflect on the weeks that had passed and the insights that had so graciously awaited my awareness. I sat out on the porch in my chair to watch the life buzzing around me and daydream about love. Each day was sunny and bright, and on this day the light breeze made the conditions almost erotic. I had my pencil handy in those quiet moments in case I wanted to write down an insight.

I thought about what it was that made things new for me, what it was that allowed me to rejoice in life. Something felt as good on the outside as it did on the inside, and it looked incredible around me, too. I was searching for the perfect theory or metaphor to explain my revelations in an enduring form. I picked up my pen: It's not a struggle with our thoughts; it's a change in our perspective. It's that easy. Look at it from a different angle. When my viewpoint changed, as it did with the feeling of Joe's love, everything had a whole new meaning as if I rubbed tarnish from the silver.

I sat in my chair staring directly onto the greenery of my front lawn. The brilliance pulled my gaze as I stared on, curious, enjoying the feeling of intense light into my eyes. The powerful exchange strapped me to the chair. In its essence we were the same and I could feel it. The energy seemed to soak into my eye sockets and I began to feel charged. I felt a strong connection with all the plant life in that moment. Then it dawned on me that plant life was a valuable source of energy and that they were our brothers sharing the planet. It was a beautiful sensation and it filled me with love.

Then I realised that somehow the plant life witnessed my attention, as if it was supporting and endorsing my awareness. It seemed to speak to me on a sweetness level all its own. 'Everything we need to know can come to us through energy exchange with nature all around us,' I wrote. 'Energy exchange can be achieved by being in natural surroundings or by resting vision on plant life, relaxing your mind.'

I felt the magnitude of feeling available to me as if it reached through the natural mediums in life. I could see this experience had infinite potential and was opening doors and windows to a light in my mind. Learning how to make use of the brilliant information was my challenge. In our most natural way, we as a species and planet would overcome any obstacles that stood between us.

My mind wandered into the romantic possibilities and I knew that I could be anything I wanted it to be. 'If we loved one another as much as we are able to, imagine what this world would feel like.' Then I heard the words. *They who are loved, will love. That is why we need to love everybody. Show them what love is, they'll recognise it, embody it, and pass it on.*

Sometimes it was a fine line to walk, knowing the answer was there, but not seeing it. Often my academic mind would step forward, pushing my intuition out of the way. I struggled with my thoughts, trying to release my objectivity and learn from the surroundings at all times. It wasn't always clear; the difference between the elusive, divine inspiration and my own thought. I wanted to be open to it constantly, consciously and considered another metaphor: 'It's not about finding how to live it in the best way; it's about loosening my grip and being led to and through to the goal of consciousness.'

But still, I wrestled with my objectives. I wanted to know the 'best' way to live life and tried to eke it out, depending on my perseverance that so often led to a crystal clear ending. I wanted the moment that would resound around me and then life would come back to the moment.

Like taming a wild horse, I worked on controlling the direction of my thoughts, only sending my attention into worthwhile areas, knowing I had the freedom to ponder on what I wished. I wanted my thoughts to be useful, more qualitative than quantitative. I wanted to magnify my power of thinking, because it seemed the most natural thing to do. Then my wishes and concentration would have more power. Goodness had the most power of all.

As I sat writing what would help humanity, I smiled and felt that everything around me listened in on my thoughts. The Universe and Nature hears all, so be careful what you wish for, and make it grand! I looked around at the trees and wondered if they could see our physical surroundings, or if they could only feel what was around them. I thought that would be a glorious way to live.

I had come to believe that in order to understand this experience fully, we needed to see and understand how energy behaved among us. I knew that energy surrounded us and we made use of it for everything we did; thought, action, word etc. We used energy. Energy was constantly travelling through us. How did that occur? How did we direct and redirect that energy? Were there levels and angles of repercussions of effects?

To become more aware of our orientation in our environment, we needed to study this energy phenomenon. We needed to attune with our higher selves and recognise our thoughts and our experiences as what they truly were: an expression of ourselves. After all, we were all using this energy; sharing it, and even competing with it, without being fully aware of its participation in our existence. We were sending it out to where it lent itself to the creation of our realities.

I closed my book, deciding it was time for an excursion. Pulling a sarong from my shelf, I grabbed a water bottle, then plopped them both in my scooter basket. Smiling at Dao sitting out front at the store, I motored onto the road and headed toward the beach. Passing tourists along the way, I waved to some. I was a resident now and my tye-dyed clothing demonstrated my immersion in the culture. I buzzed along the road near the beach and gazed out to see revellers on the sand, trying for a sun tan to take home after their week in paradise. I whirred on, past the Club Med resort, past the hanging durian and bananas at the roadside carts. I motored through the village of Kata, past the restaurants, shops, resorts, and down the winding road that led through Karon, past the hotel where Joe and I stayed along the stretch of road beside a beautiful beach.

I pulled over to park by the side of the road, and padded through the sand to sit near the shore. I breathed in the salty fresh air, communing with the sea. I stared out basking in the beauty and appreciating my perfect life. Everything was so wonderful, better than it could have been if I planned it. Life was giving me some very big gifts.

One day after a busy day at work, I wanted to cruise along to find some undiscovered byways, rolling through the jungle with the early evening sunbeams. I cruised along taking in all my eyes could see. I continued driving over the hills in the general direction of home until I saw a sign with an arrow that said swimming pool. I drove down the road surprised to find an 25 meter covered outdoor swimming pool. I pulled into the parking lot and walked to the entry way. I could see there was a restaurant just inside the gates with prices listed to swim. I spoke with the girl behind the window and I could see the location would be perfect to come for a long swim then have a thai dinner afterward. I strolled around the pool surrounded by jungle and rice patties and marvelled its existence. A lone swimmer continued his lengths. I paid for a monthly pass then enjoyed a delicious plate of noodles in the dappling sunlight. I had found a new past time. I happily hopped on my scooter to head home, delighted with my new find.

I finished another great week at the school. The other teachers were very nice and helpful and the Thai staff worked hard to keep it all together. The owner showed herself to be somewhat erratic and hot-headed so I gave her a wide birth. I enjoyed the snacks and meals that were included in the position, as well as the view of coconut and avocado trees growing in the corners of the yard.

The next Saturday afternoon I sat on the porch, feeling the warmth of sun on my legs and feet. I reclined in the chair and smiled at the bushes and trees. The great feeling that seemed to permeate the whole scene smelled like the tropics, warm and comforting. I inhaled deeply.

I stared down at my feet perched on the railing above the grass. I thought about what experience I could share with my surroundings so I focussed on the space between my feet and the grass. After a while, I could see that my energy paled in comparison to the vibrant greenery, and felt that my experience within my physical form was somehow less than the magnificence of nature. I felt humbled in that moment, as if I was merely passing through and that this great source and force of life was so strong that it shone brilliantly, eternally. It was then that I laughed to myself, realizing the vast difference between my self and Nature.

I could see the powerful energy clearly, as it waved ever so subtly. 'Energy is a magnificent form of Life.' I felt loved by the idea that something so grand opened its arms to me and held me and provided for me all the days of my physical life. I picked up my pen. Love nature actively - smell the flowers, touch the plants, and tread softly. Give it attention and love. That will help strengthen your love light. And remember to always appreciate the various forms of life.

Chapter 9 – Green Gecko

Joe's emails came frequently, expressing how much he missed me, with romantic scenarios he wanted to share with me. He wrote about his appreciation for the wonderful way I had impacted his life. He talked eagerly about my arrival and our future together. I wanted to read them over and over again.

I began a new routine after work: stopping at the swimming pool for a half hour swim, then eating a plate of noodles from the restaurant. It was time to decompress after a full day with my students. The temperature of the pool enveloped me in warmth and comfort.

Driving through the jungle on my way home the fresh, moist air washed my face as I replayed delightful exchanges with my students, knowing that their impressionable nature demanded the best from me. I wanted my words to make sense to them, to see lights go on in their little eyes when I said the words that they most needed to hear. I built on my philosophies from these exchanges, believing that their innocence allowed them to freely access the wisdom of life.

Saturday morning, I awoke early and showered in fresh, cool water, awakening my warm skin. Making my way to the bedroom with a towel around me, the warm air dried my skin my skin as I picked out my clothing and put them on. The sunlight glowing through golden curtains beckoned me to take in the day. In this refreshing moment I prepared my bag with a water bottle and snack food for a day trip.

Nodding goodbye to my landlords sitting at a table in front of their store I rode off on the winding road that led to the beach. The sea sparkled to my left as I headed north along Karon beach. I stopped at the restaurant where Joe and I had stayed. I feasted on banana pancakes, fruit and coffee. From my table I could see that the sea was bumping and churning, foretelling its powerful tow.

After finishing my meal and reminiscing about Joe I hopped on my scooter and headed through Karon, up into the hills of the island. Authentic inland Thailand lay ahead. Coasting higher into the jungle on paved single lane roads, I cruised around bends meeting only the occasional passerby on scooters or the occasional truck, appreciated by those I met as the only female tourist they'd seen in a while.

A few miles on I entered flatlands where rice fields lined the hillsides. Sky-high palm trees towered over trellised patties, sparkling water between grassy blades. I pulled over and turned off my scooter to bask in the solitude of such a serene place while admiring the lush, tropical life that thrived all around me. In awe of the simple purity of this culture that appeared timeless. I felt hypnotized in the mist and heat.

After a few luxurious moments of this indulgence, I hopped back on my scooter, turned on the tiny engine, and leisurely veered around bends enjoying the feel of the ride. Cruising down the winding roads through the jungle covered hills and plateaus I felt enamoured by all the sights that emerged. The newness exhilarated me as I had never before laid eyes on these places. The road led me along, bending and curving, breathing air into my face and filling me with sunshine.

Driving into the more populated part of the island, I approached a busy, bustling, market. Drawn by the music and excitement, I parked my bike alongside cars and made my way into the action. Choosing from the vendors who smiled genuinely, I searched out authentic gifts for my family and friends as gifts. Sarongs and textiles so colourful and soft. Hand carvings of a rich brown wood depicting Buddha, dancing women, urns and treasure boxes of all sizes and shapes. A feast for the eyes, I strolled enamoured by the items and energy of the space. Incense burned in the corners. Well fed Buddha statues dotted each home, a reverence to the energy it created among the people. There was a table full of Buddha statues of all sizes and position and I poured over them looking for just the right on to convey position peace and unity.

I made it to the beach as the day was coming to a close. I was met with salty air and a fresh breeze. I inhaled the beauty of the place. When I returned home I relaxed on my porch with a cold drink, some drawing paper and paint. In the glowing sunset sky I created simplistic, conceptual artwork that wordlessly expressed my perspective.

Sunday was warm and inviting as well, but I opted to stay home and continue my artwork. I enjoyed the time and space to create. After finishing several depictions of my state of existence I hung some of them on the wall.

Enjoying this domesticity I padded through the kitchen and into the bathroom where I plunged a pile of my light, cotton clothing into the wash basin. Swishing them around, I rubbed and scrubbed then squeezed out the water. I carried a wet armload out to the clothesline and hung them, listening to chickens pecking the earth and squawking among one another. I smiled. Bugs buzzed around in the air and every creature seemed to be having a splendid experience.

My work at the school was going well and I began to know and understand my students better. They were from Madagascar, France, England, Thailand, USA, and Germany. I worked to find ways to communicate that we could understand together. I used a lot of pictures, storybooks and enthusiasm. I tried to fill their days with joy, encouraging them in all they could do.

I began each day by sitting in the sunshine at my desk, half and hour before their arrival, reviewing my curriculum goals for the day. There was so much I wanted to teach them, expressing my love for life into their lessons. Our classroom was harmonious and tidy, a place where my students thrived.

After dinner one night at home, a delicious sticky rice and papaya salad, I went to the Internet café to check for mail from Joe. In my inbox was a message from Simon, a friend of mine from South Korea. He wrote that his sojourn was up and he wanted to visit Thailand. Was there an extra room for him to stay in? I wrote that he was welcome to visit.

It was now the end of August, and the weather had continued to remain sunny and clear, but I was told that the monsoon season was on its way. On Friday after work, I excitedly mounted my scooter to fetch Simon at the airport. The rain began to sprinkle gently on my face as I drove, but I saw grey clouds on the horizon. Balmy Thailand was about to show a different face.

Simon was burdened with a large pack and I smiled to see him. He smiled coyly, flashing his blue eyes in Simon style.

"Hi Simon. Welcome to Thailand!" We embraced and I rubbed his balding head. His light hearted, easy going manner reminded me of how much fun we had had together. Piling onto my scooter we rolled down the hill toward my abode. We tried to talk over the whirring motor, but the sound of our voices was muffled in the wind. A storm was moving in so I hustled to get us home before the rain. A few sprinkles landed on us as we pulled into my driveway, but we were inside before the real dousing began.

"Seems I picked the rainy season to visit Thailand," he laughed.

"It just started. There should be lots of sunny, warm days. It's been great so far," I beamed, enthusiastically.

I showed him around my small house to his bedroom, the kitchen and bathroom. We caught up on news about friends and the changes in each others' lives. Soon I was telling him my romantic story with Joe.

He sat pensively back on my sofa.

"Sounds like this guy is a really great. Are you going to go to Norway?"

"Yes. Well, I think so," I said, wondering why I sounded doubtful.

"You think so? After a story like that?"

"Yes. Maybe. I'm just a bit scared. I really want it to work, it would be great if it did, you know, the two of us being from two totally different cultures. Norway is beautiful I'm sure, but it is also a very cold country, very far away from here," my eyes were on the table as I pondered where my love would take me.

"It sounds like you have doubts," he stated.

"He is amazing. I just have to let it sink in, I guess."

"Sure sounds good to me," he smiled, encouragingly. "So, any hot chicks around here for me? Any nice friends of yours you can introduce to me?" He winked, showing his sideways smile. I laughed.

"I suppose. But most of them are taken. You may have to hit the beaches and roll on your original Simon charm."

"I'm all about the charm," he grinned, widely, and popped outside to get us a drink.

When he returned from the store next door with two cold Singhas I immersed him at once in my nightly rituals of lit candles, mood music and inner reflection. I expressed my increasing awareness to him, excited to share my new ideas about reality. His open mind was impressively vast comprehending my direction, even as a I struggled to express my ideas into simple concepts. I wanted to share with him the precious moments that had changed my life without alienating him, and after hours of discussion I was encouraged that my ideas seemed to inspire him.

"What is it about Joe that drew you to him?" he asked, shifting comfortably in his chair.

"I just felt like I had to know him. I felt like he was special, and I felt magnetized to him," I laughed, recalling our courting on the bus from the airport. "He has this incredible capacity to love and he's not afraid to show it. He shows me in so many new and bold ways, giving himself so freely."

"Why do you think he does that?"

"I think he has learned to love that way. Its like he knows how to trust love." I pondered more on his question. "I think that is just how he lives. I think I'm lucky to have found him," I said, feeling grateful to have Joe in my life.

"I think so, too," he smiled, showing his respect for Joe in his response. "Now, we just have to find someone for me to love," he winked.

"Yes!" I smiled. "We can take some walks on the beach, or I'll sit in a chair and cast the Simon line out onto the sand and see what we can pull in," I winked.

"I like that idea," he said, grinning.

"How long are you staying?" I asked, excited to have a visitor.

"A few weeks, I think, then I'll figure out where to go from here. I may head to Malaysia next."

When the night came to a close we went into our separate bedrooms and closed the doors. The screen along the top of the wall for Thai style air flow stayed lit as he arranged his things and settled into the space. I wondered what my neighbours would think from their traditional viewpoint about another man, who wasn't my partner, staying in the same house. I wanted them to understand that our friendship didn't include sleeping together and hoped they could see his light on in the second bedroom. I wanted to preserve their opinion of me. This was important.

As I lay down to sleep, covering myself with the sheets, I recalled the words I had said to Simon about Joe. It sounded like I wasn't clear, like I didn't know if the love we shared was strong enough to bind. It was as if the memory of him was fading and I didn't know what that meant. I wanted to visit Joe in Norway and I wanted to give us the chance to experience a real relationship. My heart felt love, my words said it, but why was I so afraid? What was I afraid of?

The next afternoon as we puttered about, reclining on the porch and in my living room chairs catching up, I began to feel more confident in my expression of love even if I was only conveying it to Simon. He enjoyed delving into my romantic experience as I divulged more and more about how I felt. It brought strength to my love. My ability to show and express love seemed to be righting itself and growing. I had never felt the kind of love I was feeling with Joe and I enjoyed sharing love in a selfless way, even as I experienced moments of ebb and flow.

"I wonder if it is a matter of finding someone who has the same capacity to show love," I ventured.

"Could be." Simon contemplated, held in the depth of our conversation.

"They who are loved, will love. That is why showing love to everybody benefits us all, because we all learn how to do more love." I read from my journal.

"Do more love?" he laughed.

"We can show people what love can be, what forms it can take, truly, and they will recognise it. We can all be less afraid to show the magnitude of love that we have inside ourselves."

"I think you need to be less afraid," he said, pointedly.

"That sounds good!" I said, and wrote the reminder in my book.

I sifted through my feelings, looking for other parts of me that I hadn't uncovered. Turning a corner in my mind, I felt a rush of sadness that Joe was gone. It gushed through me, like a torrent of water and the thought of missing him was strong in my mind. I realized I had been holding the feeling back and that it was hidden within me. It surprised me that I would do this, and I wondered why.

One afternoon after work Simon and I went down to the beach to watch the sun set. Phuket skies had the most incredible blend of surreal colours that danced across the sky enmeshed in sweeping clouds. The colours moved gradually into one another, taking witnesses along for a magical, spectacular ride. Visual delight demanded silence as we lay back on the soft sand staring into the sky.

Many tourists took pictures from the shore, the setting sun above their loved ones with the most amazing tapestry across the sky and beyond the hills behind them. Pure beauty.

"Why do people gather for the sunset, Simon?" I asked. "What happens during that time that people feel the best place for them to be is on the beach, not necessarily even watching the sunset, but just to be there while it happens?"

After some reflection, he answered, "People are extrapolating information from the sunset."

I smiled, and nodded. Looking back into the sky, I considered the idea that colours in the sunset were a form of communication. In an aware state, perhaps information was available in the myriad of colours. Even in Koh Phangan during sunset, dogs gathered out on the beach, playing and frolicking in the sand.

"Simon, what do you know about other dimensions?" It was one of my biggest questions. "Do they exist as part of this reality or are they parallel realms to our own."

He rolled over in the sand. "I don't know what you mean. What do you mean about parallel realms?"

Just then, prying eyes and ears descended on our space so I suggested we take the conversation back to my house where we could continue to explore in private.

On the way back, we picked up papaya salad from a street cart where I introduced Simon to the local cart vendors. He took an immediate liking to the several people who manned the carts and shops nearby. With his easy-going, friendly manner, they smiled easily in return. Simon was fitting in well with the scene and quickly making new friends.

When we arrived home I lit some candles and opened the windows, pulling back the curtains to let in the breeze. We sat in the living room with cold drinks and ate our meals.

"Have you heard of the fourth dimension, Simon?" I wanted to access his higher mind, giving me the random fruits of his insight.

"I haven't heard of it, that I can think of," he responded.

"Surely, you have heard of the third dimension. There is supposed to be a fourth, a fifth, maybe even more." I paused, waiting for an expression to register on his face.

"Mathematicians have proven its existence through mathematical equations, but it is yet to be explored," he recounted.

"When I was young I had thought about how life could be better. So I always listened to people who had a unique point of view," I said, recalling the various people who had helped me along the way.

Simon's gaze followed my movements.

"The experience opened me up to what I can feel with Joe. Love and a lot of it."

"Do you think I can feel this way?"

It was a sweet question, and I looked into his eyes.

"Sure. I think you have to stretch though. I had to stretch. I had to learn how to allow it. I'm still learning," I said, picking up my journal.

"It sounds like you've figured out a lot here since the days of Changwon," he laughed. "I knew you were into new things, so I'm happy you found some answers. It's really cool."

"Yeah, thanks Buddy," I blushed. "I'm really happy I did."

I sat comfortably, barefoot, covered by my sarong. Looking down at the garment's vibrant colours, I felt safe within my house, the sweet air pouring through. I wrote in my notebook, 'This is the coolest experience I could dream of having. For now.'

Sometimes while drifting through thought I could see an emotion emerge within me that I hesitated to address. What was in there? What would appear? I could face my emotions of the present, but what about the past? I considered my well of emotions deep, at times daunting and hollow, echoing. What was down there? Frightened by the depth, I wondered if I would somehow have to release all of my past pain in order to relieve myself of the burden.

Go through your feelings. They will guide you. That is where the answers are; inside. Look at yourself; uncover them. It is not a search for the answers; it is an uncovering of the answers. Be strong, be smart and stay centred. Make sure your feet are always planted in the 'reality' of this world and look at yourself.

On Saturday Simon and I packed our scooter baskets with water and snacks for a road trip up island. We buzzed off just before noon to enjoy a leisurely brunch of pancakes and coffee nearby. After finishing we continued our journey, the buzz of our engines increasing up steep hills as we travelled to the ocean side of the hilltop. With a view off the cliffs along the shore, we ascended winding hillside roads into the thick jungle.

Roadside 'Elephant Safaris' and 'Cobra Shows' called to us from large signs at the side of the road but we passed them by, enjoying the ongoing vibrant green with glimpses over the trees of blue sea.

Riders passed us going in the other direction and with an exchange of a smile or wave. It was delightful to coast through the breeze in such beautiful scenery. Tall grass and levelled rice paddies sparkled in the sunshine, delighting vistas punctuated with pockets of jungle foliage.

After travelling for some time, and checking to see that my skin wasn't burning, we came upon a sign that pointed out a waterfall. Nodding in agreement, I turned down the road, excited to spend some time up close in the cooling lush jungle and to cool myself off.

As we approached the waterfall we saw Thai tourists enjoying the area and pulled up to park our scooters. The whole area seemed still except for the gurgling falls and the pouring of water. There was a small monument and a few plaques in Thai about the history of the area. Something uncomfortable struck me about the area. I felt no resonance with my surroundings. Ignoring the unresponsiveness we prepared to take a dip in the rustic pool of rock that lay below the falls.

"Go ahead. Jump in." Simon stood to the side.

"You go first. Tell me how it is."

"Do you think there are piranhas?" Flashback of an eighties movie went through my mind. I laughed, not sure myself. I submersed my toes to test. Nothing came. I splashed around in it with my arm, gazing as deeply as possible.

"I'm going in." I sat on the edge of the gurgling pool, hesitating. I looked around at the dense jungle and rich green foliage. Nothing. Turning back to the water I plunged in quickly. The water was over my head and I burst back to the surface. It was refreshing and clean but the strange feeling remained with me as if we were being watched. I heard the Thai family leaving and I watched their departure, wanting to call out to them to stay. Just as Simon slid gingerly into the water I swam to the edge and hopped out, feeling spooked and alone.

"Simon, I think you need to get out. I'm feeling weird about being here alone. There is something creepy going on." I stood looking into the foliage like a hunted deer.

We dried off with our towels, trying not to think about it. Instead we decided to walk down toward another pool away from the edge of the forest. We kept our eyes downward on the path, cautious for any approaching creatures. It was eerily quiet as Simon and I walked alone in the jungle, staring into the dense, vibrant foliage. We spoke softly to one another, aware that something strange was happening. I looked around quietly at the verdant life felt alone. Simon felt it too.

Then all of a sudden a strange, high-pitched buzzing pierced the silence from deep in the jungle. It moved quickly through the forest toward us, a large mass, becoming louder and louder until it reached the inside edge of the forest about fifty feet ahead of us.

We could hear it just inside the thick jungle foliage. The sound was like a large swarm of bees or an army of some giant insects moving through the forest. But staring into the forest, we could see nothing. Then, as quickly as it had started, the sound stopped.

As if it was still watching us, I tried to reason what kind of insect or insects had been responsible for the sound and why it had stopped suddenly.

"Simon, what was that?" Both of us peered into the forest in the direction of the sound. I began to feel unsettled, wanting to run, the fear in me heightened now that we were alone. Then the strange sound began again behind the trees just inside the thick tropical foliage.

It stopped again and Simon shocked me by turning toward the forest and heading along a path up steps deeper into the jungle. In a split second I decided I wasn't going to be separated from him so I followed him unwillingly into the forest, staying close behind as he began to ascend the steps.

"Come on, Simon. This isn't a good idea. Let's go." He continued onward. "Simon, what are you doing?"

Simon snapped out of it, shaking his head, agreeing to leave right away. We fled to our scooters and drove away from the waterfall, shivering and cold.

Our heads down because of the rain pelting us as we drove, we hurried home, Simon in front. Passing the beach we could see a storm on the horizon, dark clouds moving in the distance. We sped on trying to escape the rain.

When we arrived at my house we didn't speak about what had happened. We were both a little spooked. I put on some Bob Marley, and the strange experience was forgotten.

"The way is everywhere, Simon. There are so many tools here to help us find the way to freedom. The possibilities are endless when I imagine what I could do with myself and my experience here. I have to remember to dream on!"

"Dream on, dream on, dream until your dream comes true," Simon sang, countering my Bob Marley with Aerosmith.

"His lyrics are so inspiring. There's a reaction, for every action, I'm so happy inside."

I sat back in my comfy living room chair until I became tired and decided to go to bed. I went to sleep with thoughts of Joe dancing in my mind.

The next day Simon went out for a ride to socialize and meet new friends while I enjoyed solitude at my house. I cleaned the kitchen, swept the porch and toured my beautiful yard, admiring all the life that thrived there. Many beautiful butterflies called my yard home and each day they floated on the breeze, enchanting me. Small gecko lizards zipped about none too interested in any close up inspection. They ate tiny bugs flying around and perched on the porch walls, a splash of green decoration. Some of them lived inside my house and used the unscreened windows as passage. It didn't bother me because I knew they were harmless to humans. I sat on my living room chair, enjoying a beautiful experience in the sunny afternoon relaxation.

"Oooh, what a life!" I said out loud, stretching my arms up in appreciation. I was listening to Sade love songs and the feeling of Joe's presence warmed my heart.

Everything seemed to be just how I wanted it, in perfect order. I was happy with my job, loved my students and the other teachers. My house was clean and fresh and the yard was filled with interesting creatures, lush and tropical. I loved my hedonistic lifestyle, finding inner peace and connectivity. My body was at ease while my mind was plugged in, seeing outside and feeling inside.

I felt a warm and wonderful feeling of pure love flow through me as my left hand moved up and stroked the left side of my face, gently and lovingly. It caught my attention immediately, because I knew it wasn't my intention. I was not in control. I was shocked.

"Who just caressed my face with my hand?" I asked aloud, feeling pushed beyond limits once again. It was a loving gesture. What force is this I thought to myself. Life was so amazing. Clearly, somebody is happy with me.

I felt buoyant and joyful as the hours went by. When the sky began to change at sunset I moved my chair onto the porch to listen to the crickets and creatures as colour spread across the sky. Deep orange, purple, red and yellow stretched over the entire sky, imbuing the land with a peacefulness. After it went down, I moved my chair inside to prepare for the week and Simon's return.

"Did you see the sunset? That was amazing!" he said, clearly delighted.

"I saw it from the porch. It's a miracle every night. I just love living here," I said, smiling.

"I met some new people. A woman named Karen from England came to the pub. She's staying for a while. I met a few others as well, really nice people. And the Thai guys are so funny," he said.

"Good to hear you are having a good time."

The next week flew by while Simon explored more of the island on his own and I focussed on school. He gained knowledge of the area so he quickly shared some new byways and insider information from the Thai guys at the pub.

The upcoming weekend was a four day holiday. Simon and I planned to take a vacation on another island, deciding upon Koh Phi Phi, a small island three hours by ferry in the Andaman Sea.

On the Saturday morning we went into Karon for a big breakfast before returning the rented scooters and hopping into a taxi back to my house to pick up our bags and drive to the pier.

While the taxi waited in the driveway I headed along the walkway beside my porch. Something moving caught my eye. It was black, fast and slithered between Simon's shoes that lay at my front door. The sight of it stopped me short, attuned to such movement from my days of hunting turtles. I could see a round black head with a red, beady eye peering back at me.

I turned back to summon my landlord who sat leisurely on his front porch. I made a snake-like hand movement and his face dropped. He turned to pick up a whacking stick leaning against the wall beside him.

I stopped Simon from going any further along my walkway as we waited for the landlord to approach with his stick. I felt sorry for what I thought was a 'little black grass snake.' I didn't want it to be hurt. My landlord walked past us as Simon and I watched him move around to the entry gate. Taking a moment to collect himself he leaned forward and poked the stick between the shoes, quickly moving one to the side.

Out shot the snake, rolling upward, revealing an eye shaped symbol on its fully fanning neck.

"It's a cobra, Simon!" I shouted, jumping in the air as the man whacked the head of the snake until it was surely dead. He moved it onto the grass so we could pass, chuckling at our reactions. He threw it into the neighbour's yard, food for chickens.

We were amazed that we had seen a real cobra, on my porch, and that it was hiding between Simon's shoes! That was a first! We talked excitedly about it for hours.

"I wanted to see a snake while I was here in Thailand and a cobra is the best I could have imagined," I said.

"Those shoes have a new meaning now. I may never wear them again," said Simon.

The three hour ferry ride to Koh Phi Phi passed quickly, recounting our story over and over again. When we arrived at the Koh Phi Phi pier we noticed there were no cars or roads, only foot and bicycle paths.

Directed by a helpful tout who greeted us on arrival we were hustled to Charlie's beach bungalows where we rented a two bed bungalow, one of many neatly packed into rows. It was perfectly appointed with a nice wide porch and hammock. A short walk through the maze of bungalows revealed a breathtaking beach. We immersed ourselves in the azure paradise gazing awestruck at the beauty enveloping us. The bay was surrounded on two sides by jungle and blue sea at the mouth. A gentle wind blew high in the palm leaves as we relaxed on powdery white sand.

Elderly Thai ladies worked the beach handing out coconut drinks with a smile, and opened on the spot carved with hand-sized machetes. Shirtless Thai boys rented jet skis and many joined in on the fun. White-skinned tourists frolicked on the beach, reclined in chaise lounges, many of them canoodled on the shore or in the water. The surroundings enveloped me in an aura of love. I felt at peace.

"Here we are, Simon, with foreigners from all over the world, staying together in blissful harmony on a tiny, tropical paradise island off the coast of South East Asia. The mood is delightful!"

After an hour on the beach we returned to our bungalow to shower and unpack. Later we walked along soft, worn footpaths that weaved through bungalows and shops into the tiny village. Several open air restaurants enticed our gaze as we strolled, each filled with triangle recliners and tourists upon them, sipping cocktails with tiny umbrellas.

Everyone was smiling and happy. We found an interesting spot to check out. At our low table we sat on floor mats with many triangle-style cushions available that encouraged maximum relaxation. Strings of colours lights adorned the ceiling while Bob Marley sang to us from the speakers. I sipped a coconut shake while Simon cooled off with Singha Thai beer. We watched as natives strolled along the pathway on foot, bicycle or wagon, and tourists who meandered past meeting our eyes with friendly smiles. The island was incredibly serene and while the day was bright and warm.

Adapting to the slow pace of the islanders we returned to our porch. Hearing voices and sounds from nearby cabins it was obvious that people were living life to the fullest. Most were far from home with only a friend or two. Some travelled on their own, wanting to meet and chat about local activities. I could hear the intensity in their voices and they seemed to be a more adventurous type of tourist, far from home on this remote island.

"This is all we could ask for and more," I said.

"This is better than I could have imagined," Simon said, his eyes beaming.

"That is awesome," I said, happy for our choice.

"We lucked out this time, Cass," he smiled.

"We sure did. Lucky we are." We clanged our glasses in cheer.

"Let's go see what excursions we can sign up for tomorrow."

"Sounds like a great idea."

Later that afternoon as evening approached we entered a sight-seeing shop, eyeing maps on the wall. Simon chatted with a tourist agent who read us a list of activities available. We decided on a snorkelling day trip on a boat at seven the next morning. After confirming our reservation we went to the beach to catch another glimpse of the beautiful sky with starlights twinkling as far as the eye could see. We returned to our bungalow for a good night sleep.

The next morning, standing with a gaggle of other foreigners on the beach, we were handed snorkels and told to choose life jackets from a pile. We were ushered to a semi-covered long-tail boat with protective sashes tied to the nose. We piled aboard with our Thai driver who started the engine that roared with life. As we got comfortable in its seats, the boat motored out of the bay between tall peaks at the mouth. The sky was an amazing colour of blue. Everything about the day was clear and sparkling.

After a short trip, waving at all passing boats, we steered into a lagoon fringed with steep cliffs that shot up into the sky. As we waited for the boat to stop I turned around for a signal from our driver. He was leaning over the water, peering into it. We started up again and pulled out of the small lagoon.

"No safe," he said grinning, as we gasped, making jokes about sharks.

The next lagoon was deemed clear of any such hazard so he turned off the engine and we coasted shoreward surrounded by cliffs. I looked down through the pristine, clear water to the bottom. It must have been about 20 feet deep. I positioned my gear securely and we all plunged in one by one, piercing the crystal clear surface.

We had entered the realm of multitudes of brilliant fish, most of which I had never seen before. Beautiful shoals of elaborately painted fish floated and darted in the water. With my face glued to the colour around me, I swam with passion and curiosity, coasting above parrotfish, butterfly fish and clown fish. It was as if each one had been plucked from the water and individually styled then placed back into the equally beautiful setting filled with vibrant coral. It was easily the most spectacular underwater scene I had ever experienced. Florescent colours in spots and stripes adorned their perfect forms as they happily soared and dipped in the tranquil waters, sheltered and safe in the lagoon. Below the riot of colour I could also see spiny black sea urchins resting on the bottom. I was happy to be buoyant near the surface high above.

At the far corner of the lagoon there was a small patch of white sand leading into a pocket of jungle. It beckoned me so I swam over, my wet body shimmering in the sunlight as I crawled onto the tiny beach. Sitting in perfect, untouched sand I imagined myself to be the first person to ever be there. I sat blissfully in the warming sun and wondered what it would be like to live like a native on this pristine island. I imagined that everyday I would discover beautiful secrets, always in bare feet, eating fresh, luscious fruit from the trees. Paradise.

Simon swam up, grinning from ear to ear. "Hello, Miss Cassandra. Enjoying yourself?"

"I am, beautiful Simon." We rolled on the sand, feeling freedom, then gradually, reluctantly, we crawled back into the shallow waters and swam back to the boat. Some of our fellow travellers who saw us returning from the secret beach asked for more time so they could share our experinence. Unfortunately, it was time to go. We were hastened back on board.

By noon we were all hungry anticipating a feast as the boat ran ashore at a long, white stretch of sand. A few other boats arrived to share the beach so Simon and I took our sandwiches further down to a secluded soft spot in the sand. The sun was hot and the sand was getting hotter so we ate our lunches quickly before submerging in the shallow water. Relaxing and floating with others, we lolled in the gentle waves.

What an incredible dream. I basked in surreal beauty, shimmering and gleaming bright light into my eyes. My mind was clear of concerns. Peacefulness purred within.

After lunch we boarded the boat again and headed out over very deep, dark water. Marked by floating buoys, we approached another snorkelling spot, and our driver stopped and turned off the engine. I tried not to hesitate and plunged into the water, looking around at other snorkellers while positioning the mask on my face. I thought about lurking, menacing creatures but quickly reassured myself that there were others swimming nearby and they were fine. I inhaled deeply and decided I wasn't going to let a petty fear overshadow the big bright part of me that had shone all day. I swam away from the boat.

Looking into the deep blue water I wondered about the larger fish that lived in the sea but almost as if they could hear my inner thoughts, thankfully, they all stayed out of sight. Others who climbed on board told stories of manta rays and large fish they had seen only meters from where I swam.

By the end of the day Simon and I were exhausted from our journey. Back on shore we returned to the bungalow and rested on the soft beds. After a restorative afternoon slumber I played some music and we lounged until evening. As darkness fell we wandered to one of the restaurants that served authentic Thai food in a unique dining experience.

Built with a bamboo frame and lined with palm leaves, the entire makeshift restaurant stood on sand near the shore. Relaxing reggae music played as we sipped our drinks while warm breezes blew gently amid the sound of waves lapping gently at the shore.

After eating, we sauntered through the tiny village and considered our options for the next day. Pausing at a tiny tourist office, we asked for suggestions.

"Hello, there," we smiled at a neatly uniformed woman, sitting next to a computer with signs of island paradise day trips lining the walls in the tiny room.

"Do you know any paths or trails we can walk to another beach?" I asked, looking into her deep, friendly eyes.

She gave us a warm smile. "I know a path go over hill to bungalow, restaurant on other side Ko Phi Phi."

"Okay." Simon and I nodded. "How long to get there?"

"Two hour."

"Perfect!"

She sketched a small map. "Find path, go this direction," she said, pointing to the right with her pencil, "find white steps. Take steps to path over to other side."

It sounded easy and I envisioned a well travelled sight seers' dream populated by tourists. Simon reached for his bag to pay her.

"No charge," she said. "Enjoy."

"Thank you!" we said, smiling, then padded away slowly, agreeing that the people on Koh Phi Phi were very warm and friendly.

The next morning Simon and I ate a filling breakfast of French toast, fruit and coffee. The coral coloured papaya tasted so sweet and the local bananas were delicious. All of the fruit we were served was grown on the island. We filled our stomachs and when we finished some time before noon I was struck with an idea.

"Simon, why don't you go on ahead? I'll meet you on the other side," I said, feeling like some solitude to take in the scenery on my own.

"Okay. If you're sure," he said.

"It's only two hours. I'll just meet you there."

"Okay. See you by three o'clock at the latest."

"Three it is," I said. We hugged goodbye and he headed toward the trailhead.

By the time I was ready to go it was noon. Wearing flip flops, shorts and a tank top, I carried in my backpack a full water bottle, camera and sarong. I started along the pathway that led through restaurants, small clubs, shops and Thai foot traffic. The village was quiet and peaceful. Most of the tourists were already out on excursions or at the beach. The sun shone down brightly casting shimmering light between towering palms that lined the pathway.

As I carried on past bamboo structures the pathway became overgrown in grassy patches so I looked from front to back to see if I was even on the trail. The narrow path curved past a swamp and a small gathering of wooden shanties where children played on steps. It weaved past a small factory where men stood outside smoking, watching me as I passed by. The path was not at all what I had imagined. I wondered if I had taken the wrong route. Then I came upon a staff of white cement steps leading up a steep, jungle covered hill. I breathed a sigh of relief.

I trudged upward for a long time before ascending to the lookout point. I passed one lone Thai man coming down, who stepped quickly and fled past me. No one else was to be seen.

Arriving at the top I had to stop to catch my breath. Ahead there was only a tight grassy opening with a small sign that read, 'Lookout' stating the obvious. That was it. I walked across the mound with distant views where I could see the stretch of sand that bridged the two pieces of land that made up Ko Phi Phi: Phi Phi Don (big) and Phi Phi Lei (small). Palm trees grew in neat rows along the stretch of sand that joined the two islands in Thai-style planned development. In among the palm trees were the roofs of the shops and restaurants, conveniently sheltered from the sun.

After a few minutes enjoying the view I decided it was time to continue. I began to look around for the path leading down to the other side but no obvious path appeared. The surrounding bush was thick and looked like it hadn't been traversed in years. I laughed at my predicament, shaking my head, wondering where Simon had gone and how I would meet him on the other side.

Then a sudden movement caught my eye. I walked over and saw a small gecko dart into the underbrush at the head of a small trail. I recalled the words of Paulo Coelho in *The Alchemist* about lizards being a good sign. I trusted the signal and went in.

As I walked along the narrow path, thick, deep, jungle, surrounded me. Penetrating silence peeled through the space even as sunlight beamed onto my path. The green foliage appeared energized, pulsing, urging me onward. The path became thinner and thinner as I walked, less worn, and I wondered if I was headed in the right direction. The dense jungle foliage packed moisture as I moved deeper into it, somewhat worried I looked up at the tangled vines of the forest canopy knitted tightly together. I was all by myself, walking further and further into an unknown jungle, with no idea what lay ahead. The calls and cries of birds echoed through the trees, reaching my ears in melody. The cobra story was still fresh in my mind...

I tried to focus on the positive: I was in love with nature and nature, I believed, returned the love. No sharks had nibbled when I'd thrown myself into the sea so I walked into the jungle's embrace with the same confidence.

I traversed along the pathway, eyeing the ground with cautious optimism. To build on this feeling, I started voicing Sing a Song by the Carpenters. It helped me relax because I had to concentrate on singing which kept my imagination from running wild. I laughed, reminding myself to, 'Get a hold of yourself, Cassandra. Find that calm, safe place inside you.' I told myself to appreciate the beauty of the lush scenery thriving around me, untouched, completely natural.

After a while the path began to slope downward and to the right. I had no idea where I would end up but I figured there had to be somebody at the other end. It had to come out *somewhere*. So I walked on, singing and becoming more relaxed in the surroundings. I looked up to see light streaming through magnificent leaves and foliage, the sun sparkling high overhead and a few creatures leaping about. My first jungle trek, all alone in the deep, dark, tropical forest, on a path with an unknown destination. What an adventure!

I came to a fork in the path with two signs fixed on a tree. One had Thai writing on it which I didn't understand. Scribbled on the other sign with an arrow that pointed up to the left was written 'Lookout point.' I surmised that led back up from where I had come so I chose the other direction and kept on. I wondered about Simon and if he had chosen as I had and whether I would find him on the other side.

I saw another gecko which helped reassure me that I was on the right path. Despite my confidence I was aware that nervousness lingered just below the surface. I pushed these thoughts away and kept listening for signs of warning. But there was nothing to alert me to danger so I trusted the feeling of strength and carried on.

A little ways further, I stopped and stood on the path, listening hard to the buzzing that surrounded me. Was it in my head? What was I doing? Where was I going?

I looked back in the direction from where I had come. I considered turning back and weighed the known destination I'd travelled versus to unknown distance ahead. I took a deep breath and continued on the path.

Singing to myself as I walked, I carried on until I caught sight of a large camouflaged net to the right of the path. There was a big hole in the bottom.

"Oh great," I laughed to myself. "A tiger trap." I didn't even know if there were tigers in this jungle! I told myself that I wasn't a suitable sandwich for any large and toothy jungle creature. It was another opportunity to exercise my trust in life and I wasn't going to give up now.

The sun was moving west in the sky and after a while I came to a high point on the path. I could see blue sea through the trees straight ahead. I was nearing the other side of the hill! I breathed a sigh of relief just to see it. Then I saw a third gecko. It was as if they were leading me through the jungle.

The path started to head downward so I quickened my pace to accommodate the angle. I called out ahead to creatures to watch out for my fast moving feet. Reaching a bend, I slowed down and heard loud cracking noises. The cracking was coming from a group of tall bamboo trees clustered together. Upper parts of the bamboo had fallen on other branches creating pressure and the whole group of trees were leaning forward from the added weight. Creaking and cracking loudly, I imagined they were about to tumble down the decline directly ahead of them, and me, just where the pathway led.

I stopped for a moment to survey the situation. I waited and watched. I didn't want to stand there all day so I took a deep breath and motored down the hill while listening for anything coming behind. Thankfully, nothing did. I rounded a corner safe and sound and released a big sigh of relief.

Moving steadily downhill at a comfortable angle, the thick bush around the path gradually started to retreat and I came upon an open area. Tall shoulder length grass to my shoulders replaced dense jungle as the path threaded through it. The ground levelled out and I could see only a deserted beach. Finally, I caught sight of two Thai men building a rustic bamboo structure, relieved to see other people.

The path continued to weave through thick grass before opening up at the edge of the most breathtaking, pristine beach I had ever seen. To my left I saw Simon talking with an old Thai man in front of another small shack, his backpack still on.

I smiled to them and Simon met my eyes with a look of relief. I walked directly into the embrace of the beautiful sea, having exited the jungle entirely unscathed. The whole process had made me a different person, a stronger, braver version of what I had been. I strolled into the shallow water and felt the warmth on my skin.

Chapter 10 – Fresh Coconut

Simon and the Thai man smiled widely as I walked toward them. We laughed together, a common language. The old man picked up a coconut from his large pile and chopped it open with a machete, dolling out fresh coconut to each of us, handling his big knife with ease. As we ate the delicious coconut meat he handed us two freshly cut coconuts so that we could drink the milk. Then he gestured for us to use the tree swing hanging in his front yard. Simon and I sat down on it, laughing with the old man and his family, using hand signals to communicate as we swung back and forth over the sand.

The beautiful moment silenced us as we gazed at the white powder beach, glowing in the sunshine. I was filled with appreciation and Simon was relieved too. The sky was clear and a gentle breeze was blowing. I wondered what it was like to live on this beach, gathering coconuts, spear fishing, in an isolated idyllic scene with the vibrant sea only footsteps from your door.

It was hot on the beach even under the shade of the big tree. I asked if I could use a room to change into my bathing suit. Two women, one elderly and one younger, who sat at a nearby table nodded to me. When I emerged in my colourful swimsuit with large flowers they laughed heartily. I blushed and smiled then moved toward the crystal clear sea. I would meet up with Simon later.

Placing my things on the sandy shore, I waded in and lay back to float. My mind wandered back to the fear that had emerged within me while I travelled through the jungle, not sure if I would end up at my destination. My intuition had led me through unscathed. I sat up in shallow water, lulled back and forth by the gentle waves, as my eyes took in the length of the beach. At both ends it was contained by natural rock outcropping.

My curiosity was peaked by the sight of a shack further down the beach nestled in from shore. I saw a blonde man with a grocery bag walking along the beach in that direction.

He approached the shack and disappeared inside. I stood up and tied my sarong around my waist. Soft sand and bubbling waves met my feet as I walked along the shore. Basking in serenity and tranquility, with the warm water rushing over my feet, I sauntered the length of the beach. As I passed the tiny abode, I saw flippers and a mask hanging on the wall. I continued on exploring the length of the beach, then on my return, I strolled up to the shack.

"Hello," I smiled. Two men seated at the table in front smiled at my approach.

"Hello. I'm Martin," said the blonde man with an English accent, "and this is Dang."

I walked toward him to shake his outstretched hand.

"Dang lives here," he explained, "and has graciously offered me a hammock here until he moves out in a month or so," he said, grinning respectfully at the Thai man who said nothing but smiled.

"Sit with us," said Martin, who gestured to the bench at the table. I sat down taking in the surroundings.

"This beach is amazing," I smiled. "You are both very lucky to stay here," I said, the intensity of the beauty enveloping me.

"I am learning how to live here," continued Martin. "There is no stove or sink, only one hot plate and a bunk and a hammock. I have been travelling for months with my girlfriend who is on another island at the moment, but she will travel here and stay with me. She's writing a book so I have moved to this place for her inspirational benefit. And of course, because its beautiful."

"Where will you go from here?" I asked, my gaze on Dang, who was absent from conversation, staring only at the sea. As soon as I asked it I knew it was meaningless to him. He shrugged. His vacant expression told me he was listening to something deep within. I understood what was happening and adjusted my seat, knowing I had found something unusual in this moment. I could see why Martin was so enthused about spending time with Dang.

"He's twenty five. But he's wise enough to be an old man," Martin laughed, talking about Dang who seemed ageless and continued to stare out at the horizon. After a long moment, his gaze met mine.

"I move on when its time," Dang said, ending any sense of questioning that bubbled inside me. A comfortable smile took form on his face, a peaceful clarity in his eyes. I smiled back.

"Tell me more about living here," I purred, wanting to know more. They smiled kindly and my inquiries turned into an intriguing conversation with both Martin and Dang who chose his words carefully.

Later in the afternoon, Simon joined us at the table where we had been peacefully enjoying the beach. I made room for him on the bench as we invited him to sit down.

I listened deeply to Dang, fascinated by how his words resounded within me. His knowing perspective silenced us all. I imagined the magnitude of feeling, living alone on this beach with such an incredible view. I wanted him to pour enlightenment into me in words I could understand.

"I'm from Koh Phangan, from child," he explained in clipped English, relating about his youth on the island, living in the jungle, and his experience with a King Cobra. Many a day was spent playing in the jungle with friends, exploring and climbing trees, foraging through bushes and picking fruit for his family.

"One day, giant King Cobra snake follow us, we hear it move in bush. We run and climb tree and watch as snake rise up to height of small boy. Big neck and very mad. We throw rocks and make snake hiss and spit. We know nest must be close. We leave and no come back."

We shivered to hear his story. Dang just laughed at our reactions.

"What about snakes in this jungle?" I asked, twisting in my chair.

"I don't know all kinds that live here. Some poisonous, but only bite if you step on. Be careful and watch path ahead," he said, with a gleam in his eye.

I let my eyes wander over the incredibly vibrant sea and sky. Green trees and branches hung over the shack, rustling lightly. Dang spoke of many things. I gathered insight from his words because there was depth in the pure truth of his meaning. I continued to listen intently, wondering if he had become somehow enlightened while living on this glorious beach.

"Full moon rise last night. On horizon. Same again tonight," Dang said.

"Wow! It must have been beautiful!" I said.

"You can see it, too," Dang smiled.

"Yes, we would love to!" I said, smiling to Simon.

We watched a small power boat drive toward the shore filled with tourists. They plunged off the side and frolicked in the shallow water. A woman walked through the water and over the sand toward us.

"Do you mind if I join you?" she asked, dripping. Martin got a chair for her to sit on and she towelled off, explaining her arrival.

"We have been snorkelling all day. I had to get out of the sun," she said, squeezing water from her brown hair. "I am Lydia, from Israel."

Her deep voice was purposeful and her forthright manner intriguing. As we adjusted to our expanding group a man walked from the water to our table. Now we were six.

"I am Aaron," he said, greeting us all with a smile.

"He is from Israel, too," Lydia said. We all smiled. After a few minutes their boat motored off without them. They just laughed.

"I guess we're here with you!"

"You can watch the moon rise with us!" I said.

"I will make us something to eat," said Dang, who rose from the table to fix us some food. Martin joined him in the tiny kitchen. I was hungry and happy to hear this.

In a while, the two chefs handed us each a bowl of white rice with vegetables. We enjoyed our impromptu gathering, eating every morsel, anxiously awaiting nature's evening show.

As the sky darkened it was evident that we were on a lonely stretch of beach surrounded by jungle.

"How are we getting back to our bungalow tonight?" I asked Simon, who shrugged and looked toward Martin and Dang.

"You could take the trail back through the jungle. I have one flashlight," said Martin.

"It is black as night in there!" Lydia exclaimed.

"It's the jungle! At night!" Simon echoed.

"Another adventure!" I said, a little uneasy at the thought but feeling confident to have others with me.

"But with only one flashlight, we may have some trouble seeing the trail," offered Aaron.

"I don't think it's a good idea with only one flashlight. We won't be able to see," said Lydia.

"There is a man with a boat down there," said Dang, motioning down the beach to the family who had greeted us with coconuts. "If you pay, he will take you back."

There was no light coming from their windows.

"He may be sleeping," Lydia said, as the moon remained a mystery.

"Just pay him well," Dang smiled.

"Okay, let's do that." We nodded in agreement and settled back to watch the sky change. Soon the sun was below the horizon and a sparkle of stars spread over us. It was very dark.

"Maybe, it won't come tonight," I offered.

"It must get very dark first," Dang said. "Be patient."

We squirmed with anticipation wanting something spectacular, knowing it was just around the corner. Then, responding to our wishes the moon crested the horizon, white, full and magnificent. Within minutes it was full on the horizon, demanding of our attention: a glowing white circle of beauty in the night sky.

A magical sight to behold. We sat in awe of the moment. Peacefulness permeated us: six strangers listening to the quiet of the night. The ocean lapped gently at the beach in small ripples against a magnificent deep blue sky. Crickets chirped as the forest charmed us with sounds. We rose, one by one, pulled into a surreal moment on the beach, meandering and moving about without words. I breathed in the night air, looking down at my feet on the soft glowing sand. A gentle rain shower passed overhead, delighting us with fresh sprinkles.

Immersed in serenity, enveloped by darkness, I felt at one with life.

"Hello," spoke the gentle voice of Dang standing beside me. "You like it here?"

"Yes. This is so magical," I smiled.

"Yes, magical," he smiled, then moved from my side to the table where he set up drinks for us. Martin joined him. I turned back toward the sea and thanked it for everything, then smiled up at the stars and moon, thanking them, too. One by one everyone returned to the table. We lit candles in the shelter and gathered, all six of us from different places, around the world, coming together easily as friends.

The moon rose higher in the sky, taking us into dreamy worlds until we were satisfied. It was time to go. We pooled our money, gave some to Dang for the meal then gathered our things.

"Just go to the house and knock on the door. He will take you home."

"Thank you so much," I said to both men, conveying my deep gratitude. "It was a night to remember."

"One special moment we shared in time, one we will always remember," said Lydia.

We padded across the cool sand in moonlight. Silence enchanted us walking along the edge of bubbling waves. When we arrived at the shack Simon knocked on the door and spoke with the man. Simon returned to us with good news.

"He will take us back to Ton Sai. He just has to get dressed first." We laughed, waiting by the shore, bright moonlight on our faces. The moonlit sand lit up the deserted beach, in an otherwise black night. The sound of lolling waves danced in our ears.

When our driver appeared we waded into the shallows to climb into his boat. Offshore another gentle shower sprinkled our faces as we motored along the edge of the island, around the bend and into the electric light of the tourist area. He slowed the motor and pulled onto shore.

"Thank you," we smiled to his happy face, paying him in baht. He thanked us then motored back into the night. Simon and I hugged Lydia and Aaron goodnight and goodbye knowing we would forever share our special evening together.

"Have a good life," we echoed to each other upon parting, Simon and I walked back to our bungalow at Charlie's.

The next morning we awoke early to catch the ferry to Phuket. After breakfast Simon and I went to the pier and climbed aboard the boat, finding a spot on the deck with reclining chairs.

"What a crazy adventure that was," he began to laugh. I began to laugh as well and we carried on, reliving the memories. After arriving in Phuket, we took a taxi to the scooter rental and picked up two scooters, then drove to my house to continue life at the beach in Kata.

When we arrived at my home, butterflies fluttered everywhere in the vegetation, skipping through the air from one bush to another. It was serene, unspoiled, ours. I sat on the porch with a cold iced tea, drawing pad in hand.

"I envy that you have artistic talent."

"Everyone does, Simon. You just have to find what you like to do."

He smiled, shaking his head at my optimism.

"You sure are one of a kind," he said.

"I think there are others like me," I smiled.

I began to draw, starting without a picture in mind, with only a desire for a stroke here and there compelled to express myself this way. Passion in the exchange took me up into it, immersing me entirely in focus. When the lines were complete, the picture yielded a metaphor. I was astounded and stepped back from the work. I could see meaning as if the answers were emerging, floating just beneath the surface of my consciousness.

Simon could see the metaphor, and found another one. It was deep, yet so simple.

Soon, I was finished and a new idea emerged, beautifully non-descript, non verbal but lucid in a manner that subdued me for the moment of interpretation. What was I creating here?

I began to display my artwork on my walls, syncing the colours and placing a picture of a desert in the spare room, the pinks and oranges agreeing. The two small people stood in an embrace in the distance, their hats only a dot. Overcoming a desire to be perfect, I just wanted to share what I had made and because I believed it was beautiful. Simon thanked me for the addition, saying it brought life to the room.

Taking in the life that glided along the top of my hedge at the front of my yard, cars and trucks but mostly scooters whizzed past. I saw that everyone had the same purpose - to love and be loved. Everyone wanted to be accepted by their peers, to be appreciated, to contribute something good. It was natural. And here we were, all one, doing the same things to survive. It is really so beautiful, so special, the life we share.

"Subtle behaviour in others speaks loudly. Pay attention to their subtle cues. What are they saying?" Simon and I sat in the flicker of the candlelight that I had brought out onto the porch. The moths fluttered on the tiles as we sipped our beer.

"We have the power to heal ourselves. The world shows us what we were doing with our energy. This world is a mirror of our thoughts. If I experience something I don't like, then I can change it. And I can look at what I am doing to create the manifestation," I said.

"So you think we are creating our world, by how we are thinking about it. Like if I'm pissed off I'm only creating more negativity," Simon responded.

"Yes, and the answers are always within. We live our thoughts and beliefs. The way life speaks to us is true and simple," I said, feeling comfortable.

Revelations poured into me from the familiar intimate place inside, opening me somehow. I knew now that my answers came from deeper understanding that I held inside me all the time.

"Uncover the secrets of the subconscious. Bring it all into consciousness," I said, feeling expansive.

"So, you think I already know all of this," Simon asked.

"Somewhere within you are all the answers." I smiled, not sure where these answers were coming from or and eluding to.

The next day, when I returned from work I sat in my chair on my porch. Everything beamed with energy around me, green vibrant pulse of life, waving and wiggling in the breeze. As I sat appreciating the beauty, I felt enhanced by the feeling of love, as I looked at the plants absorbing the essence of their expression. As if with my loving friends, we shared this beautiful afternoon together. My notebook had to be here. 'The more I see life's beauty, the more beauty I see of life; the nature, events and experiences.'

Simon returned and suggested a new restaurant for dinner at the beach. We went and enjoyed a great meal as the breeze rolled in from the nearby sea. The club next door lit up the night with red and green flashing lights, gyrating entertainment for us. We listened to the hoots and hollers of the tourists here for a party and Simon told me about a new English friend he had met named Karen.

"Tomorrow night Karen wants to share an omelette at the beach," he confided.

"Hmm, this could be just the right thing for me right now. I would love a boost into the unknown," I said, excited by the opportunity.

"She wants to have a celebration for her arrival into such a cool place." He smiled his endearing smile.

"This place is like no other. Never again are we going to be living an experience like this. This is a once in a lifetime, Simon," I said, feeling grand.

"Yes, it is. So, lets funk out!"

"Okay, I'm in for my last go around on the mushroom highway."

"Knock it out of the park," Simon and I cheered our glasses. It was nice to relax and allow myself some simple pleasures.

When the next evening came, we headed down to meet Karen at the relax café. She was a spirited girl with interesting conversation and an easy going manner. Her brown hair fell on her shoulders and she was pretty, but I felt that Simon was only interested in her friendship. We spoke excitedly about the evening ahead as we sat at a table for our meal. Locals who had made the omelette gathered around us smiling at our soon to be heightened awareness, assuring us they had eaten it several times and that we were in for a fantastic ride.

After a few bites, we finished most of the plate, and soon began to giggle lucidly. Soon, my visual reality began to roll in waves. I reached over to Simon.

"I've got to get out of here. The visuals are becoming intense," I said, standing.

"Me too. I'll get Karen."

The three of us crossed the road to the beach and sat on chaises facing the shore. The wind was blowing, and we could barely hear each other talk so we returned to the café. But moments after we were inside and I told Simon I was going back to the beach.

I walked toward the beach, looking for cover where I could sit in nature. I saw a wooden bridge over the sand to the beach so I sat down on the steps. I took in a deep breath there but then I noticed a subtle sensation tugging me forward.

I laughed to myself feeling the pull, then said, 'Okay, where do you want me?' I stood and walked along the bridge, trying to remain lucid to feel the sensation. Halfway down, the sensation stopped, so I sat down on the wood railing.

"What is it about this place?" I asked aloud, then I laid eyes on a large, leafy tree directly in front of me. It was the only one beside the bridge, providing protection from the wind. Had the tree itself beckoned me?

In calm surprise, I laughed. The purity of the moment engulfed me as my perceptions expanded, until I could feel the peaceful pulse of nature all around me. Lightness and love filled my feeling as I connected with my surroundings, feeling as if I became one with them. The dark night swirled wind around me but I was safe, protected by the tree, being whispered to by life.

Happiness welled up inside, freely lifting my attention upward – I was an instrument of pleasure. Floating high, feeling good, I saw blessings all around me, flowing through me. I was at peace with myself. The surroundings enveloped me and I felt love coming from outside of me, as if I relaxed into a grand feeling of joy.

"Should I believe in this?" I asked myself. "Is this real?" My hearing zoned in on the response of Bob Marley's lyrics playing at the bar. "Oh, darlin', darlin', I'm callin', callin'."

I felt reassured by the words, feeling comfort and expansiveness around me, my every thought heard by this space. And so it responded, blowing my awareness out even further into the unknown. Increased perception recognised the synchronicities that made me laugh, hard. I was rolling over with laughter, as tears of joy rolled down my face. Loving and kind, the experience provided just what I wanted and the jokes I needed to feel more free inside myself.

I looked up at the tree in front of me, appearing to enjoy the moment, involved in something spectacular with me. Leaves shuffled in the breeze, the dark sky sparkling starlight upon me, between clouds on this windy night. In the distance, lights flickered behind palm branches, echoing the waves on the beach.

A figure approached and I saw Simon's form moving across the road toward me. He sat down, piling into the moment.

"I just came to check on you. Are you okay down here by yourself?"

"Yeah," I said. "I'm in my own world."

"Okay, I'll be at the pub. Come up when you're finished."

"Okay," I said, and he padded back to the pub.

After he left, I felt comforted by what a good friend I had, appreciating Simon and the wonderful people in my life. My thoughts went into the other brave humans with whom I shared my life, the wonderful spirits who stood by me on my journey, who loved me and were always there.

I journeyed on within myself, feeling the expansiveness within, laughing because it was all inside me. I needed deep breaths to steady myself. The images from beyond opened me, again with more depth of understanding I was realizing that I was not just my body or my body just me.

I repositioned myself on the rail and turned myself toward the sea, where I could see the long stretch of beach with light posts lit up in the distance. I drifted deeper into non-sensory experience, into a vision of another time, another reality. Then, I couldn't feel my body but I knew it was sitting on the rail, awaiting my return.

Out there, somewhere inside myself, I didn't need vision. Sensation told me that wisdom that resided there - the power immense. Beyond context in this world of illusion, I was in a space with lots and lots of love, where I didn't need to do anything but just Be. In this realm of finer vibration 'nothingness,' I saw my existence in more detail, from the observer's point of view, riding the wave further into the unknown. Did I sit in the Supreme Consciousness classroom?

Moving deeper into my emotion, I saw my feelings for the people in my life as a pie graph, as I was shown where I was putting my energy. The image zeroed in on slices of the pie as whom I was loving. The largest piece of the pie was Joe – and the amount of my love for him surprised me. Then next largest was my Dad, which didn't surprise me, and my family then the rest of the pie as my close friends and the others in life. I saw the many special people whom I loved.

I woke up to myself on the rail and looked down at my hands. I really did love Joe. I wasn't just imagining our love, or living a fantasy. Where was this love hiding within me? Why did it elude me at times? I felt ashamed that even I didn't know who I loved.

Then I sensed that judging myself was futile and unnecessary. I was a child of the Universe learning to love and be loved, and that I wasn't alone. I always had help in the Universe, and there they were beside me helping me to understand more about myself. I was in the presence of my wise invisible teachers, who were showing me immeasurable qualities of myself, until I was brought to tears of gratitude. I could go into this feeling more deeply, experiencing more, wondering where the information was coming from, feeling love thousands of times stronger than ever before, more encompassing than any love I had ever felt in my life. But how far could I go before I would lose myself?

Just then, I was pulled back into my consciousness by the weight of the fear - A stark feeling of standing on the edge of something irreversible. I inhaled to steady myself. I looked up to the tree and the beach. The road was quiet. Who would know what I was experiencing?

I laughed out loud at the thought of explaining it. My God, what is happening?

Gazing toward the sea my mind went out into it, past the night sky, past my vision of consciousness and out of my body. I was in the same place as before. This time I saw an image of Earth and the nature of experience there as if I sat observing on a star. Time was a concept held to in my reality, but it doesn't exist. It was not as I had believed my whole life. I could see how time was necessary to fulfil our destiny in life as we know it. Time is a tool of our awareness and doesn't exist outside my consciousness.

Wow. Amazing.

I came into awareness of my body again. This meant that I had enough time to do everything! I took a moment for a breather. I could hardly retain it.

But this time I had prepared my mind for this consciousness, this knowing, building my understanding as a foundation for growth. I was strengthening my ability to digest more information and more profound concepts – the same truths I was being shown on the island with Mark.

At the time, I hadn't prepared foundations for this kind of knowledge. It had served only to open me in fascination, but was beyond my ability to recall. I laughed at the brilliant plan to release me into more of myself.

I went up again by placing my vision on the beach and letting my mind go into the space beyond the sights and sounds that normally held my attention. I surrendered to the experience, releasing the confines of my physical life.

I saw life on Earth and my experience within it taking place inside a large tube with open ends. The starting end was behind me, the beginning of my experience of life on Earth. The end was bright green, or yellow and it pulsed just beyond the lips of the tunnel. It fanned out and I was in it: a virtual tube. Then, it appeared that I was standing near the end of the tube.

Huge energetic brilliance shone beyond the exit. Something loving was waiting patiently for return. But who? What?

I sensed pulsating vibrant green energy, thick with approval for my speculation and introspection. I could sense three beings with the unconditional love of a proud parent. Was it the Father, Mother and their creation, a Son? Who was holding space for me to learn and discover the truth of my reality? Who was outside the exit? I leaned forward for a better look.

The moment caught me with the realization that the exit would mean the end of my relationships on Earth with my beloved family and friends. A stark awakening returned me to my place on the beach.

Energy as intelligence, love and peace embodied the space around me. How did I not know this? How was this secret kept from me when it existed in plain sight? Knowingness flooded my awareness as tears filled my eyes. Deep gratitude entered my feeling in coming back my reality at the beach. I dabbed the corner of my eyes with my sarong, the depth of awareness engulfing me just as the wind began to stir. I knew I would never be alone again.

I wrapped my sarong around me and thanked the night sky for another breathtaking experience. Turning back to the boisterous music and the life I had left behind, if only briefly, I was never to be the same again.

I silently stepped through the crowd to where Simon was standing, with a beer in his hand. He was taking it all in from a space along the wall, then smiled when he saw me.

"Are you ready to go?" I said, when I reached him.

"Yes, I could go," he said, and poured back the rest of his beer. He set the bottle on the table and we headed for the door. We said goodbye to Karen on our way out, waving to others we had met.

Arriving home after the drive along the beach, I snuggled up on the sofa with my notebook and lit the 3 candles of the silver candelabra Joe and I had bought on Koh Samui. Simon prepared for bed, then smiled at me from his bedroom door.

"Did you have a good time?" he asked.

"Yes, an amazing time."

"Let's catch up in the morning. I'm really tired."

"Sure thing, Simon. Goodnight."

He quietly closed the door and turned off the light as I stared into the flickering light of the candle. The wax dripped down onto the base, reminding me to treasure what was beneath the surface, the foundation, the base. Nothing else mattered.

'There is no mystery to life,' I wrote, 'What is, is what is. This is, what is. Look at this.' I laughed at the vagueness of my words, but they were best left as they were; describing fully and completely what I felt in the simplest way.

'Is there another dimension? What had I really seen in going up into heightened awareness?'

'This power that is, is BIG. Just Be; Feel, Experience, go through those. You can go there with your mind. I caught a glimpse.'

Gratitude filled me until I permeated everything, then I was ready for bed. I tucked myself into the bed I had shared with Joe, thinking of his piece of the pie. I closed my eyes and went to sleep content, embraced by life.

The next day I felt extremely settled inside, like a big ocean without any ripples. My inner emotions felt in unity with my surroundings, resounding, while hens clucked and roosters crowed in my yard. Ants marched single file across my wall, drawing my attention to the window frame where they continued onward through a tiny hole under the sill. In formation, trotting across the wall, I admired their dedication to the task.

I got up and opened the windows. Then, I heard Simon stir in his room. He offered to get our morning coffee through the wall. So when he returned I was sitting on the front porch chair. He handed me the coffee as he sat down beside me.

"Thanks," I said.

"No problem," he replied.

We sipped silently enjoying the morning air and the sound of nature. Tears came to my eyes for the beauty of the expression of nature all around us.

"There's a place you can take your mind, a place that's so big, where our time system appears mere human creation, a system in order for us to understand this experience."

His eyebrows raised.

"I was in the pub so I couldn't get that high. There was too much noise and people moving around," he said, repositioning in his chair. The sunlight shone down on our knees warming our skin, as insects fluttered and buzzed about. The birds sang in the trees and joy was the order of the day.

"You can be in a place that feels peaceful, high and light, from where you can look down and see that your family and friends are humans too and not the centre of life but a social system we have believed in."

He looked toward the lawn in contemplation.

"You can recognize that we humans have created a system of relating to one another. Our life seems similar but miniature to the larger systems you can sense by being in that state. I took steps to the edge and glimpsed something so awe-inspiring - Exuberance only comes close."

"Wow, that wasn't the kind of experience I had," he said, chuckling.

"I felt that I wanted to hear what was going on inside me, so I went to a quiet place. You chose the social element."

"Yeah. The guys at the bar were pretty funny," he smiled, causing me to smile, imagining.

"I saw another world, I looked into a different time," I reminisced.

"You could see things. Awesome," he said.

"I wonder if it was another dimension that I saw."

"Mathematicians say it exists," he said.

"But what kind of existence is it? Did I see into another dimension? Another world in this world?"

"There are other worlds in Science Fiction novels," he added.

"I haven't read many but George Orwell. I read 1984."

"I've read a bunch. It's a guys thing, I think."

"But have you ever seen one yourself?"

"I could say Yes. You know how some of those nights you just know something unusual has happened, in a good way. Yeah, I've experienced that."

"Okay, good," I said, feeling we were on the same page.

After sharing breakfast of fresh fruit and toast, Simon buzzed out for a scooter ride while I cleaned the house and washed some clothes in the bathroom. Kneeling over the cement basin, I appreciated the feeling of the refreshing water and dunked my hands in. I enjoyed the fresh scent of clean clothes, even as the water ran down my arms in shades of blue from my new freshly dyed clothing that had no staying product.

Five loads later there was water all over the floor from my trips out to the yard to hang them on the line. I walked around the house on the uneven sidewalk that defined the space. Vines grew along the wall and fresh eggs lay randomly on the ground near hens clucking about. I rounded the building to the washing line with handfuls of wet cotton clothing.

While I was hanging it on the line I listened to the many sounds around me. I surveyed the neighbour's home, a build similar to mine made of cement. There were chickens running in their yard, too. Leafy trees overhung from their yard into mine above a rustic fence. Both lawns were sundrenched and sparsely covered the ground.

The lady behind me lived in a tiny thatch hut made of rattan. Among a few other huts that lined the jungle edge, she sat on a wood plank porch and waved in my direction. I waved back. Day after day she wore delightful colourful cotton dresses and always looked relaxed. She grew vegetables in the small garden in and raised chickens in a pen. Word was she was a relative of my landlord and stayed for free. Her chickens wandered across our lawn pecking and parading with complete abandon. There were two peacocks living among the chickens, their plumbs mostly held back.

A bee buzzed around my head as I continued to lay the clothing over the line. 'It is just looking at you,' I reminded myself. Everything in life seemed so simple. Everything was easy, really. It was our limited perspective that made things difficult. In those precious moments of awareness the answers to my questions were crystal clear.

Remaining in bliss was my eternal goal. In abundant moments, I understood so much of what life was offering. Opening up to something much larger than myself, I experienced a deep sense of safety and love. How could I live in that awareness and immense understanding always?

I raced inside for my notebook. 'It's not our will; it's our way. It's our destiny.' I sat down feeling more and continued.

Choose what you want, love yourself, and know what you're thinking. Then look at what happens and follow the signs. Allow yourself to be led into situations you choose. Read the signs and work with your inner feelings. They will lead you. Listen to others, as they will identify themselves to you. Hear what they are saying about themselves and decide if you want that in your life. Choose from what presents itself and trust in life.

It was all in front of me. Life was ready to be understood, I felt, as I washed the kitchen table in the sunlight pouring in and the sound of birds ringing happily in the surrounds. I practiced moving into the grand feelings of appreciation that accompanied this sense of knowingness, transporting me into understanding.

Feeling myself rise to a higher level of being from which life appeared clearer, I saw living in paradise as a springboard, allowing me to feel joy and bliss because of this peaceful setting.

The sound of beer bottles jostling shifted me from euphoria. Simon was moving chairs on the porch fresh from his ride. He was speaking with another man as I wiped my hands on a tea towel and headed to open the door. Simon introduced me to his new friend.

"This is Espen," he said, as the man reached out to shake my hand. "He's Norwegian," Simon grinned.

"Nice to meet you," I said, winking. We spoke briefly about our individual plans for the island and I discovered that Espen had just arrived on his first journey to Asia. Then would continue traveling to embark on his lifelong wish to visit India. It was a big moment for him. He was visiting Thailand to relax and get ready. They had brought beer and offered me one. I smiled and accepted.

"It's all about the party!" Simon joked, grinning and swaying.

"There is a party at the Safari Club tonight. Do you want to go?" Espen asked.

"A night out on the town sounds great!" I said.

"Let's leave in an hour," Simon suggested.

When the time came we poured onto our scooters and zoomed along the beach in the early evening. We watched as the sky darkened after sunset as we followed the beach road into an adjoining district. Our destination was the Safari Club high on a neighbouring hill.

Perched high on the hillside with a dazzling view, we entered into a wild place. The club was filled with tank-top or bikini wearing tourists and Thais. Indoor palm trees flashed with coloured lights, lining a wooden dance floor with couples of all ages. Sun kissed foreigners grooved to familiar music with smiling friends and a handful of prostitutes. The place was a hopping Saturday night disco.

Moving to the beat Simon and I wove through the crowd and sat down down with Espen at a high top table. We sipped beautiful cocktails with tiny umbrellas and skewered pineapples. What a sea of humanity! We laughed and laughed at the myriad of activity in this twilight zone of multi layered extravagance.

"What do you think?" I asked Espen over the throbbing music. "Here you are half a world away from your home with some crazy Canadians, in some nutty hillside disco club with flashing lights and funky music, along with all sorts from all over the world, in a lost paradise of South East Asia, at the shore of the Andaman Sea."

"I feel that this is like a dream. More than a dream," he smiled. We both laughed.

After swaying to several songs amid flashing lights and thumping speakers we tired of watching the wildcard partygoers and decided to head back.

Cruising along the two lane highway road, winding over hills in the balmy breeze, I inhaled the idyllic utopia. We soared along up high before descending to the beach road along the shoreline, kissed by the sea spray on our faces. We veered lazily along the curves of the road until finally reaching my drive and turning off our engines.

We piled onto the porch laughing, recounting the strange scene. I lit candles and put on music then sat down to snack on sweet papaya salad and sticky rice that we had picked up along the way.

As I was clearing our plates after we finished eating, Espen began to confide in us. "When I first arrived in Phuket, the weather was warm and sunny. Everything was great so I paid for ten days. But since then, the weather has been rainy almost everyday."

"I think the rainy season has just started," I volunteered.

"I have learned that in late August the monsoon season begins on the west side of Thailand," Simon offered.

Espen frowned. "The owner of the bungalows will not refund me the money so I feel that I am wasting time."

My intense focus on Espen as he told the story led my feelings into his until I began to feel stressed and upset. I could see that my concentration on him had enabled me to tap into his emotional field.

At once, I stopped myself by changing my opinion about the situation from his back to mine. I took a deep breath as I searched for the right words to say.

"You know, ride the wave," I said, smiling at him. It was all I could think to say, trying to demonstrate peace with my calmness, but he just looked at me. He continued to talk about the problem, more to Simon, who was agreeing with him that he had received a bad deal.

The mood soured and we began to look at one another, wanting to feel happy again. I suggested we go out to the porch and get some fresh air. We went outside and plopped into my comfy chairs for a while but soon the breeze became cool. We were at odds with something. The evening came to a close and Espen went home. Simon wished me goodnight and closed the door to his bedroom.

Over the next few days, Simon spent most of his time with Espen, touring on scooters and exploring more of the island. "The bungalow where Espen is staying is really great. Its really social, with lots of tourists coming and going. There's action over there!" Simon was excited, having enjoyed many hours at Espen's bungalow.

"I guess because I'm in love, I want to stay home," I smiled.

"I'm thinking about where else I'd like to go in this area, and wondering when I should go to Malaysia."

"I have heard good things about Malaysia," I said, recalling stories from the tourists.

"Yeah, I think that's where I want to go," he explained.

A few days later Simon and I were on the porch having a few laughs together and talking about his travel plans, knowing the time had come for his onward travels. I was wistful, not willing to say goodbye to my companion.

Just then, Espen showed up on his scooter.

"Let's go to the beach!" he said.

"Sure!" we replied.

We hopped on our scooters and headed to the beach where we sat down comfortably on the warm sand. Looking out in the surf I saw something struggling in the waves. As I got closer I could see it was a small sea bird, gasping for breath. I rescued it from the waves, placing it gently on the sand. It continued to gasp.

"Oh, will he be okay?" I asked, concerned.

"I don't know. It may have swallowed a lot of salt water," Espen said.

I packed the bird carefully into my basket and we drove back to my house. I rinsed it off in the bathroom sink and tried to pour small bits of fresh water into his mouth. It wasn't swallowing, only gasping for breath. I wrapped it in a towel in the spare room to rest. I wished it love and closed the door.

Espen was preparing to leave the island. "I'm on my way to India to fulfill my lifelong dream," he said, proudly.

"I'm happy to have met you on the eve of realising your dream. I wish you good luck and enlightenment," I said, hugging him.

"I am lucky to have met you. You are inspiring. Thank you for everything," he said, his chest welling up.

"You are welcome. Have a magnificent journey," I smiled and watched as he mounted his scooter.

It was Simon's time to leave too. He smiled his sweet, charming smile at me as he stood on my porch with his bags packed.

"It's been a blast, Cass," he said, reaching for a hug.

"Me, too," I said. "I had fun with you."

"Thanks for letting me stay here. And thanks to Joe." He smiled.

"Oh, Simon, you are so sweet. It was my pleasure."

He climbed onto his scooter, balancing his heavy pack. They started their engines in unison.

"Stay in touch," I called out.

"I will," Simon said, winking.

"Bye," I called out, waving, as they made their way to the road.

"I'll email from Malaysia," Simon called out.

"Okay," I said, and we parted, knowing a special part of our journey was ending.

I closed the door and went to the spare room to check on the bird. As I approached the door I knew it had died. Even though I was sad at its passing, I was happy it had been safe and warm when it exited this world. I carried it outside to the Thai lady who lived behind me. She carefully gathered the bird in her hands while speaking Buddhist prayers in Thai before ceremoniously burying it in the earth.

I sat on my porch that afternoon reviewing the three endings I had witnessed. Three changes, really, nothing to be sad about. A reflection of Joe brought a smile to my face. I missed him so much, even as I was happy in solitude.

I went inside feeling the strong all-encompassing love I shared with Joe. I had never before felt anything like it. It was strong even when we were apart. I felt like that pot of gold at the end of the rainbow as if all the colours led to him.

Chapter 11 – Red Rooster

School started at the beginning of September. My classroom bubbled over with twelve 5 and 6 year olds from France, Germany, Madagascar, America, Thailand, and Japan. Each child on their first day of primary school stared bewildered at the activity around them. Yellow and blue objects riveted their attention, as they sat cloistered around white tables on green and red floor mats, gazing helplessly at one another, and me.

I welcomed them all by name, smiling and greeting each student individually. I walked around the table shaking hands and making jokes. Sitting on a stool at the front of the classroom, I spoke of things they needed to know about the life they were about to live. Wide eyes wandered around the room at the treasures that awaited them with barely enough will power to stay in their seats. A few were brought back to the table with gentle gestures of my assistant, and the sound of squirming children.

I began to talk about what words they needed to use and six play stations they would have the opportunity to visit. Each of the centres around the room had a different purpose, equipped with wall displays to engage them visually. A large paper tree had been pasted to the wall and I told them of items we would place on its branches together.

I began teaching from my new curriculum as if it were a launch pad and the children, rockets. The ideal program: building intellect, language and confidence weaved well-being through interactive and engaging exercises. I began with hand puppets and songs to capture their attention, then one of my favourites, animal identification by sketching.

I set up the afternoon craft while the children lunched in the outdoor play area. Benches accommodated about 25 children with four Thai supervising staff. I ate lunch at my desk while reviewing my notes to make sure I was on track. The curriculum was only eight weeks so my plans were crisp and concise. Before I knew it, the students were gathered back into the classroom to begin the afternoon craft. Art supplies were set up in the outdoor classroom with five colours of paint and glass jars overflowing with paintbrushes.

As I ushered them into the outdoor art room the excited buzz of children's voices filled the school. Two classrooms had art in the afternoon, while the third class of younger children had naptime. Later I collected many pages of beautiful expression, and hung them with clothes pins along a line that strung between pillars of the art room to dry in the breeze.

Back to the classroom we went, where tired children were gathered with their elbows on the table. Then, we sat in a circle as I read books until the faces of their mothers and fathers appeared in the doorway to pick them up. As I waved goodbye at the tiny, happy tired faces I was warm inside. Priceless!

Driving home with the breeze in my hair I felt the day complete. The first day of teaching from my own curriculum! I loved it! How would it unfold in their mind's talking about seasons and pastimes? Would they learn the underlying lesson I was teaching them, that life loved them?

The first weekend break from school I awoke to the crowing of roosters penned in the back yard. Listening to them I discovered there were about three or four who did most of the crowing, seemingly saying, 'Hello, everybody wake up. Are you awake? Are you awake?' I would have to answer Yes!

The rising warmth made me throw off the sheet and pull back the curtains to the day. Opening the windows to the breeze, floral scents wafting in as I watched bees buzz all around. I toasted bread for breakfast while accepting the industriousness of ants that made tracks to every food item on the counter. I had tried squirting detergent soap in a thick line to prevent the ants from accessing my edibles, but they had simply waited until it dried then climbed over it. The bread had to be moved and ants shooed constantly. I contemplated a refrigerator and a shower water-warmer, but eschewed them for the simple life.

I walked over to get a coffee from the shop next door and chatted with Dao about her life. Fascinated to hear about Thai culture, we shared stories of love and family. She explained the closeness of her family, their shared acceptance of each other. Mutual respect held them from interfering with opinion or judgement. A Buddhist mentality in practice felt soothing to me. They experienced a freedom within those relationships to explore any and all parts of themselves.

Respect operated as a boundary, living so closely together, this created harmony and a life worth living. Breathing room, living in confined quarters, was enough. Being able to afford a cement structure for a home was an esteemed accomplishment in this neighbourhood as many still lived in thatched huts.

After a good chat I returned home where I sat on my sofa wondering what to do with the day. I felt my attention drawn to the open doorway, the sunlight and my lush green yard beaming with energy.

Gazing out the door I stared at a bush that shared space with me, in full view of the opening between us. As I focused my attention on its beauty I could feel a pulsation, as if it was pulling on me. I moved my chair outside to sit with the plant. It appeared so full of energy. It was like we were friends, living side by side for two months, passing it by on every entrance and exit to my house. It had been witness to the greatness I was feeling living there and I thought it seemed equally as happy. It felt good be observe it so I relaxed, enjoying the stimulating feeling that moved through me. My mind wandered among thoughts of all the great things I wanted to continue to see the best in my life.

I looked out at a tree on my lawn, its leaves energized by the light. Another dimension of 'personality' and looking around I saw many more. The yard was filled with unique individual trees and bushes, each with a different expression, like the people I knew as part of my life. I laughed out loud because I had ignored them for so long, when they were just as real as my human friends, but more subtle.

I wondered if those who studied energy were aware of the things I had experienced. We could study our friends in life and learn from them. Maybe they could help us heal. What patterns existed between them? How do they utilize energy?

I enjoyed the space to paint and write on the porch all afternoon. In silent communication with my leafy neighbours while I created a few more pictures to hang on my walls. Delighted with the colours and multi level meaning, I tacked them to the living room walls. It was time for a change. I packed the basket on my scooter with my sarong and wallet then went down to the internet café.

Another letter in my email inbox romanced me, Joe telling of his yearning for me, his wanting of me in his arms. They were perfect letters, rich with meaning, seduction and heated desire. I relished opening them, letting the words spill on me like rain, knowing he was waiting for me.

I drove home feeling elated and saw the full moon in the deep blue sky. After arriving, I moved my comfy chair out onto the grass to view the night sky. The sound of crickets filled my ears, then the croaking of a frog. A symphony of sounds enchanted my senses as I relished in the feeling of new permission to love all of myself. Loving life is loving myself. Everything in my experience is in me. How could I best love myself? How could I best live? Life is in me, so I can love myself thus love life.

Taking time to look at nature grew into a greater respect and larger understanding of the depth of this system of life. The more love I shared, I showed, especially in nature, and the more beautiful my experiences became. How could I actively implement the greatest love I felt into my life constantly? How could I exercise my greatest loving capacity in the best way?

I lay in bed the next morning inspecting ants marching up and over the window sill. Their flawless system allowed them to march steadily, side by side in a line that wavered only slightly at places, pausing at moments, where small groups stood to the side. What were they communicating?

The tiny creatures were made up of three balls joined together, six feet and two small antennae that were constantly moving. Picking up information in brief moments of checking antennas of others heading in the opposite direction, they headed onward diligently.

I hopped up from my bed and headed to my bathroom. Entering the kitchen, I saw a small brown snake in the middle of the floor heading toward the back door. When I saw it, it saw me and we both froze. Who was more afraid of whom? I tossed a tissue toward it to see if it would move. It did, slightly.

I did an about-face, dressed then strode out the door to my neighbours, who sat in a small group on their porch. After my brief story one young man rose to the cheer of the others. The brave man, laughing nervously, followed me into my kitchen for a look but the snake had disappeared. He searched the space and found it curled under my sink beside the leftover paint cans. We recoiled.

The man left and returned with a bucket and stick and forced the snake inside. Then he carried the bucket to the grate at the edge of the road and pushed the coiled intruder through the crack. It was gone. Finally, we could go back to our day.

I sat in the living room with all the windows open. A nice breeze poured through and fluttered my sarong that hung loosely in the doorway. Candles flickered and soft music played while I drew diagrams in my notebook, looking for answers I could see but had to make sense of. I wanted to create something that demonstrated the key principles of universal brilliance so we could see our reality with more skill. I wanted to find a word, a phrase, a picture that showed the metaphor in simple, digestible form, explaining the forces and how we interacted with them.

I realised the possibility that other realms existed independently and having entirely different systems of understanding, different paradigms, and that maybe ours was unique to our locale. I imagined the possible variety of belief and my thought went to ancient symbols, depicting one in my notebook with a cross and eye at the top. The diagram could be a person with only one eye, turned on its side. Our vision viewed life horizontally but what was in between, existing as the meridian of our selves? What was there to know about the 'third' eye that sat atop of that meridian?

I knew that balance played an important part in this existence. There were two poles, but how did we manoeuvre ourselves in relation to these poles? Did the earth have to be one of the poles? Where was the other? Was it the sun? Did it matter, finding an answer to that?

Water is a majority of our physical makeup. Water is reflective. Therefore we are reflective. What is inside us, is outside of us, and vice versa. We would find outside, what existed inside. And what part did we have control over?

Fantasizing about the nature of experience expressed metaphorically, I considered our daily life. We slept horizontally. What side did most people sleep on? Did the position of the body relate in any way to the dreams a person had? Why did Egyptians bury their dead facing East? What did the Egyptians and other peoples of our past on Earth truly know about this experience? What about the Pyramids?

I had endless questions when it came to finding a metaphor for this life and toward this end, I had been eyeing the pyramids intensely. Their mystery, like life's mystery, held something simple yet elusive.

I picked up my pen and reminded myself, Look at life. The successfulness of your thoughts manifest in your experience. I wrote these words and looked around at my house, pleased with my life in my safe abode. My life was enjoyable: successful.

Excitedly I pondered the experiences that still awaited me. I knew there was still more work to do and I envisioned my future in the grandest terms imaginable, seeing the effects of success in my immediate surroundings.

Life is so funny. It is incredible. If I give in to it, paying constant attention to its subtle cues and humour, I can just laugh and laugh. When all the people of this world can laugh together and share love, we can get where we need to go. We could get to where we would feel incredible all the time, and to me that was a place worth finding.

Love was the answer I had been looking for and it had been there all along, just waiting for my attention. Loving my self became endlessly rewarding and enjoyable, so I had more love to share with others. I realised, after many days of working at the school, that it wasn't about trying to do lovely things, it was about being love.

The children could 'be' love, without knowing any barriers to its expression. This made me feel even more love, until all I could do was smile and laugh. But I kept this to myself. Who would believe me? Who would understand?

When I thought of the greatest feelings I had ever experienced, the biggest and happiest in my life, I saw my favourite times in life. Recalling happiness lifted up my state of being, relaxing me and enhancing my feelings of bliss. I needed to remind myself what I wanted to feel and to be aware of the emotions that I was experiencing.

I had been given a gift in this life: the ability to probe, unravel and inspect myself in life, and I savoured this opportunity. My skills developed daily so if I came to a point where I did not feel pure and loving, I knew there were thoughts blocking my perspective, like dark splotches on the kaleidoscope of this colourful world.

Upon closer inspection, I could see judgement or a recent event hanging in my thoughts, taking up space and drawing my attention. After seeing what was bothering me, I could release the issue with my breathing into the space expanding it, putting the situation into a larger perspective. I could feel more love and then saw what was needed to resolve the problem. So, I followed the cues inside and released whatever came for attention.

While teaching at school, I encouraged the children to be true to themselves. In everything I praised who they were, and their attempt at any task. I found the things they did well and mentioned it. I asked for improvement in areas they needed to develop. They listened and worked, enjoying the classroom and our dedicated effort to work on developing new skills.

At playtime they receded into their own worlds of games and fun in the yard. Sometimes, I watched through the window to see who was playing with whom, and who served whom. Some children walked alone and this concerned me. Language barriers needed to be overcome while others needed more self confidence.

Each student had their own unique version of wisdom and divinity. The classroom would revolve around one child at a time, learning to know each person and their gifts. The children naturally supported one another, teaching each other the skills they needed. This complemented my efforts as a teacher. My Thai aide stood by, smiling approval and helping the children understand events. Speaking Thai for some, she comforted those who had no idea where they had arrived.

The daily routine was reassuring for my students and they began to show more confidence in the classroom, speaking up and being noticed. The children became more at ease with each other and joked and played together. I smiled from my chair at their natural behaviours then drew their attention in to the colourful storybooks.

Each day after I got home from work a rush of thoughts poured through my head. I recalled the events of the day and evaluated the successfulness of the lessons I was working to achieve. My lesson plans were progressing well, and the children developed their English skills more and more every day. The students were enjoying themselves in the learning environment provided.

Safely nestled in my abode with music playing from my speakers a magical feeling made me laugh out loud as I watched the sun set against a brilliant pink sky. Life loved me so much it entertained me. Working through my thinking, I heard the words, 'I love you.' A gentle voice always there within me, lending support and encouragement, reverently.

This love feeling is bigger than anything, I wrote in my notebook, as the words rolled from my pen. My attention synchronized perfectly with moments that bespoke my connection with life: it was speaking to me, directly. I was being listened to and responded to like loving parents who stood around me, pervasively all the time. They waited for me to become aware of the freedom of living consciously, of being aware of my conscious connection to my wonderful essence.

I sat energized on my chair watching my vibrant green yard, bursting with positive emotion. I was truly loved by life and I cried from the awareness. Tears streamed down my face as I smiled, feeling safe in a moment of peaking inner emotion. Immersed in love climax, blissful excitement rolled through me. Beaming bright with energy I opened more to the sensation of love, feeling more thoroughly our connection.

Elated, I stood to feel that I was still in my physical body, feeling as if I had won the lottery of love. I could feel my blissful state in my body so I sat down again. So light, the connection so strong, I cried from pure pleasure. I was the richest woman on Earth in my simple green tye-dyed dress, on my blue sofa in bare feet.

'Love is seductive,' I wrote. 'It pulls you into it.'

Life was showing me many ways to feel and know love. I lay down on the sofa and my attention tuned to a motor in the distance. A fear passed through about the longevity of this joyful experience, as if it could slip away.

Then, the words sang to me, 'I'm going nowhere.' More reassurance. Bliss.

I thought about plant life in my yard and whether plants experienced life like I did. Were they using senses to perceive their surroundings? We slept when the plants slept and we were awake with them too. Did we dream with them? Humans lived side by side with plant life and treated it like a form of scenery. I could feel love with the greenery, appreciating its beauty. I told it so.

The earth needs our love, were the next words I was inspired to write. Feeling full of emotion I turned my thoughts to what I could do to help. I felt Earth call to me, pleading me to educate people and open them to the life that awaited them: joy, happiness and love, all there, ready to be embraced. The feeling was so real that I wanted to run into the street, throw up my arms and shout out that life loved us. We could make this place so incredible if we became aware. I could just feel it.

I stared through the doorway where bright light was flooding in. We needed to heal ourselves, and in doing so, we would heal Earth. I just knew this was true. Everything around us was speaking to us loud and clear. Life was symmetry on a grand scale. What was here was there and there was no escaping that. There were endless forms of expression but we would only become truly free when we woke up to see ourselves expressed clearly in our environment. The answers to our questions were everywhere. Our situations, on all levels, were looking us straight in the face.

'Love is so grand! Life is so great! Look at what we have! Look at the brilliant mysteries! Life is full of wonder and amazement!' I can love life because I am part of it, I am closest and easiest to love because I am always here with myself! Every person can love themselves and reap the benefits of a life filled with love. I knew life could be experienced in this Joy at all times. I wanted to know how. I wanted my life to be Joy.

It was mid-September and that meant one thing: monsoon season with torrential downpours everyday. The space at home and school was moist and cool. Each morning before leaving I put on my silver rain suit and powered through puddles on the way to work. The rain suit held up well, but the buttons and sleeves were too short and rain leaked onto my clothes. Often I was half soaked by the time I arrived at school.

After a few weeks of commuting in steady rain I developed the flu. I was ill at home for four days and I barely moved from the bed. After three nights cooped up in my bedroom, I needed a change and I wanted to communicate with Joe.

All afternoon I gathered my energy to drive down the road to the Internet café. Hoping letters from Joe would lift my spirits. I parked my scooter at the restaurant where I regularly used the Internet. The owner, a friendly Thai lady, greeted me with hello and a smile, using her few words of English.

When I sat down she asked if I was feeling well. When I explained my situation she offered to make a remedy of chicken broth soup with rice to take home. I had barely eaten for days so I was grateful to have something homemade. As she prepared the food I scrolled through Joe's loving words. They were just what I needed to hear!

After a few minutes she came out of the kitchen and asked me if I wanted to take a shower, telling me she could prepare a basin of warm water in her bathroom from which I could rinse myself. I gratefully accepted. The cold showers at my house had been excruciating during the fever.

Kneeling on a folded towel on the warm tile floor of her bathroom I ladled warm water over my back, relishing every moment. With each scoop the warm kindness poured over my skin, comforting me in my hour of need. I felt so grateful to be offered this help, just when I needed a loving person to come to my rescue. I revelled in the sensation of love, then dried off and dressed, feeling much better.

"Thank you so much," I smiled to my helper when I was finished. A container of chicken soup had been placed in my scooter basket.

"Get well," she said. She would take no money and smiled at me like a mother. I thanked her and got on my scooter. With my basket full of delicious takeout food, I drove home full of appreciation beaming at life's love for me, feeling held in a tender embrace. Once home I bundled up on the sofa eating warm rice soup, appreciating the kindness of the lady who helped me. It was true that kind and helpful people were a part of my life. I went to bed feeling satisfied and nourished.

After doing light housework the next day I felt better and I spent some time on my living room sofa. As candles flickered the day quietly ebbed into the early evening. Listening to Finley Quaye sing about 'hyper planes.' I imagined them to be a state of mind where a person could operate in life with wisdom and clarity, floating with life while fully enjoying the experience. I was sure that reaching 'hyper planes' would benefit our experience. I wondered if there was such an enduring, pleasurable and spiritual state available within our experience. It felt to me as if there was, and I wanted to find it.

During this pondering I could feel that my energy level was cutting short, the circuit breaking. Insights weren't flowing as endlessly and easily as usual. I realised that my recent illness was causing my early burnout, because my body was tired from combating the virus. Despite my fatigue I still wanted to spend my time thinking about the mysteries of life. I had never worked so hard on anything in my life. I was bound to take my experience higher and higher into what was unknown to me, answering the call.

I was still feeling weak the next afternoon but I forced myself to go outside, take a ride and enjoy the scenery. I drove along the ocean witnessing familiar teal sparkles. I smiled back at its beauty. I rode into the beach area to get some rice and sweet papaya salad, taking in the sights and new faces bubbling about. A few meters from my favourite street side stand, I came up behind a car that was moving slowly for a left turn. Coasting comfortably just behind it, I decided to veer around it rather than stop so I moved toward the right side in order to pass.

As I came alongside the car I was startled by the proximity. I felt like I was losing my balance and veered toward the car. Then, some unseen force pushed me upright and away from the car. I drove away stunned, excited, breathless.

What was it that had helped me regain my balance? I parked my bike safely at the side of the road and shook my head at the strange occurrence. Who had helped me? And where had they come from?

The event was one of the most unique I had ever experienced known. An external force had sprung into action, taking me from bliss, through danger, to safety and bliss again. Remarkable. I was humbled and awestruck.

By Sunday evening, I was feeling restless and needed some conversation and the pleasures of human contact. I headed down to a beach side club where I knew there would be some tourists to share some time in English. Soon after I arrived I was introduced to someone new who had been staying on the island for about two weeks. His name was Eric and he was from France. We began chatting, working on our combined knowledge of French and English. He was interesting and told me that he worked for the 'dooble vay, dooble vay, eF' in France. Oh the WWF? He warned me not to pet the stray animals on the island because of the possible afflictions. He was also an Astrologist.

Eric and I decided to leave the thumping music of the club and crossed the road to the land bridge that lay over the sand to the water's edge. We sat on the rails and I watched him prepare a cigarette from the tools inside his belt pack. We ended up talking there for hours while looking up at the night sky full of stars. I told him that watching the stars made me feel calm inside and I liked the opportunity to sit quietly, observing the sounds of the night and the stillness in the air. The stars and their role continued to perplex me as we supposed the meaning of their presence. I couldn't help feeling some connection to them.

Eric said that Astrology was a useful system and that I may be able to understand my tendencies better then he offered some valuable insights. He told me some things about my star sign, Scorpio, and his sign and the types of things he dealt with as a result of being a Libra. 'Libras are into balance, but we aren't rooted anywhere. It can be frustrating', he said. 'A Scorpio with a Sagittarius can be a good match because you are both seekers.'

About eleven o'clock, I decided to head home to get a good night sleep. I had made a new friend in Eric and was happy to have found someone with whom I could discuss some thoughts about the stars. Again, a stranger had come at the right time and was able to give me information so that I could again take my thoughts forward. We said goodnight and I headed home.

At home that evening I sat on my chair listening to music. A reggae beat with rhythmic sounds made me want to dance but I didn't feel like standing. My hands were propped on my elbows that rested on the wooden arms of the chair and my hands moved to the music naturally as I watched them.

After a short time I noticed the movements of my left hand were smooth and flowing with a certain charm quite different from my right. I studied them closely wondering what was going on and why they weren't displaying the same passion of movement. My left hand moved and turned elegantly with the beat of the music. It seemed to have a mind of its own, dancing with pleasure. My right hand was sloppy and moved haltingly.

I rested my right hand in my lap and focused on the movement of my left. It seemed all I had to do was desire it to dance and it moved of its own accord, easily to the beat, graceful and pleasant to watch.

Then I rested my left hand on my lap and encouraged the right. There was a profound difference in the movements of both hands. I had to consciously control the movements of my right, like a puppet master with a distracted pupil.

This made me want to explore the experience of my left and right hands. I sat in my chair with my arms up and hands clasped behind my head. I leaned the chair back against the wall, knowing my thumbs would touch first and I would rest there. I couldn't see the wall behind me, but I knew I would stop at contact. I leaned back and was surprised by the contact my right thumb made with the wall as if it was shocked to make contact with the wall so soon. But then I thought about my left thumb and I realised that it touched the wall gracefully and gently, as if it had known all along the outcome.

I thought about something I had I made up as a teenager, a phrase that was like a riddle. And I turn to the left, ah, thank you. It seemed to behold a secret somehow. What was there to discover about the left side of my body, or the left side of life?

I sat in the chair, then thinking there was a bug on my shirt, I pulled out the folds of my shirt. I found a small silver star. Smiling, I took it as a sign to go out and see if there were any stars in the sky. I got up and went to my porch and looked up to see a bright star, one just for me. The world was a beautiful symphony playing together.

Looking up at the stars and night sky, admiring the natural beauty all around me, I thought about the Western society in which I had been brought up. I considered our incessant consumerism and the teachings that led us in that direction. Was that what we really wanted? Had we gone too far with consumerism?

Then I laughed, imagining a future where we would tear down all the stores and malls we were now feverishly putting up, reducing excessiveness in favour of a life more true to our spirits.

I wanted to see a life around me where humans lived a simple joyful existence, a life with meaningful conscious connection between people, animals and the earth where we lived. I wanted to see us get back to nature and enjoy a more natural and free way of living.

I heard the neighbour's gate close, perhaps the last person in for the night. I watched my neighbours sometimes, all turning in together at the end of the day. I knew Thais shared sleeping quarters, lying on mats side by side on the floors, close and comfortable. They had each other at night, sleeping together in their cozy homes, while my feeling of loneliness crept in.

My mind wandered to others alone like me, to the woes of the world - the malaise of our minds as the malaise of this planet. I was troubled by stumbling over the same obstacles, jousting with others in my experience, being confused about my place and purpose. Now, finally, I was beginning to see an end to my suffering. This made me think of others who continued to suffer with no end in sight.

I knew that our 'sickness' stemmed from errors in thought, which represented itself in physical illnesses, showing us that something was going wrong. Healing our selves needed to take precedence. We needed to come together with our minds and bodies and become aware of the connection between people, our individual physical experience and the energy of our thoughts. Everything was intimately connected and this was becoming clearer and clearer. We needed healers, we needed risers who would take our intelligence higher, then we would necessarily heal ourselves, our environment and our planet. We needed to heal our minds and our selves: mentally, soulfully. We could do it. It was a matter of desire and I knew I was ready to see a change.

I could see clearly that Earth was a large perfect organism. We were only part of that organism. I could see how people believed that we were the only thing that mattered. I looked at all that we had done to the Earth and could see that she still loved us, even after all. Mother Nature continued to grow and produce for us. Now that is love! Knowing a love like that was how I was sure we could all feel. And in some moments, it was easy for me to feel that way.

I knew that if we could become aware of the intricacies of our lives, as we weaved with others around us, we could open up to a much larger awareness in this experience. I knew it was a process. Everyday I worked at relieving myself of a lifetime of fear conditioning, as I watched beautiful newness open up to being known to me. My helpers never tired of teaching me what I most wanted to learn.

I have got to fully believe in what I believe in, or else there is no point. I must go for what I want. I just wanted to experience it as 'perfect,' because in my clearest moments, I knew it was perfect.

Practice being there, in the feelings you want.

In my clearest moments, deep within a journey of my mind, I could see that what I was experiencing in my physical reality wasn't 'real' as I had believed. My life was something I was experiencing in response to my desires. I could choose to live and perceive it in any way I preferred. It was all for me, and up to me.

I breathed a sigh of relief knowing the 'seriousness' of life had been removed. Chuckling at it now, I could see that I had been living with its limitations planted deep within my psyche. It was fear that had caused my dim outlook on life. Now I pulled back the curtains and bathed in brightness. I could be as bold as I wanted to try the wonderful things that came in to my thoughts, especially if 'it' wasn't real anyway.

I was seeing how deep my processes could go. My thoughts were strong and powerful as they developed and improved. Examining and postulating into great freeing experiences, I reached further into increased awareness. I knew there was a state of mind where I didn't have to think so much, where I could flow and experience living life fruitfully. I knew that one activity replaced the other but I still spent most of my time examining life. It was so fascinating.

I rose from the chair and moved onto my porch. I said goodnight to the stars and the night sky and went inside. I picked up my notebook and wrote a few words. The trees told me something today that is between us. It was incredible to feel as if I had friends in the trees. It was as if the tree were a loving parental figure wanting to help me feel free and experience true love. A brilliant force caressed my experience as if I were being played like an instrument, coaxing me into feelings of exuberance.

The next morning I moved the chair on the yard to observe life in the daytime. Scooters buzzed beyond my hedge, helmets whizzing past, but the yard was mostly private. I curled up my legs tucked in my tye-dyed dress and began to be entertained by the creatures around me. There were many beautiful butterflies surrounding my fluttering over flowering bushes, unrolling their long pink tongues to taste nectar in the heart of the flower. Coasting on the breeze from branch to branch, contentedly enjoying their existence, I watched them in awe.

Hand washing my clothing connected me to the local women. I knelt beside the washing basin on my bathroom floor sloshing the water as I worked the fabric with my hands, in moments of quiet time making my clothes clean and fresh.

I dashed outside with my wet clothes to hang them on the washing line. Resting on the wire was a beautiful green dragonfly so I slowly walked up close, speaking softly, asking to inspect it. It was brilliant green with black patterns and I watched as the middle of its body, moved in and out, breathing. The body was the size of the tip of my finger holding a pair of slender wings and a long narrow tail, shimmering impeccably with translucent colours of the rainbow. Tiny threadlike veins ran the length of the wings while they glistened in the sunlight, moving up and down, slowly.

Large independent bulbous eyes examined me. Its head turned on a spindle neck. Then its gaze lifted as the buzz of other bugs flew overhead, its eyes moving to follow them. So tiny and compact, yet complete. The moment was bittersweet.

Examining life around me was like riding a wave of consciousness way up high above it all. I began to hold within me an understanding that permeated this environment: invisible but magnificent, communicating but not demanding to be heard, subtle and on all levels. The Earth as my real mother and the sky as my real father, and I, a child of the Universe.

I thought about the purpose of experience to test limits to see what we could become, how good we could be, how great we could become. I thought that was a nice option. Being good in my own way felt right. People had many ways to be good and to show the essence of their goodness. I had come to understand that I need not worry that I didn't yet possess habits that enabled me to always demonstrate goodness. I had witnessed many kind ways other people had shown me. I gave the best of what I had to offer, by being the most genuine me, and as I threw off judgements and opinions that had restricted me. Being my truest self was getting easier and easier.

What you see and think is what you get, I had written in my notebook. Know what you are thinking. It's all in your perspective. I knew this to be true and it concerned me when I felt negativity or an undesirable thought passing through my head. I reaffirmed my position and my strength in choosing what I wanted as part of my reality. I don't let it get me. Negativity may be there, but it is not here. There are many things there and that is one. There are many good things here. There's only a relationship between me and what is there if I choose there to be one, via thought and emotion. With no thought or emotion concerning that, that stays there. I held the power to my experience.

The communication between 'self' and life had continued to expand me and I moved around during the days smiling to myself, knowing I had become aware of a big secret. Life's nuances in cryptic and poetic forms enchanted me. The more I appreciated the nuances, the more they came, rich with meaning about abundance and love, freedom and bliss. Just what shell was cracking, around what?

Each day I worked on opening and trusting in life, and I had seen my doubts truly diminishing. I seldom felt fear inside and whenever I did, it was easier to release its power over me. I had almost given up doubting the extent to which my senses could take me. Negativity just seemed like a waste of time.

I studied with my rational thought processes, comparing what I had heard with what I was seeing. I wanted to be sure I wasn't drifting somewhere that didn't make sense to me. I needed to learn about the path I was on, and to know how I had gotten to where I was. In this place my thoughts were much more creative because I knew I couldn't be held back. They were like balloons with varying wisdom hanging in space all around me. I could pull down any one of my choosing for closer inspection.

Gail invited me to the Vegetarian Festival. She had been talking about it at school for weeks and wanted to know how I would react to the unusual sights. Dressed in white we drove down to the busy locale where crowded processions brought Phuket town to a standstill. Delicious vegetarian food was served from street carts. Absolutely no meat was eaten for the nine day festival. Chinese in origin, the festival's roots told the tale of an travelling Opera troupe from China stricken with malaria that was restored to health by eating only vegetarian meals.

The gods were invited to descend to street level by following lantern poles set up in temples. Many people participated in the religious ceremony. They wore flowers around their necks, dressed in their best clothing as they walked in processions. A ritualistic cleansing was demonstrated more dramatically by those wearing bizarre costumes with knives, swords or other sharp items pierced through their cheeks. These displays were religious, to bring blessings in their search for redemption.

We walked along the streets in silent amazement. We came upon a man a man in a complete trance, dancing like a shaman, eyes rolled back in his head. The sight caught me by surprise and I knew he was doing something unusual and unsettling. His body shook and moved in the middle of a circle others made for him, as if they benefited from his display.

Gail and I ate delicious snacks from the street carts then headed back to the beach with another new experience to expand our minds.

One afternoon I was painting and drawing, using my creativity and feeling encouraged by the outcomes of my concentrated efforts. There was one painting I was hesitant about working on because I ran out of paint and the new shade looked off. I wondered if I should stop or continue with it. It was a picture of a girl looking up at the moon with her blonde hair falling back onto her neck. I named it Sister Golden Hair. It reminded me of a friend so I continued with it, blending the paint as best I could. In the end it turned out well and I made a note in my book reminding myself not to give up and that the finished product would always look different at the end of the process.

As I sat on my sofa, leaning over the painting using the colours that appealed to me, I listened to the endless crowing of the roosters that lived in a pen in the back yard. I had never lived near chickens before and came to know the drawbacks. During the day they were let out to wander the yard freely, crowing and pecking at the ground with their sharp red beaks. Often they ended up meandering across my grass, taking in what seeds I had to offer. I watched them through my window, having been roused from my concentrated efforts, as they strolled like royalty across the lawn.

This day I decided to go out and shoo them off the yard, feeling as if I needed some quiet time after hearing them crow for hours. I walked out onto the grass as I had seen my neighbour do many times and waved my arms above my head. The score of hens ran for cover but the rooster stood its ground, looking me directly in the eye. It appeared human-like, stiff and poised with bright, well-groomed feathers, holding what seemed to be an expression of defiance.

Then, gallantly, slowly, and ever so assuredly, he strolled toward the back of the yard. The whole while keeping its eye on me, seeming to stand down only because of the overwhelming size difference. I left him walking toward the back of the yard. But within an hour they were all back!

The season continued with many days of rain but one afternoon, the weather suddenly turned sunny and warm again. Everyone was outside enjoying the weather immensely, our moods lighter. All around, I could feel the energy as light and permeable. If we could consciously take our feelings higher into this state, we would benefit from the change. I imagined the feeling we could generate collectively to the point of physical, psychical climax and it excited me.

Sitting in a chair imagining our human potential, I experienced the familiar feeling of physical glee characteristic of my highest moments. I recalled the feeling of my extraordinary experience at the beach with Simon. It seemed as if I had gone through feelings of joy and pleasure to some kind of climax and then I was over the top. Just where were these feelings taking me?

I was being coaxed onward, inward, somewhere into the unknown. In these higher reaches I could see that life on earth seemed pretty interesting and lively. Here we were living in these incredible, self-maintaining bodies, having a life that we could lead anyway we liked. I dreamed of all the wonderful things I wanted to do as a free person in this existence, smiling, feeling safe and ready to do them. Higher love was the feeling of a complete battery recharge. I had to know and remember that I had the power and tools to free myself from any thoughts that held me back, in any situation.

The rain had stayed at bay so I went to the beach to watch the sunset. Surreal colours throughout the sky, permeating one another, making something greater, transcendent, our prayers answered by the beauty of the dance.

After returning home I found a quiet peacefulness and settled in to enjoy the evening. As the night descended I moved my cosy chair out onto the grass to watch the darkening sky in all its wonder. I sat down and wrapped a sarong around my legs to keep out the chill.

Whenever I was in natural surroundings my mind went to the other incredible experiences I had had within nature. It was as if it loved me to think about its mysteries. I wondered why I was able to have that incredible experience by the beach, and why it had happened in that way. I wondered whether the water had something to do with it. Then my head started nodding, moving up and down on its own. I immediately thought 'What is this?' Then it dawned on me. That's my answer! Yes, the water did have something to do with the experience.

Understanding the communication silenced me and I sat back, closed my eyes and slipped passively into my senses. My hearing unbridled, I registered the sounds of the night as they breezed over my skin to my ears. I focused on the sound of insects from deep within the jungle. I heard their rhythmic existence, in buzzing harmony. For no reason my eyes popped open to the light of a firefly high up in the sky. I saw its light three times until it stopped then I saw transferred my attention to a star in the night sky.

Looking out at the galaxy, I wondered about civilizations beyond our reality. I wondered how close or far away they actually were. I wondered about other realms, other dimensions living here on Earth, knowing energy vibrated at different levels, rendering only some vibrations visible to us. My mind ran with possibilities that other existences shared Earth with us, and I looked around into the dark night, smiling at the possibility.

The night got colder so I picked up my chair and went back inside and sat down to write. When I do things with loving intent, embodying my truest idea of kindness and caring, I love life more. It appears to me that life wants to be loved. I smell the flowers, inspect the creatures, and admire the systems around me and this feels good.

I wanted to communicate with life. I wanted to build on the intimacy of my experiences within it, appreciating it ever more in new ways, knowing it was always there for the experiencing. I could touch life by touching bushes, trees, leaves and other things that breathed air, while I enjoyed and admired their differences. I loved to inspect the insects as independent forms of life, fascinated by their miniature capsules, unique and self-contained. Taking care to see life in these ways I could give positive attention to my surroundings, while lending an ear to the voice of life.

Saturday I drove into the Kata Beach area. I became ensconced in the tourist world again, shaking my head at the bizarre transition. I headed to an Internet café to connect with friends online, hoping to see some interesting foreigners, nicely tanned and looking relaxed. Gorgeous people filled the scene, smiling and dancing in the streets. Most were returning from Scuba Diving or snorkelling day trips. Sliding through the scene with ease I returned to my scooter, feeling the need to get away for a longer ride.

I toured out onto the main road and drove in the damp toward the other side of the island. I needed this new scenery and joy filled my heart as I cruised along. As I neared the town, evening traffic began to fill the road as the rain clouds built along the horizon. I looked up in the distance, lifting my eyes, and saw the most beautiful rainbow spread across the sky. Lightness and laughter spilled from the people who lined the road as they gazed up at the sight. In my rear view mirror I caught sight of an orange hue. I pulled my scooter over to the side of the road, and stood in awe of the beautiful moment. Ahead of me shone a brilliant rainbow gracing the sky in full view, a glistening arc of light. Behind me a deep, rich sunset cast orange and pink colours from horizon to horizon. The sky lit up with the majesty of a symphony, all before our very eyes. Everyone stopped to smile and gaze up at the lights. I stood in awe of the sight. Inside my body a feeling reached deep within my soul, down into the abyss of forever within me, resonating with a memory of truth and brilliance. It was God's gift to my eyes and I received it into my being as fully as I could. Tears came to my eyes. I had been chosen to experience this spectacular delight. I accepted it as a personal token of love.

Cars continued to move along the road, a few stopping, but mostly the movement continued as people pressed on with their duties. Others who observed the miracle shared a smile with me. I returned to my scooter forever changed by a new moment of truth.

I drove home delighted and prepared my living room for a night of solitary communion surrounded by candles, soft music and relaxing ambiance. My own company was worth the extra effort as I snuggled into my philosopher's chair, titillated by incense smoke tendrils, and mellow music with lyrics sung especially for me.

The smoke danced delicately with intricately changing forms never duplicating its manifestation of beauty, freely moving from one shift to the next. A feeling of bliss encompassed me as I watched and felt it fully. Life was communicating with me directly with the greatest love. I knew I was only beginning to open my eyes to the love that was available to me. A gentle breeze joined me in revelry, fluttering my purple sarong in the doorway. Joyful awareness rippled through the room. The lyrics echoed around the room, 'Try to make the fantasy come true.' I was in a love dream.

Listening to the music, feeling love inside me, bliss permeated my experience. I could feel it surrounding me and infiltrating through me, seduced by life in the most loving, fun way. It romanced me, directing my attention to the words in the song at just the right moments to tell me about its undying love. I felt so beautiful.

I thought about Joe and I wondered if he was missing me as much as I was missing him. I wanted to call him, to hear his voice. My mind ran off into doubting thoughts about whether it would work for us in the future. Fear crept into my thoughts and turned everything negative. Then the sound of wax dripping on the table from the three tiered candelabra broke the dark spell. Keep the balance I said to myself.

A stiff breeze chimed my ceramic fish and fluttered my sarong in the doorway. It was a sign that said "Pay attention to the subtleties, you'll be shown what you are doing and reminded of where it is you want to go. Just be aware."

More and more my mind was going somewhere, lulled somewhere unfamiliar, but beautiful. Unfamiliar, yet familiar. I was in a playful relationship with life where it made jokes for me. I was only beginning to open to the communication. I was learning from the experience as if it were an open book. I eagerly flipped through the pages, needing to read and inhale the meaning.

Just ask the questions. Listen to life and when you think about it, you will get the answers.

Even though I didn't understand everything presented to me, it felt good to be in the presence of beautiful teachings that I could digest at my own pace. The more I trusted life, the more belief I had, and the more I could let go of the reins and let life lead me into the bliss of its magical mystery. I rode in a sweet saddle of my faith.

I wanted to know about the pyramids and the secrets they held. I always visualised the Pyramids at Giza, thinking they were the most magnificent structures on Earth. I felt a great deal about them that could instruct us about our present reality. They seemed to behold something far greater than what we knew and I yearned to know more. I felt sure that they held powerful secrets of this existence.

One day sitting comfortably on my sofa I began drawing a reference diagram in my notebook, as I forged onward to find a more revealing metaphor. I drew a cross that seemed to demonstrate balance and pointed to the four cardinal directions. It seemed that the pyramid was a tool that may help us understand our destiny. The pyramids were signposts to a heightened experience, unique and perfect metaphors of this world.

Looking at the word pyramid I saw a reflection of the last three letters against the other three, with the starting point of the alphabet, 'A', as the centre point. 'Mid' struck me as meaning, 'me', and 'pyr' stuck out in my mind as meaning a reflector, totalling finally as a mirror to the self. Shocked by this conjunction I thought about the actual pyramids and their purpose and function on the planet. I considered them as reflectors of our state of being, reverberating messages of our 'selves' across the planet and up into the sky.

I could see that life was constantly demonstrating itself in clever metaphors and the more I looked for them, the more I found. I realised I could regularly gather more information from any situation, objectively reducing each situation to its base elements, then seeing clarity in its presentation.

Looking at my own surroundings I could see that my thoughts and approach to life had improved. I knew this because I could see a better environment around me. To me the changes and benefits were obvious, as now my life seemed to be something quite enjoyable in comparison to the struggle of my past.

I was happy to now be solving the conundrum of my life, realising that part of my problem had been the perspective of my situation; another part was the lack of understanding of my level of responsibility; and thirdly that I needed to appreciate the good things that I brought myself. Looking back where I had been versus where I was now, I was filled with joy and a pleasurable feeling that I intended to carry with me the rest of my life.

Since there had been so much rain on the island lately the nights took on a different feel. I discovered that there were many frogs living in a tiny stream that ran alongside my house, trickling down from the jungle-covered hills in my behind. I could hear a chorus of frogs croaking during the evenings. One night in bed I listened closely to their sounds. It was then that I discovered something magical. To my joyful surprise the frogs took great care with their melodies. One frog had a very deep voice and acted as bass. It seemed to be the foundation for the rest which would join in rhythmically, one by one. They all sounded different, some higher in pitch and some lower in tone. I could separately identify them from their sounds! Together they croaked as if happy, pleased with their collective melody. All at once, a new frog joined in randomly and threw off the whole bunch. They all noticed right away that something wasn't right, and struggled on for a few more bars. Everything crashed and came to a silent halt. Then they would start up again, one at a time, re-establishing their rhythm and melody. And again, one of them would croak off key or out of place and they would stop, dedicated to perfection as if performing a perfect symphony. I listened, riveted to their choruses, convinced they were conscious of their goal of making music. It was truly magical to hear and it sent me to sleep with a smile.

Chapter 12 – Blue Sky

My house sparkled with light the night my three girlfriends came over. Eunice had come down from Bangkok to stay for the weekend, so I invited the two close associates - Gail and Nadine - from the school to join us for a 'hen' night.

We gathered around my coffee table drinking beer that Gail had brought, talking about life and love. Candles flickered in the gentle breeze that also fluttered my purple sarong hanging in the doorway.

Bjork shouted out her Islandic melodies while we shared perspectives of the world around us, laughing with our beverages. After a while we retired to the sofa set and talked about living in the village area of Kata and Karon, on the South West corner of Phuket.

Nadine was from Australia, and her bright turquoise eyes shone as she spoke in a smooth Sydney accent. "I've seen angels," she said, widening our eyes. "They're all around us. They have a shimmery appearance and they are always near you, and always believe in you. They help you when you ask, they come when you call."

"But how do I know they're there if I can't see them?" Gail asked, astonished.

"You can feel them, if you try," she offered.

"Something helped me with my scooter that day," I said, remembering a time of need.

"That was your angel," Nadine smiled. I smiled, too.

"I can feel them. If I see a feather or a dove I know it's a sign." Her angelic expression captivated us. We all sat back to contemplate her words, looking up the walls at my artwork.

"That sounds like religious bunk," Eunice retorted from across the coffee table. "I was raised Catholic and I have been told so much rubbish, you wouldn't believe it."

We sat dumbfounded at her bold confession.

"Angels exist," said Nadine. "I've seen them."

"Tell us what they look like," Gail entreated. She was on the edge of her seat and I leaned in.

"The face is so clear, you can see through it. They look at you with love. They shine so brightly you can't see them. They just stay there in your space, floating," Nadine explained.

"Above ground?" Gail gasped.

We all laughed at her reaction.

"They're in the angelic realm so it looks like they are elevated." We needed time to absorb the presence of angels in our awareness. Our eyes wandered up the walls lit by flickering candlelight.

"I like your artistic style," Gail said, looking at my art.

"Thanks," I said, feeling grateful and appreciated.

"The paintings are simple, yet deep." Gail said.

"Do you know what you are painting when you begin painting it?" Eunice asked.

"No, I don't usually have a plan. Something just comes out on the paper," I said, feeling more comfortable about displaying them.

"They come alive in the most interesting way," Gail continued, eyeing the five pieces. "In this one I see pyramids with the four elements of life: water, air, earth and fire. I can see energy in motion, waves under the Earth. I see lifeforms under the ocean: aliens, love, and prosperity; cycles and waves, ebbs and flows."

Nadine nodded in agreement, smiling at me brightly.

"There's a change coming in humanity, where we move toward an experience of life where everything is good." When Nadine said the word 'good' there was a prolonged sense of comfort and truth in her meaning.

We sat quietly to ponder her words, recalling prophecies and discussing our own perspectives on where humanity was headed. We paused, deep in introspection, then all snapped out of it at exactly the same time.

What caused this lucid moment of connection, all of us glued to the spot within our own spotlights? No one else mentioned the synchronicity. What did we share in those moments?

It was late and my guests started to ready themselves to leave. I thanked them for their compliments and kind words. We hugged one another and said goodnight. Eunice kissed my cheek goodnight then went into her bedroom.

I prepared for bed and sat with my journal, my mind buzzing with excitement. They really liked my art! Gail's words held so much meaning when she spoke about my craft. What had I connected with? What potential was waiting for me?

Truth showed itself to me in a powerful way so I endeavoured to speak my truth, knowing others would gain from my words. I knew that we could share truth and love honestly with all that surrounded us.

What I will do will involve all things. What ever I want to do, I must put together. Look at me now. I write, I paint, and I listen to my feelings and my body. Everything is developing beautifully for me. I feel extremely happy with myself. It was simply magical experiencing life right now, and most importantly, I was living in the moment.

I learned that being aware was important but I hadn't figured how to best do so. To what extent did I need to observe and what was the best way to remain open? I plodded onward knowing I would understand more in time.

Saturday afternoon Eunice and I went to the beach. Her orange bikini suited her svelte frame. She wanted to suntan so we planned for a few hours in the sunshine. It was something I seldom did because the environment was so hot during the day. I had aquired a tan just from daily activity living in the heat. At the beach we found an umbrella and settled onto some chairs in the shade.

"How long do you think you're going to stay in Thailand?" she asked, adjusting her bikini. I didn't have an answer and my indecision caused me to gaze out toward the water.

"I haven't decided yet," I answered, looking down at my sketchbook and black pencils.

"You'd better go to him before he finds someone else to love," she said out of the blue, then scampered off to the water's edge.

I stared at the horizon, sure that Joe's love for me was true and that he would wait for me. But I knew he was becoming restless, anticipating in my arrival.

I sat alone under the umbrella pondering the blank page that lay on my lap. My hand hovered over the paper as I looked down. Then it came to me, a drawing ready to be made. Shadows danced across the paper, beguiling, teasing. My pencil followed the lines that were generously given. As I worked my mind travelled to other worlds of sound and space.

The heat was enveloping us and we soon felt the need to retreat. We packed up our things and lightly padded over hot sand to my scooter. We travelled home where I spent the rest of the afternoon completing the drawing with watercolours. As I painted I realised that life was a bountiful harvest and it could be really easy, that creation was simply wonderful and that time was as elastic as we needed it to be.

I sat on my porch painting, filling in the shape of my hand with flowers, making the trim of the umbrella a waterfall. The pencil became a solid, creative sword, while the white space carved room for infinite possibilities waiting to take form. The colours came alive and the image burst from the page.

Eunice and I went to get takeout dinner from a restaurant that had caught her eye. We ordered the best tom yum coconut soup I had ever eaten. It was fresh and spicy with juicy tomatoes and mushrooms, fragrant lemon grass, and was served in a large tub. We bought two orders and motored back home.

"Have you heard from Joe?" she asked, excited about my romance.

"Yes, he writes almost everyday."

"What are you waiting for? You must go to him," she said, between mouthfuls of soup and coconut jasmine ride. She was single and her yearning for the 'right' relationship was evident in her encouragement.

"He could have stayed here in Thailand and we could have been living here together. Now I have to go all the way to Norway where its cold and he's at school," I said, feeling disappointed that we hadn't been able to run off into the sunset from the moment we met.

"You have your university degree, he's trying to get one. He wants to build a future for himself and you," she said, between slurps.

"We could have made it work here in Thailand. I would have helped him. He wouldn't have had to work. My teacher's salary is more than enough. We could be living the dream right now," I said.

"Did you tell him you felt this way when he was here?" she asked.

"Yes, I asked him to stay here with me, but he didn't listen. He insisted that we go back to the real world."

"You have to swallow your pride and go," she said.

"I know." Somehow I knew the decision had already been made.

Eunice left the next day on a bus to the Phuket airport. As the bus pulled away she leaned out of the window and blew kisses shouting 'I love you!'

As the bus pulled away, I returned the salutation then looked around at nearby eyes that had been watching the scene. I smiled then I motored back to my house for the evening. Her words about Joe rang in my head.

The next weekend I decided to cruise into town to check out the newest batch of tourists snuggling up to one week of freedom. Some were intoxicated and this was amusing as I drove along past them to the Internet café. I parked my bike and noticed someone standing across the road.

Captivated by his clarity, astounded by his presence, I stood staring. He held my gaze. His white cotton shirt billowed gently in the breeze that also sent dust particles into the air. We examined each other. Striking blue eyes shone back at me, his kind face framed by sun kissed shoulder length hair. His eyes were fixed on me, reflecting calmness. Time stood still.

I pulled myself from the exchange to enter the café. All the terminals were occupied. I exited the shop wondering why. As soon as I approached my bike another man appeared beside me, smiling. His blue eyes dazzled charmingly as he spoke. All the while the man across the road stood, his eyes still focussed on me.

"Welcome to Kata," said the man at my side, his words demanding my attention. "I'm Tariq. I work at the scuba shop," he said, pointing to the sign above the store.

"Hello," I said, noticing the man across the street approaching. His proximity demonstrated a friendship with Tariq.

"Come with us to a restaurant," he said, decidedly.

I paused to consider his proposition.

"You need to eat, right?" he probed.

I felt fine about joining them in a public place and smiled while he fixated with penetrating eyes. We started walking and he held his arm behind my back to lead me down the sidewalk to the restaurant. We went to the patio and sat down at a large table.

"This is Mario," said Tariq. "He is from Italy, I am from Egypt," he boasted, drawing me in. I searched his eyes for Egyptian secrets.

Within moments we were handed colourful cocktails. Other tourists said hello to Tariq and Mario as a few more people joined our table.

"Cassandra, I have not seen you around here," Tariq said, staring at me. "I work at the dive shop. We go diving everyday, taking tourists to all the best places to dive. Do you dive?"

"No," I said. I noticed Mario gazing at us as we spoke, silent. I turned again to Tariq. "You are from Egypt?"

"Yes, I am Egyptian," he smiled, his eyes boring through me.

"I want to know about the pyramids."

"Oh, the pyramids are incredible structures. And they are so beautiful. There are many mysteries surrounding them. You need to go and see for yourself," he said, grinning at me.

"Tell me some of them," I asked.

"The shape of the pyramid has healing qualities. If you have a headache and wear a hat in the shape of a pyramid and it will go away. It's true. That is just one of the mysteries." His penetrating blue eyes held secrets I wanted to know, but there was something else.

A tall Danish girl sat down beside Mario, who shifted over for her. An American man, an Australian man and a German woman also joined us. Tariq suggested we take the gathering to his place.

"Let's go, now," one person said. "We can pick up some beer on the way." Everyone except me was in agreement.

I sat and decided what was best for me. "Cassandra, are you coming?" Tariq asked, leading the way.

I could think of no reason not to join, so I answered, "Okay."

"Don't be too excited," he laughed, causing the group to focus on me.

"I just wasn't expecting an excursion right now," I said.

Several people hopped in the back of Tariq's truck and I followed them on my scooter. We arrived at a row of bungalows with entryways under low hanging tree branches. We went inside to a small living room where we all crowded around a low table on the floor. We were a circle of ambassadors representing various countries from around the world: South America, North America and Europe.

Mario fascinated me so I sat beside him at the table. He spoke only a few words, but appeared fully present in all that was being shared. He gazed appreciatively and smiled at me.

Quietly, he asked, "You are a seeker?"

"Yes," smiled.

"I am, too," he smiled at me. It was all that needed to be said and made us friends. Tariq directed the attention to me.

"Cassandra, what do you do on the island?"

"I'm a kindergarten teacher. And I'm writing a book," I smiled at the inquisitive faces.

"A book?" he exclaimed in surprise as the others tuned in. "What is it about?" Eyes focussed on me as I searched for words to describe the view from a kaleidoscope.

"I'm unfolding and observing the process of life, so I write about what I see."

"Nice," they chimed.

"And so," Tariq probed.

"I write about ways I understand the world," I answered, not wanting to reveal much.

"So, what have you understood?" he asked, zeroing in on my expression as the group leaned forward.

"That life is truly beautiful if you want to see it that way," I said, hoping to close the questioning.

Heads nodded, eager. I was encouraged to share more.

"Lately, I've been considering the gaze in the eyes of babies, how they seem to hold so much behind their new eyes," I offered.

"I have a two-year-old and he is incredible. He can do so much," said Dan, the American surfer. This surprised me and I wondered where the child was now while he was sitting with us.

"I have one too," said another, a new surprise.

The conversation escalated as each person described their unique experiences with babies, talking over one another fervently as to how much they knew about them. It went on and on while Mario and I observed the exchanges.

"Babies eyes are just amazing," Dan finally said, drawing the conversation to a close, passing the forum back to me.

"Yeah, I believe that's what I said," I said. Everyone laughed uproariously.

"Yeah!" Mario cheered. The drinking continued and voices got louder so I finished my drink and announced my departure. Mario walked me outside to my scooter.

"It was nice to spend time with you. I'd like to see you in town more often," he said.

"I'm sure we'll see each other," I smiled, before powering over gravel onto the paved road.

The next day Mario stopped by to surprise me, having tracked down my house from the description I had given him. We sat on the porch sipping ice tea that he had brought. He told me stories about travelling the world for years: sailing, scuba diving and surfing in many countries in South East Asia; Shark encounters, month-long Mediterranean sailing trips, meaningful inter-dimensional meditation, all very interesting to me. But my feelings for Joe didn't waver.

"Why did you look at me the way you did, the day I met you?" I asked.

"Don't you know?" he asked, returning power to me. I looked at him, wanting his answer.

"Your energy is what I saw. I have never seen energy so beautiful. It was all around you, encompassing you. I could only stare at it," he said.

Shocked that someone could see me for what I felt inside, the power and strength of loving life, I could only smile.

"I love that you could see my experience of love," I said, feeling special.

"Your love? Are you in love?" he asked.

"Well, yes, but I meant in life. I'm in love, yeah. I met the most amazing guy here in Thailand named Joe. He's Norwegian. He's blond and brilliant and I'm leaving here at some point to go to him," I answered.

"You don't have your ticket?" he asked.

"No. Not yet. I haven't decided the exact date." I felt the moment heat up as he scanned me with his eyes. I saw his eyes moving up my leg. I crossed them.

"We can go for a ride and visit a woman named Karen. She's English and just moved into her own place up the street," he offered.

"Oh, I know her! That's great. Sure, let's go see Karen," I said, somehow relaxed. We hopped into his truck. He put in a Madonna CD, Ray of Light. Surreal sounds vibrated through us as we drove, enchanting the moment. I enjoyed being a passenger riding with the windows down listening to music.

We arrived at Karen's suite at the back of a larger house owned by her landlords. We knocked on her door and she opened it with a smile. We sat down in her living room on a white cushioned sofa surrounded by tealight candles and incense that swirled throughout the room.

"One day I will have my own place down here. I love it," she said, surprising me with her boldness to ask for such a large gift. I listened to her story of life in England, as she chatted easily with Mario and me. We laughed and entertained each other, discussing what our lives were like on the island.

As Mario spoke he seemed ageless and timeless, but carried himself with charm and down-to-earth genuineness. He was real. No facades, just truth. We were inspired by his presence and told him so.

"Go to Italy. There are more of us," he said, waving us off.

I contemplated the residual effect of centuries of history and innumerable beautiful works of art on the Italian people. What a difference between New World and Old! Mario's gentle movements and shoulder length sun bleached hair highlighted his turquoise eyes. His smile lit up the room and I could see that Karen was smitten. She told us of her meditation pursuits, yoga and spiritual practice. The ethereal music she was playing in the background added to her mystique.

"Do you believe in a fourth dimension?" I asked to no one in particular.

"Yes, there are other dimensions," Mario answered casually, as if he had told me to pass the butter.

"How do you know?" I probed.

"Because, I have seen them," he said, unblinking.

"Where? When?" I asked astonished.

"When I mediate I go through different visual realities that are other dimensions. It's like I can see into other times," he said calmly.

Karen and I exchanged glances. I couldn't find the words to ask another question.

"How do you meditate?" Karen asked, with trepidation and awe.

"I lay on my bed with my eyes open and listen to my breathing. I quiet my thoughts, but my mind stays alert while my body relaxes. Then I drift and release into the reality surrounding me and end up seeing all kinds of things." He smiled at our expressions.

"There's a story about a little black ball that lived in the third dimension. It had shape and form and could roll just like a ball. Then it rolled into a two dimensional world so people could see it as he really was, a three dimensional ball. But people in the two-dimensional world looked at it and said, 'No, it's not a ball - it's a spot moving around.'"

We pondered the imagery.

"Did the people ever see it as a ball?" Karen asked.

"Some did, some didn't." He smiled, watching us process this perspective.

After the sky began to darken Mario and I thanked Karen for her hospitality and left. He drove me home and I thanked him for the remarkable evening. I waved goodbye from my door.

Inside, I was missing Joe so I decided to drive to the Internet café. An email was waiting in my inbox from Joe. He missed me and wanted me to come soon. He said he was enjoying school and learning and studying hard. There was something in his yearning that told me to hurry. He was becoming impatient. I knew I didn't want to give up on our love and I knew I had to make a move.

A few days later Mario came by for another visit. We sat on my porch drinking coconut juice he had brought. Our friendship was growing as my curiosity for his knowledge continued. I knew his feelings for me were developing. We sipped our drinks in silence.

"Have you talked to your boyfriend, Joe?" he asked.

"We've been emailing," I answered.

"Does he still want you to go to Norway?" he asked, looking away.

"I think so." Just the thought of Joe brought a smile to my face. I wanted to talk about him.

"When do you think you will go?" I could tell he was wondering if I would actually leave the island.

"We haven't set a date," I confessed.

"Do you want to leave your job?"

"Not really because I love it. I love the children." Mario knew that went straight to my heart. "But, I can't stay here forever. I have to move on with my life." I wanted to go to Joe.

"Let's go for a ride," he said.

We got into his blue truck and he turned on Madonna, laughing and bringing a smile to my face. Then he drove us to the beach.

We got out and walked along to the beach. I stepped mindfully on the soft sand that had been my home for months, knowing that our time together was coming to an end. Mario walked beside me.

"This place will always be here. You can come back," he said.

"Yes, but what I have here will end when I leave. Everything will be different."

"You have to trust that what you could make here, you could make anywhere. You have to believe," he reassured.

I looked up at his kind face, his silhouetted form framed with wisps of blond hair, wild and free. He looked like a pirate with a heart of gold.

We watched the rolling waves of the tide for a long time. Then he drove me home.

"The water always soothes me," I said, standing at his truck door. "Thank you," I said, smiling.

"Yes, it's soothing," he said. "I'm happy it helped."

He drove away as I waved goodbye and entered the sidewalk to my house. As always, it was clear of sticks and leaves. The landlords were diligent in beating back the jungle. They were always helping me in subtle ways, watching over me, guarding the space. I lacked for nothing, really, and what I needed was always brought to me quickly. Life was loving me back.

I imagined my life with Joe, what it would be like living in the mountains. I had never been to Norway or northern Europe for that matter. The closest I had been to was France. I knew it would be a new world of adaptation. I was looking forward to the cultural immersion, and I knew I would enjoy learning a brand new way of life.

It rained during the days more than I had ever seen before. I drove to work through thick sheets of warm rain, avoiding large puddles. Chunks of earth washed from the side of the road, continuous erosion, daily.

Saturday morning I awoke early to loud, continuous pounding at my front porch. I woke with a start and jumped out of bed as the sound of a torrential downpour filled the room.

I ran to my front door and pulled it open to see my landlord crouched on his knees, frantically nailing wooden boards into my door frame to stop the flow of rainwater from the porch. A giant torrent of brown water was gushing from the hill in front of my house. It was a desperate situation.

People shouted nearby as plastic lawn chairs began to float and large umbrellas toppled. My landlord quickly pounded the boards into place and stealthily jammed putty between them to seal cracks. The two foot barricade held the water back momentarily but the floodwater grew and grew and soon breached the barricade.

"Move! Move!" he shouted, waving for me to leave the house and head to his house on higher ground. I dashed around my house as water flooded in, sloshing at my feet as I ran to get important things and clothes to wear. The water pouring in was relentless. I shrieked.

The whole area was flooding, the brown rainwater levelling grass and plants in the yard. I could hear people screaming as their houses were invaded by the deluge. I waded through knee-deep water to my porch where I could see the flood pouring down the hill. I pushed through the deepening water over to my neighbours yard and higher ground.

I stood with others who had gathered, arms crossed in silent embrace as water stealthily flooded our homes.

"This, first time," said Dao.

"Never before?" I asked, incredulously.

"No. First time."

We watched brown water flowing past us with items washed from peoples' yards and houses. The scene was punctuated with desperate screams as my neighbours tried in vain to save household possessions and wondered when it would stop.

After what seemed like forever the rain began to cease and the flood water lessened. I walked back home to see my landlord and the little Buddhist lady busily bailing my living room with buckets.

"I'll help," I said, reaching for a bucket but they shooed me out, indicating that something dangerous could be in the water. I begrudgingly agreed and returned to the porch of the nearby store to wait.

A couple of hours later I went back to see them wiping the floor clean with cloths. It looked almost spotless, like nothing had happened, except for the walls which showed a faint brown high water mark all around the room. I thanked them profusely.

As if on cue, the day began to brighten and the sun came out with a clear blue sky. Everyone in the village sighed with relief. Most people spent the day putting their houses back together, fetching items that had ended up down the road.

I went out for a ride to the beach for a much needed change of scenery. I sat watching vacationers playing in the surf, appearing to live picture-perfect 'brochure' lives. Life on the beach was marvellous. Everything felt easy, relaxed, and calm. I wanted my life to feel this good everyday, surrounded by beauty. Would I be able to create this outside of paradise?

I returned home to find Mario waiting on my porch. I asked him if he knew what had happened and he said he hadn't seen the flood. He lived in another area of Kata that had not received torrential rain.

"Where have you been just now?" he asked. My eyes flashed at his.

"Kata Beach," I said. "I wanted to buy some fruit and hang out on the sand. You?"

"At home. Let's go to Kata town," he suggested, then stood up, jingling his keys. I went inside to drop off the fruit then back outside into his truck.

We drove into Kata town and parked. Surrounded by a suspension of stillness, crossed the street to Tariq's scuba shop. The door chimed as we entered. Heaps of snorkelling equipment hung on the walls as customers milled about eyeing large colourful maps. Tariq greeted me with a hug and mesmerizing green eyes that bored into me, pulling me aside to talk.

"Are you enjoying yourself, Cassandra?" he asked, dazzling me with his snake-charmer eyes. I needed to find my footing.

"Yes," I answered, knowing there was something more in his words.

"Now you are meeting new friends, finding your crowd on Phuket. Stay with us and enjoy," he said, making me feel strangely uncomfortable. His eyes were spinning like saucers and for a moment, I felt pulled into his line of thought.

"I have to go to Norway," I replied.

"It's too cold in Norway. Its much warmer here. You like the sun?" he asked, standing too close.

"Of course I like the sun," I replied, not sure what was happening.

The entry bells chimed as my eyes were then drawn to the doorway as three sturdy fair-haired men entered the shop. They began to converse with Mario in English, with thick Norwegian accents.

I laughed out loud and Tariq recoiled, confused. I knew what I had to do.

I excused myself and left the shop telling them I had to send an email. I went to the internet café and wrote to Joe, telling him I was ready to come. I felt as if a huge yoke had been lifted from my shoulders. It was time.

Mario was standing outside the Internet cafe when I exited.

"Are you okay?" he asked.

"Yes, but I should go now. I have some things to take care of."

Mario walked me to his truck without saying a word and unlocked the doors. He drove me home in silence.

My hand reached out the window catching the wind as we drove. I was flying.

"Here you go," he said, pulling up in front of the house.

"Thank you," I said, hoping out.

That was it. His truck drove away, red tail lights weaving down the road.

I walked to my porch pensively, pulling out a chair to sit down and listen to the sounds of nature. An idea came to me and I went inside and found a postcard with cows on it. I wrote a message to Joe telling him all the reasons I loved him and that I would be there soon.

I went next door to mail it, handing it to the girl behind the counter who smiled when I gave it to her.

"You go to him," she nodded. "You go to Norway."

Her intuition was so strong. I smiled at her.

"Yes, I'm going. But, I don't know when." I exhaled.

She smiled, knowing. "Soon."

I walked back to my house and padded out onto the grass, looking around at my beautiful life: fine palm trees, my peaceful space, my house. Gratefulness flowed within me as my thoughts flew to Norway. What would life be like there?

The next day after work I buzzed to the Internet café to see if Joe had replied to my message. I opened my email account to see one reply in my inbox.

'Buy the ticket' was repeated three times in his lengthy love letter to me. I went home radiant with love and planned to go to the tourist office the following day.

The next day after work I drove to Kata, enjoying the fresh breeze along the way before parking in front of the tourist shop I had been eyeing for weeks. I entered into an air conditioned room filled with colourful maps, my eyes drawn to waterfalls and blue sky vistas. I sat down in front of a smiling Thai woman dressed in a blue uniform.

"Hello," I said.

"Hello," she smiled. "Do you need a ticket?"

"Yes, I do. I would like a one-way to Oslo, Norway."

"Okay and how will you fly?"

"It doesn't matter which airline. When do you have a seat available?"

"Let me check for you."

She tapped on the keys in rapid succession. Many keys, many taps. Finally, she said, "You travel by bus to airport in Phuket Town, then you fly to Bangkok. Bangkok to Prague, Prague to Oslo."

"That would be great," I said, feeling relieved that the route existed.

"Yes. This one leaves Tuesdays and Thursdays."

"Thursday," I said.

"You go for work?" She continued clicking the keys.

"No," I paused. "Love."

"Then it's worth it." She smiled a beautiful smile.

I glanced around the room at the places I had seen and many that I had not. My eyes roamed over vibrant photos of Thai style boats, the Bangkok floating market which I didn't see, more tropical beaches and endless coconut palm trees. I looked down at my white cotton pants, my blue cotton flowing shirt, my beaded bracelets, my simple flip flops and my perfect bronze tan.

From here, I would be moving to Halden, Norway, a small town on the eastern fjords of Norway, across the bridge from Sweden. I was making a giant leap of love.

She handed me a printed ticket with my name on it that read 'Destination: Oslo, Norway.'

I had two weeks to prepare.

At the end of the next work day I handed in my letter of resignation. I knew saying goodbye to my life in Thailand would be hard so I savoured every last moment on the island. I drove the long way home, went to the pool as much as possible, toured through the fishing village of Rawai, past other fruit stands and noodle carts, past boats in the harbour and other white sand beaches.

On the southern road heading west, the highway led up to hilly range through thick jungle foliage into a triple canopy rainforest. Moist air hung in condensation, clouds moving in from the forest as dusk approached. I wanted to soak up the scene and never forget it.

I came upon water buffalo lounging in a shady marsh. The vision was breathtaking as the horned, wild herbivores lounged in streams of sunlight, standing and lying on a wet patch of ground. I slowed down to park at the side of the road, joining them in the quiet moment.

As I peered through the foliage, the cold, dense air hung over me as the jungle pulsed with life. The round, grey buffalo stared lazily over at me from their grassy slope, horns held high. Such majestic creatures, they gazed upon me as I gazed upon them in appreciation.

I mounted my bike and headed to the next panoramic vista. The sun was setting as I approached home so I pressed on past my house to take in some of the beautiful colours. I purchased som tum salad with sticky rice and took it with me to the beach, where I munched, dipping rice in the salad bag to get the juices. Sitting on the sand I took in the view of all the people who had come to be enchanted by the highlight of the day.

Families frolicked at the shore, some tossing their little ones up in the air amid shrieks of delight. The beautiful endless sky displayed colours like never before, revealed in amazing movement across the horizon. I watched the giant golden ball as it slipped down into the horizon, taking colour with it.

At home in the moist night air I jumped around catching mosquitoes before bed, before settling in to the sound of the distant ocean, waves upon the shore.

Early morning came with the crowing of roosters and I silently thanked them for waking me up on time.

I drove to school where the children played in the yard. I sat at my desk writing a goodbye song to share with the children to teach them about endings, remembering that one never leaves completely when a mark is left on the heart.

I explained that I would be leaving to carry on my life in another country. They listened and learned the song that we shared everyday until I departed.

As I drove home feeling good about my teaching and my day, replaying the lovely events one after another, I saw some butterflies at the side of the road.

I pulled over and turned off onto a pathway where I parked my scooter. More and more butterflies appeared, scores of species in more colours and patterns than I had ever seen in one place. They surrounded plants with open flowers, drifting, taking turns at the nectar in perfect harmony. Brilliant, colourful plants and bushes grew beneath the flowers as many unique bugs crawled on stems and leaves. Here at the side of the road was a bounty of incredible life, flourishing under the sun.

Some of the plant leaves were so huge that I laughed, feeling tiny by comparison. This pumping, pulsing realm of life, totally independent from any human involvement bloomed in brilliance, undisturbed. Time stood still as I appreciated this beautiful expression of life. Was I the only one to have ever seen this?

I was beginning to see a connection between life and the way dreams played out in my mind. What was I being shown subconsciously? Was I seeing in my dreams the reality to come?

On my drive home I considered my passion for Joe - a warmth of togetherness that enriched my life and made me want to be a better person. I loved to live in passion, understanding life and being open to love. It seemed the most natural way for me to live, the purest way, and the most satisfying way. I was living life exactly how I wanted, and life had true meaning for me.

I visualised a future world where we gave freely to one another: truth, love, and friendship. I wanted to contribute to a beautiful collection of societies living in peace and harmony, together fascinated by the incredible world surrounding us.

My consciousness was thrilled and piqued daily and I could see insights weaved into every part of life. My experience of life was transforming. The way love danced throughout my experience opened me up to a greater and greater understanding. My mind and senses were opened up by brilliance, enlightenment.

I moved my chair onto the porch as the sound of Mario's truck came from the driveway. I sat quietly as he made his way to the porch and sat down beside me.

After a while in silence, I began to share my passion.

"Wise people through the ages have tried to share with us their insight, using their best words to teach us how to live in a pure and divine way. But we have idolized them and put their words in stone, instead of seeing our own way. Those prophets were strong enough to follow their own paths and they had all been led to wonderful places. They were showing us how we could grow and exist, as they demonstrated the way they achieved their greatness. In doing so they showed us that we could find our greatness the way they had found theirs."

Mario nodded.

"'This is where you can go', they said to us. And we knew that what they had embodied was our deepest desire as well. But in naming ourselves 'followers' we had told each other it was best to take their path, walk to their destination the way they did, and we came to a dead end, lost in the fog. In our aim to capture their wisdom in an eternal form, we have made untouchable those who have tried to show us. And in our self-deprecation, we made them our saviours and lost their message altogether. We had become lost sheep when we were all of the same great potential and capable of achieving our own personal destinies, truly as great as any other."

He smiled at me, nodding.

"In our efforts to crystallize the teachings and make permanent the possibility of anointment, we formed religions around those who succeeded in embodying bliss and brilliance. And then, as we fought with each other about whom to follow, and what words to use, we lost sight of where they had been leading: ourselves."

"A beautiful woman with a beautiful mind. A rare combination," he said.

"You know what I have learned? If you think about something, do it, jump. Life will catch you. Allow it to. Trust in it."

"That means we have to go to the beach because this was my idea," he said.

"Let's go," I said, needing a view of the ocean.

We drove to the beach and parked on a sandy street then found a place to sit on the sand. Mario reclined and I sat pouring sand through my fingers.

"It's like time through the hourglass. Each piece of sand is a moment. And we have so many moments," I said, feeling the relief of the sea.

"Remember this when you are in Norway," he instructed.

"I will," I said, smiling.

"You will come back one day. Maybe with Joe and your kids!"

"Aha! That would be nice." I smiled with the imagination. "Where will you be?"

"I don't know. Maybe I will become tired of this lifestyle and go home to Italy." He grinned, suntanned and relaxed.

"You will find someone to share your love," I said, looking him in the eye.

"I know. Tell Joe you will make a good wife," he said, looking out over the sea.

I blushed, nodding.

I rose from the sand and padded to the shoreline. The ocean gently flowed to my toes, as if kissing them. I inhaled the beauty of the sky, the serenity of all that had embraced me while I unfolded my inner being. Mario stood beside me.

"You will come back one day," he said.

"Yes, I will," I said, as teardrops formed. I wiped them with my sleeve, overcome by emotion, turning away from him. We walked slowly back to the truck.

He drove me home in silence, then stopped in front of my house.

"I have a gift for you." He reached down and pulled out a copy of Madonna, Ray of Light.

"Thank you for this," I smiled, and gave him a hug.

He smiled at me, his blue eyes lingering on mine.

"Goodbye and good luck," he said, finally.

"Goodbye. And good luck to you too," I said, then hopped out of his truck. The sound of tires on crushed gravel faded into the dusk.

In the darkness I saw the familiar form of Gail saunter up to my porch. She was holding a gift.

"This is for you," she said, sitting down beside me on the porch. Inside was a pink scented candle.

"I love it. Thanks."

"I knew you could use that." She smiled. We sat on my porch as the crickets played their music.

"Are you excited to be going to Norway?" she asked. "It's supposed to be stunning. Many of my relatives have visited and rave about its beauty."

"Yes," I smiled, looking at my hands, twisting slightly in my lap.

"Oh, those lousy crickets making all that noise. Can we just have one quiet evening?" she shouted at my lawn. The crickets were momentarily quiet. "They are all around my house, little buggers, keeping me up at night," she complained.

"I like the sound. I find it comforting," I said.

"You know Cassandra, life can be pretty lousy at times," she stated.

I paused to consider my reply. "I believe that the more I endeavour to be positive in my thoughts, words and actions, the more I will reach an even more loving place and feel better about myself. And I want to feel good, so I hold firmly to that belief," I explained.

"But how do you remember this when the world turns upside down around you? At school you never seem frazzled, while I am constantly pulling my hair out." She made a face.

"I pay attention to the insights, the good things that encourage me. I look for the good in all ways."

She stared at me.

"Life tells you things all the time. It's a matter of listening. The more aware you are, the more you pay attention and your consciousness expands, heightening your pleasure of this experience and improving your ability to expand your awareness." I said, feeling excited.

"My awareness," she repeated, postulating on what that meant to her.

"There is a cyclical nature to everything. Life repeats itself, over and over again. But its a spiral, so when you make a change, it amplifies it and moves you forward into your future."

"A spiral," she repeated, trying to understand where to apply this picture.

"When a person speaks, we need to listen their truth, whatever truth is to that person. A person's truth is entirely subjective, but it is truth to them," I said.

"My truth must make your ears shudder," she joked.

I laughed, recalling some of her zingers.

"I know life is listening, so sometimes I cringe when I hear people use negativity, talking about their displeasure of their view of life."

She frowned.

"I want to plug the ears of life at times so that negative words will not form any part of reality."

"Good luck with that," she teased.

"We need to listen to life, continue to ask questions and stay in touch with our inner voice. There are moments during my day when I have feelings of sublime calmness and life seems to float, carrying me along. In that bubble of peacefulness, I know I am doing the right thing because my intention is to enjoy life, and so I let it happen," I explained.

"If only people could feel what you are feeling," she said, wistful.

"I want people to feel what I am feeling. I love to imagine that," I said, looking at her deeply, knowing she carried the spark within her to light her own fire.

I sensed a resonance within myself when I spoke as if the words came from somewhere else, as if my reality slid back and forth between realms, becoming pliable, lucid in a way that felt surreal and magical.

"You are a mystic," she said. "I think you have a lot to give. I wish we could have had you here longer. You bring up such interesting ideas."

"It's been great getting to know you. I hope to see you again someday," I said, knowing she would be a good friend to keep.

"Maybe in England. That's where I'll move back to one day," she said, the image drifting in space.

"I'll keep it in mind," I said, smiling.

With that she got up. "See you in school tomorrow."

We hugged goodnight.

The last two weeks went by quickly. There was much to do and many people to hug goodbye, but I felt I was ready to leave. As I packed the final things on the day of my flight, some friends came by to wish me farewell. I was reminded of all the beauty that had come to me through the people I had met. I wished them all the very best and showered them with positive words and encouragement.

When Gail came to drive me to the airport, pulling up into the driveway in her red sports car, I was excited and ready to go. Everything was packed and my house was tidy and clean. A wave of excitement overcame me to know that Joe was on the other end of this ride.

She helped me lift my full bag of treasures from Thailand into the trunk of her car. Then, I hugged my neighbour Dao goodbye and thanked her for all out chats. I asked her to thank her family for renting me the house, and watching over me. She waved many times, standing on her porch watching me get ready to leave.

I stood at the door to my abode for the final moments. I inhaled the scents of a beautiful life, taking it into me for the future. I thanked my house and yard for providing me with a safe and happy home. Then I looked around for the last time, and climbed into Gail's car.

I enjoyed the ride through the hills, a sweet breeze sweeping over us as we passed the jungle on the way to the airport.

When we arrived she was teary, and we hugged.

"Do you have everything then?" she asked.

"Yes, I'm sure. I've got my ticket, passport, I'm all set."

"Have a safe flight. And maybe see you in England sometime," she said, hoping back into the driver's seat.

"Yes, will do," I said, waving goodbye.

She pulled away from the curb as I turned and entered the terminal to check my luggage. My plane awaited.

I walked out onto the tarmac, just as Joe had done, and climbed the steps to the plane. From my seat I looked out the window in awe of the wonderful experience I had shared with this majestic place: Thailand.

I felt ready to learn how to express the knowledge I had come to know about life, thanking Thailand in my heart for supplying me with everything I needed to explore my experience and for loving me so kindly while I took my initial steps into freedom.

Life is a symphony of elements and when I listen to the individual notes, I hear my own voice, a bittersweet reflection of myself.

I walked through the stunning windowed corridor of the terminal in Oslo, elevated over passageways, my senses calm and ordered. Dressed in colourful Thai style clothing, I marched amid handsome, conservative Norwegians in grey and black suits that hinted at their studious manner. The shuffle of people engulfed me as I drifted along with my bags toward two big white doors at the end of the hallway.

Hearing the voices of the arrivals lounge, I took a deep breath, then stepped through the door. A crowd of people hungry for their loved ones stood together with eager faces, leaning into the crowd. Some waved signs of people's names while I walked along, searching for Joe's smiling face.

I headed through the mass of people until I saw those beautiful blue eyes shining at me through the crowd. A wide grin met me as Joe scooped me up into his arms, lifting me from the floor, squeezing me tightly. I held onto him, feeling that our bond was intact, knowing the strength of our love.

I was overjoyed.

We chatted easily about small things as he picked up my bags and led me to a beautiful sky blue vintage Mercedes waiting to drive us home. I smiled.

I was wide awake in my dreams.

To Be Continued...

C.L. Wilson lives in Vancouver, British Columbia, Canada. She teaches and practices yoga and energy healing. She writes articles and books and is an active member of her community.

33863169R00144

Made in the USA
Charleston, SC
25 September 2014